Contents

C++ For Programmers

Second Edition

C++ For Programmers

Second Edition

Leendert Ammeraal
Hogeschool Utrecht, The Netherlands

JOHN WILEY & SONS
Chichester · New York · Brisbane · Toronto · Singapore

Other Wiley Editorial Offices

John Wiley & Sons, Inc., 605 Third Avenue,
New York, NY 10158-0012, USA

Jacaranda Wiley Ltd, 33 Park Road, Milton,
Queensland 4064, Australia

John Wiley & Sons (Canada) Ltd, 22 Worcester Road,
Rexdale, Ontario M9W 1L1, Canada

John Wiley & Sons (SEA) Pte Ltd, 37 Jalan Pemimpin #05-04,
Block B, Union Industrial Building, Singapore 2057

British Library Cataloguing in Publication Data

A catalogue record for this book is available from the British
Library

ISBN 0 471 95486 1

Produced from camera-ready copy supplied by the author using WordPerfect
Printed and bound in Great Britain by Redwood Books, Trowbridge, Wilts.

Preface

The C++ language is 'a better C'. Now that very good C++ compilers are available, any new programming task that would previously have been done in C can be done at least as well in C++. Although C compilers will also remain in use because of existing old-style C programs, not accepted by C++ compilers, newcomers in the C programming world should now seriously consider learning C++ instead of C.

I have tried to explain all C++ language aspects, including those shared by plain C, by means of simple programs or program fragments. There are a great many exercises, both at the end of most chapters and in Appendix A, which will be particularly useful if you are using this book as a textbook.

It is also intended for professional programmers who are already familiar with C or some other language and want to switch to C++. Those interested in object-oriented programming will pay special attention to Chapters 6 and 7. Chapter 10 is for easy reference; it is about the ANSI C function library, available to anyone who programs in C or C++.

A note on the Second Edition

Two new chapters, 11 and 12, cover templates and exception-handling. Appendix C, which is also new, is about the advanced subject of defining manipulators with parameters. Finally, there are numerous possibly inconspicuous but important changes and additions in this second edition. To mention just one example, the discussion of the *qsort* library function on p. 317 now also covers sorting an array of pointers to strings. The need for this addition and many others became clear to me when I was teaching. For a textbook writer, there are few things more useful than frequently asked questions from students.

Leendert Ammeraal

1

Introduction

1.1 About C++ and Other Languages

The C++ programming language was designed by B. Stroustrup and published in his book *The C++ Programming Language* in 1986. C++ has been derived from the well-known programming language C. The name C++ is related to the expression **C++**, which we can write in a C program to increment a variable **C**. The original version of C was published by B. W. Kernighan and D. M. Ritchie in *The C Programming Language* in 1978. The second edition of their book, published in 1988, is about a revised edition of the language, known as ANSI C. The languages C++ and ANSI C are closely related, and both are successors to the original C language. Although C++ is a much younger language than C, its use is already widespread, and its popularity will no doubt increase considerably as a result of the excellent quality of many popular compilers.

One of the attractive aspects of C++ is that it offers good facilities for *object-oriented programming* (OOP), but, as a hybrid language, it also permits the traditional programming style, so that programmers can shift to object-oriented programming if and when they feel the need to do so. In this regard, C++ differs from some purely object-oriented languages, such as Smalltalk and Eiffel. Viewed from the angle of many C programmers, C++ is simply 'a better C'. Besides the important *class* concept, essential to OOP, there are many other useful language concepts and facilities that are available in C++, not in C. To mention just a few, related to functions, we have *function overloading, inline functions, default arguments, type-safe linkage, function templates* and the very simple requirement that functions be declared before they are used. In ANSI C, the old practice of using undeclared functions is still allowed in order to keep many existing C programs valid; in C++ it is not.

The point just mentioned and some others make C++ much 'safer' than C, but unlike Pascal, C++ offers the same flexibility as C. This use of the word *safe* refers to what happens with incorrect programs. In this regard, *assembly language* is extremely 'unsafe', but this does not mean that programs written in assembly language cannot

1

be perfectly correct and reliable. They can, and so can C programs. Most experienced programmers want as much control over the computer system as is possible and will therefore prefer C or C++ to Pascal or Basic. It is fine if a language is safe, as long as this does not make it restrictive. C++ is safer than C and less restrictive than Pascal.

The oldest well-known professional programming languages are Fortran and Cobol. They have been very durable: revised versions are still widely used by application programmers. These two languages are not popular in computer science, although the newer versions of Fortran, that is, Fortran 77 and Fortran 90, are much better languages than Fortran II and Fortran IV, which were widely used before 1977.

Fortran and Cobol already existed in 1960, the year of birth of Algol 60, which was a milestone in the world of scientific programming languages. In the sixties, Algol 60 was a very elegant and modern language, and it was as popular in academic circles as Fortran was in industry. For many years, new algorithms written in it were published in *Communications of the ACM* and in many other scientific journals. This language and its defining *Report on the Algorithmic Language ALGOL 60* (the first document to use Backus Naur Form) inspired many experts to design successors to this language. The best known among these are PL/1 (also based on Fortran and Cobol), Pascal, Simula 67, and Algol 68. Because of the extreme complexity of its defining report, Algol 68 was far less popular than Pascal, for which good compilers and books were soon available.

The notion of data hiding by means of *classes*, as used in C++, has been borrowed from Simula 67; the possibility of defining operators for new types, another important feature of C++, was already available in Algol 68. Some newer languages are Modula, designed by N. Wirth, and ADA, from the American Department of Defence, which was also the birthplace of Cobol. Modula and ADA are based on Pascal, while C and C++ have more in common with Algol 60 and Algol 68. For example, conditional expressions (to be discussed in Section 3.1) were available in Algol 60 and Algol 68, but not in Pascal, Modula or ADA; the compact notation used for them in C (and C++) is similar to that in Algol 68. Another common aspect of Algol 60, Algol 68, C and C++, not shared by Pascal or its successors, is the fact that values returned by functions can be ignored so that such functions can be used as procedures. As for their general acceptance outside the academic world, those of the above languages with a purely American origin (Fortran, Cobol, PL/1, Basic, C, C++, ADA) have done better than most of the others (Algol, Simula, Pascal, Modula).

In general, realistic and easy-to-use programs are not always easy to read. It is very difficult not to make errors when complicated programs need to be modified. With C++, this situation is much better than with some other languages in that we can define our own language *extensions*, known as *classes*. We write these in separate modules (called *implementations*), and simply use such language extensions in our main programs, or rather, in our *application modules*, which can then be kept much simpler than would be the case otherwise. For example, a program that performs arithmetic with complex numbers is likely to be complicated if it is to be programmed in a language that does not support type **complex** with its associated operators +, −, *, /. Although C++ has no built-in facilities for complex arithmetic, we can define these ourselves in such a way that application programs can be written exactly as if such facilities were supported by the language itself. We can say that in this way we are extending the language. User-defined language extensions have the advantage of greater flexibility. The alternative of built-in facilities often leads to the availability of things other than what we actually want. Before discussing all this in detail, we must be familiar with more elementary language aspects, most of which are also available in the C language.

Not all important programming languages have been mentioned in the above discussion, so it is possible and even likely that you have missed some. In this book C++ is sometimes compared to Pascal, because this language is extremely popular in elementary computer science and therefore possibly known to most readers. If you belong to this category, the compact notation of some program fragments will surprise you, and you will soon appreciate such notation.

In case you have no experience with other programming languages, you have the advantage of not being confused by language differences, but you must know that it takes time to be a skilled programmer; programming can only be learned by doing, so don't ignore the exercises. Incidentally, this also applies to those who have such experience. There are many exercises in this book, but you can also use other sources, or invent programming problems yourself; the more programs you write the better.

If you are already familiar with C, you will find many things you already know, but there are some typical C++ subjects in each chapter. Most new material (not available in C) is to be found in Chapters 4, 6, 7, 9, 11 and 12.

1.2 Our First C++ Program

Let us begin with the C++ program EXAMPLE1, which reads two integers a and b from the keyboard to compute both $u = (a + b)^2$ and $v = (a - b)^2$:

```
/* EXAMPLE1: A program to compute the squares of both the sum
             and the difference of two given integers.
*/
#include <iostream.h>

int main()
{  cout << "Enter two integers: "; // Displays input request.
   int a, b;
   cin >> a >> b;                    // Reads a and b.
   int sum = a + b, diff = a - b,
       u = sum * sum, v = diff * diff;
   cout << "Square of sum       : " << u << endl;
   cout << "Square of difference: " << v << endl;
   return 0;
}
```

After typing this program using a program editor, we save it as the file *example1.cpp*, that is, if we are using some compiler for MS-DOS, such as those from Microsoft, Borland and Symantec. For C++ compilers under the UNIX operating system, the filename extension *.C* instead of *.cpp* is normally used. Most C++ compiler packages for the PC actually consists of both a C and a C++ compiler, and it depends on the filename extension which one is used. Since our program contains several elements that are specific to C++, it must be compiled with a C++ compiler; a compiler for plain C would display many error messages.

After compiling and linking, we can execute the program. Then the following text appears on the computer screen:

```
Enter two integers:
```

We can now enter, for example,

```
100 10
```

After we press the Enter key, the following appears:

```
Square of sum       : 12100
Square of difference: 8100
```

We can easily check these values: with **a** = 100 and **b** = 10, it follows that **sum** = 110 and **diff** = 90, and by squaring these we find 12100 and 8100 as the values of **u** and **v**, respectively.

We will now briefly discuss some C++ language rules, which apply to our example. It is good practice to start any program with *comment*. This can be done in two ways. The notation also available in C is to let comment begin with the two characters

```
/*
```

and to let it end with the same characters in reverse order:

```
*/
```

These two character pairs may or may not be on the same program line. By contrast, there is a way of writing comment that is new in C++: we let comment begin with the two characters

```
//
```

The end of the line is then simply the end of the comment. As you can see, both ways of writing comment have been used in program EXAMPLE1.

After the final characters */ of the comment at the top of this program, we find the following *include line*:

```
#include <iostream.h>
```

We say that this line 'includes' the file *iostream.h*, which is a so-called *header file* (hence the file-name extension *.h*) for 'stream input and output'. The contents of this header file logically replace this include line. Include lines always begin with **#include** and

they require a program line of their own. For example, you cannot write the program
text **int main( )** at the end of an include line.

In this regard include lines form an exception to a general rule that says that, as
far as the C++ compiler is concerned, program text may be split up over several lines
as we please. For example, we can replace the line

```
int sum = a + b, diff = a - b;
```

with the following two lines:

```
int sum = a + b,
    diff = a - b;
```

We can even split these lines further, but that would obviously not improve readability.
When splitting a line into two new lines, we say that we insert a *newline character*.
Similar characters are the *blank* (that is, the *space character*) and the *tab*. Collectively,
these three characters are called *white-space characters*.

Every C++ program contains one or more *functions*, one of which is called **main**.
(Note that we do not use the term *function* in the abstract, mathematical sense; instead,
a function denotes a concrete program fragment, that is, a sequence of characters!) In
our example, the **main** function is the only one. It has the form

```
int main()
{   ...
    ...
    return 0;
}
```

Functions may or may not have parameters. If they have, we write them between
parentheses, as we will see later. If not, we still use the parentheses, with nothing in
between, as is done here. The 'body' of every function is surrounded by a pair of
braces { }. It is good practice to write the two braces of such a pair in the same
(vertical) column, with everything in between indented as shown in EXAMPLE1.

After the open brace { of a function, we write so-called *statements*. As long as we
are not using compound statements (to be discussed in Section 2.4), any statement ends
with a semicolon. You can count seven semicolons in program EXAMPLE1; each is the
end of a statement. We very often write precisely one statement on a line. However,
there may be more than one statement on a line, and a statement may take more than
one line, as this statement shows:

```
int sum = a + b, diff = a - b,
    u = sum * sum, v = diff * diff;
```

This statement type is called a *declaration*. (The idea of a declaration being a special case
of a statement is new in C++. In C, declarations are not statements, and they must
precede them.) It says that the variables **sum**, **diff**, **u**, and **v** have type **int**, which means
that they denote integers. Their range is limited: for example, with most micro-

computers, the **int** values range from –32768 to 32767 (where 32768 = 2^{15}). In the above statement, we not only *declare* the variables **sum**, **diff**, **u**, and **v**, but we also *initialize* them, using the values of **a** and **b**. As is usual in programming languages, the asterisk * denotes multiplication. These variables **a** and **b** are declared themselves in the statement

```
int a, b;
```

without being initialized: immediately after this declaration their values are undefined. A completely different statement is

```
cout << "Enter two integers: ";
```

It is the typical C++ way of displaying some piece of text on the video screen. (If you are already familiar with C, you will be pleased to know that the standard library functions **printf** and **scanf** and the header file **stdio.h**, used in C programs, are also available in C++; they will be introduced in Section 2.2.) We say that **cout** is the **standard output stream**, to which we can send characters by means of the operator <<. Note that this operator is written as a character pair which looks like an arrow head that points to the left. It therefore suggests that the characters between the double quotes in **"Enter two integers: "** are sent to the stream **cout**. Instead of saying that we 'send characters to the output stream **cout**' (or to the video screen), we sometimes say that we *print* these characters. Analogously, the statement

```
cin >> a >> b;
```

reads two values from the standard input stream (that is, from the keyboard), and stores them into the variables **a** and **b**. The character pair >> may be associated with an arrow head pointing to the right, so the values go from **cin** to **a** and **b**. When executing this statement, the machine will be waiting for input, so we can now enter the two integers as requested.

After **u** and **v** have been computed, the values of these variables, preceded by some text and followed by a newline character, are printed by the following statements:

```
cout << "Square of sum        : " << u << endl;
cout << "Square of difference: " << v << endl;
```

We use **endl** to indicate that we are at the end of the line. Instead of **endl**, we could have written '**\n**', or "**\n**", as we will see in Section 1.5. The notation **endl** itself will not be explained until Section 9.2. In the meantime, we will freely use it. If **endl** (or one of these alternatives) had been omitted in the first of these lines, the output would have been

```
Square of sum        : 12100Square of difference: 8100
```

In the actual output, shown in the following 'demonstration' of the program, you may notice that the numbers 12100 and 8100 are not properly aligned: since their first digits are in the same position, their final ones are not.

```
Enter two integers: 100 10
Square of sum       : 12100
Square of difference: 8100
```

1.3 Memory Organization and Binary Numbers

Both compiled programs and data are stored in (the computer's) *memory*. In addition to this, our computer has registers, which can *temporarily* contain data. We can regard the memory as a long sequence of *bytes*, each consisting of eight binary digits or *bits*. A bit can only have two values, 1 and 0. There are also computer types with memories that primarily consist of *words*, each of which contains, for example, 16 bits. With the IBM PC and compatible machines these two types of memory organization are combined: although the memory consists of bytes, we can group two bytes together to form a 'word' of 16 bits in which an integer can be stored.

The contents of memory locations (either bytes or words) are variable: they can frequently change during program execution. In contrast to this, each location has a fixed number, its *address*, to indicate its position. In high-level languages we do not normally know the addresses of our variables. This also applies to C++, but in this language we use a symbolic notation for such addresses. For example, **&a** denotes the address of variable **a**, as we will see in Chapter 5 and elsewhere.

Let us assume, for example, that values of type **int** are stored in words of 16 bits. We number these bits 0, ..., 15, from right to left, as shown in Figure 1.1.

15	14	13	12	11	10	9	8	7	6	5	4	3	2	1	0
0	0	0	0	0	0	0	0	0	1	0	1	0	0	1	1

Figure 1.1. A word of 16 bits

This machine word contains the following bit sequence:

00000000 01010011

We can interpret these 16 bits in (at least) two ways: either as two characters (each represented by 8 bits) or as one integer of 16 bits. Which of these interpretations applies depends on the program that manipulates this word. If the word should be regarded as an integer, we use the 1 bits to compute its value. Omitting leading zeros, we have 1010011 here, which is the binary representation of 83. This value can be computed as follows:

$$1 \times 2^6 + 0 \times 2^5 + 1 \times 2^4 + 0 \times 2^3 + 0 \times 2^2 + 1 \times 2 + 1 = 83$$

Instead of 'the binary representation of a number', the shorter (but less precise) term *binary number* is more often used, and we will conform to this usage. The value of a binary number is found by using powers of 2, as this example shows. We say that 2 is the *base* or *radix* of the binary number system. Similarly, 10 is the radix of the usual decimal number system. For example, we can compute the value of the 'decimal number' 8241 as follows:

$$8 \times 10^3 + 2 \times 10^2 + 4 \times 10 + 1$$

If we use all 16 bits of a (16-bit) word the same way, the 2^{16} numbers that we can represent are

```
00000000 00000000 = 0
00000000 00000001 = 1
00000000 00000010 = 2
00000000 00000011 = 3
         ...
11111111 11111111 = 2^16 - 1 = 65535
```

We use the term *unsigned int* (or, briefly, *unsigned*) for this representation. In many applications we also want to use negative numbers. The usual way of doing this is by means of the two's-complement method. Using 16 bits, we can in this way represent the integers −32768, ..., 32767 as follows:

```
10000000 00000000 = -2^15 = -32768
10000000 00000001 = -(2^15 - 1) = -32767
         ...
11111111 11111110 = -2
11111111 11111111 = -1
00000000 00000000 = 0
00000000 00000001 = 1
         ...
01111111 11111111 = 2^15 - 1 = 32767
```

If the numbers we are dealing with can also be negative, as is the case here, the type of these numbers is *signed int*. As integers are signed by default, we usually write **int**, rather than **signed int**. Note that, with word length n, the unsigned and signed interpretations of any bit sequence with a 1 bit at the extreme left differ by 2^n. For example, using word length 16, the value we associate with the bit sequence

```
10000000 00000000
```

is 2^{15} if it is interpreted as unsigned int and -2^{15} if it is interpreted as signed int. The difference between these two values is $2^{15} - (-2^{15}) = 2 \times 2^{15} = 2^{16}$.

There are also 'long integers', which usually consist of 32 bits. In that case, their maximum values are $2^{32} - 1 = 4\ 294\ 967\ 295$ for type **unsigned long** and $2^{31} - 1 = 2\ 147\ 483\ 647$ for type **signed long**.

We conclude this section with another important way of interpreting bit sequences, namely by means of the *hexadecimal* representation of numbers. We can divide the machine word into groups of four bits. In the hexadecimal number system, the radix is 16, so there are 16 digits, which, with their binary representations, are given below:

```
0000 = 0
0001 = 1
   ...
1001 = 9
1010 = A (= 10)
1011 = B (= 11)
1100 = C (= 12)
1101 = D (= 13)
1110 = E (= 14)
1111 = F (= 15)
```

Now consider, for example, the following word of 16 bits, divided into groups of four bits:

```
1111 0000 1010 0011
```

These groups, in the given order, correspond to the following hexadecimal number

```
F0A3
```

Recalling that we have **F** = 15 and **A** = 10, we can use this to compute

$$15 \times 16^3 + 0 \times 16^2 + 10 \times 16 + 3 = 61603$$

This is another way of computing the value of the given 16-bit word, when interpreted as an unsigned binary number.

1.4 Identifiers and Keywords

As we quite often use names, technically known as *identifiers*, we need to know how to spell them. An *identifier* is a sequence of characters in which only letters, digits, and underscores (_) may occur. Its first character must not be a digit. It is wise to choose only identifiers that begin with a letter (not with an underscore), because there may be system functions with names that begin with underscores to distinguish them from other identifiers. Upper case and lower case letters are different, so there are 52 distinct letters. All characters of an identifier are significant. Here are some examples of valid identifiers:

```
a
largest_element
table1
```

The following identifiers are reserved for use as *keywords*, so we must not choose them for our own purposes:

```
asm, auto, break, case, catch, char, class, const,
continue, default, delete, do, double, else, enum,
extern, float, for, friend, goto, if, inline, int,
long, new, operator, private, protected, public,
register, return, short, signed, sizeof, static,
struct, switch, template, this, throw, try, typedef,
union, unsigned, virtual, void, volatile, while.
```

1.5 Constants

Besides variables, there are also *constants*, an example of which is the number **123** in the following statement:

```
x = a + 123;
```

There are various types of constants:

Integer constants

Here are four examples of integer constants:

123	(decimal)
0777	(octal)
0xFF3A	(hexadecimal)
123L	(decimal, long)

If the first character of a constant is **0** and is immediately followed by another digit, the constant is interpreted as an octal number (with radix 8); only the digits 0, ..., 7 may then occur in it. If the constant begins with **0x** or **0X**, it is taken to be a hexadecimal integer. We use **A**, ..., **F** (or **a**, ..., **f**) as hexadecimal digits with values 10, ..., 15. A letter **L** (or **l**), which means *long*, at the end of the constant is a *suffix*. We can also use the suffix **U** (or **u**), which means *unsigned*. The order of **L** and **U** is irrelevant if they both occur. The unsigned suffix means that the number in question has type *unsigned*. As we have seen in Section 1.3, the value of an unsigned type can be about twice as large as a value of the corresponding *signed* type but cannot be negative. A suffix **U** does not increase the *size*, that is, the number of bytes it needs. This may be different for a suffix

L. With many compilers, the types **int** and **unsigned** take two bytes, whereas the types **long int** and **unsigned long** take four bytes.

If no suffix **L** or **U** occurs in a very large integer constant, the type of that constant may yet be **long**, **unsigned**, or **unsigned long**. The precise decision rules for these cases are somewhat tedious, and it is unlikely that we will really need them because they have been carefully devised so that they are in accordance with what is both convenient and efficient. Nevertheless, they are included here for the sake of completeness:

-   If a *decimal* integer constant without any suffix is too large for type **int**, it has type **long**, unless it is even too large for that type: in that case its type is **unsigned long**.

-   If a *hexadecimal* or *octal* integer constant without any suffix is too large for type **int**, its type is **unsigned**, if possible. If its value is too large for **unsigned**, its type is **long**, if possible. If this is not possible, its type is **unsigned long**.

With many compilers, the types **int** and **long** take two and four bytes, respectively. In that case, 32767 is the maximum **int** value, so that **32768** has type **long** and therefore takes four bytes. On the other hand, **0x8000** (which also has 32768 as its value!) has type **unsigned** and therefore takes only two bytes.

Character constants

We use single quotes at the beginning and at the end of a character constant, as, for example in **'A'**. In C++ character constants have type **char**. This is different in the C language (in which they have type **int**!). However, we can easily use the numerical value of a character constant. This value is simply that of its internal representation. Although, strictly speaking, such values are system dependent, with most C++ implementations they are as listed in the ASCII table, included in this book in Appendix B. For **'A'** we find the value 65, or 41 in hexadecimal. The latter is useful if you want to write down the actual bit string quickly: 41 hex = 0100 0001 binary (= 65 dec.). In C the notations **65** and **'A'** are really equivalent. This is not the case in C++, but we can write **'A'** + **'A'**, the value of which is 130. A more sensible thing to do is to compute **'A'** + **i** in a loop, where **i** runs from 0 to 25. In this way we successively obtain the values 65, 66, ..., 90. Converting these integers to type **char** gives the characters **'A'**, ..., **'Z'**. How *type conversion* is done will be discussed in Section 3.7 and elsewhere.

Some special characters can be represented by *escape sequences*, in which the backslash character (\) occurs:

'\n'	newline, go to the beginning of the next line
'\r'	carriage return, back to the beginning of the current line
'\t'	horizontal tab
'\v'	vertical tab
'\b'	backspace
'\f'	form feed

`'\a'`	audible alert
`'\\'`	backslash
`'\''`	single quote
`'\"'`	double quote
`'\?'`	question mark
`'\ooo'`	octal number
`'\xhh'`	hexadecimal number

Note that the 'newline character' should really be written as '\n'; the notation **endl** can only be used after << in output operations.

In the final two constants above, *ooo* and *hh* denote at most three octal and two hexadecimal digits, respectively. We can use these forms conveniently if bit strings are actually given. For example, we can write '\x4F' to denote the bit string 01001111. However, we must be careful if the leftmost bit of such a bit string (of length 8) is 1. If type **char** is converted to type **int**, the eight bits of type **char** are extended on the left to the size of type **int**, which is 16 bits. If the compiler regards characters as 'signed' (as is usual), the leftmost bit is used as a 'sign bit'. The value of '\x80' may therefore be −128 instead of 128, because extending the corresponding bit string 1000 0000 to 16 bits may give 1111 1111 1000 0000 instead of 0000 0000 1000 0000. Fortunately, this problem does not occur with 'normal' characters, since their leftmost bit is always 0.

An important special case is '\0', the so-called *null character*, which consists of only zero bits. Note that '\0' has the value 0. By contrast, the ASCII value of '0' is 48, as Appendix B shows.

Floating constants

A *floating constant* represents a real number. It can have a fractional part, and its value can be much greater than those of integer constants. However, in its internal format it normally only *approximates* the real number it represents. For example, the constant **0.1** may be stored internally as a value that is actually closer to 0.0999999999999999 than to 0.1. When writing a floating constant, we always have to use a period or the letter **E** (or **e**), as, for example, in

```
82.347
.63
83.
47e-4
1.25E7
61.e+4
```

These constants have type **double**, which means 'double-precision floating point'. We can insist that they be (single-precision) **float**, by writing a letter **F** (or **f**) at the end of the constant. By contrast, we can write **L** (or **l**) at the end as a request for more precision than that of type **double**. If this is done the constant has type **long double**. Actually, the distinction between the types **float, double** and **long double** is used more frequently for variables than for constants. With some compilers, the types **double** and **long double** are identical, but with others they are really different. For example, the values in the following table the following table are very usual:

Type	Number of bytes
float	4
double	8
long double	10

String constants

A *string constant* (also called a *string literal*, or, briefly, a *string*) is a sequence of characters written between double quotes, as, for example, in

```
"How many numbers?"
"a"
```

The string constant **"a"** must not be confused with the character constant **'a'**. As we will see in Chapter 6, a string constant is, technically speaking, an array of characters. Internally, a null character **'\0'** is always stored after the final character written in the string constant. We will see that this null character is essential in detecting the end of the string.

If we want to write a double quote inside a string, it must be preceded by a backslash, so we write **\"**. We can also use other escape sequences, as in

```
cout << "The character\n\\\nis called a \"backslash\".";
```

This statement produces the following output:

```
The character
\
is called a "backslash".
```

Without special measures, we cannot write a string on more than one program line. However, two or more successive string constants, possibly with white-space characters in between, are logically pasted together. For example, writing

```
"ABC"    "DEF""GHI"
"JKL"
```

literally in our program is just another way of writing the following string:

```
"ABCDEFGHIJKL"
```

As we will see later in this book, we normally use indentation when writing our programs, so it may happen that a long string constant, which starts, say, at the middle of a program line, does not fit into that line, especially if we want our program lines to be rather short. Then we can simply use two double quotes in the same way as those between I and J in the above example.

The facility just mentioned was introduced only in ANSI C and C++. In the original version of C there was another method, which is also valid in C++. It consists of writing a backslash at the end of the line that is to be continued, as, for example, in

```
cout << "This is a string that is regarded \
as being on one line.";
```

A drawback of this older method is that we must not indent the second of these two lines: any blanks preceding the word 'as' in this example are inserted between this word and the preceding word 'regarded', in addition to the blank that there is already after the latter word. The newer method is therefore to be preferred. For example, the following two program lines have the same effect as those just shown:

```
cout << "This is a string that is regarded "
        "as being on one line.";
```

1.6 Comment

As we have seen in Section 1.2, comment can have two forms:

```
// ...
/* ... */
```

A comment that begins with // terminates at the end of the line on which it occurs. If, instead, it begins with /*, it ends with the character pair */. The latter type of comment is not restricted to one program line. Within a // comment, the comment characters //, /*, and */ have no special meaning. Similarly, the comment characters // and /* have no special meaning within a /* comment, so comments cannot be nested. If you want the compiler temporarily to skip program fragments in which comments occur, you can enclose that fragment by the line **#if 0** at its beginning and **#endif** at its end, as will be discussed in Section 4.11. These two lines have the same effect as the character pairs /* and */ would have when nested comments had been possible. This method is to be preferred to using a special compiler option (available with some compilers) which enables nested comments. It is always a good idea to use standard language elements rather than special features that have no real advantages.

Comment cannot occur within a string, so the statement

```
cout << "/* ABC */";
```

causes the following to be printed:

```
/* ABC */
```

Exercises

1.1 Write a program that prints your name and address. Compile and run this program on your computer.

1.2 Write a program that prints what will be your age at the end of this year. The program should request you to enter both the current year and your year of birth.

1.3 What numbers do the following bit sequences represent, with two's-complement method and 16-bit word length?

   a. 00000000 00001111.
   b. 11111111 11110000.
   c. A sequence of $16 - k$ zeros followed by k ones ($0 \le k \le 15$).
   d. A sequence of k ones followed by $16 - k$ zeros ($1 \le k \le 16$).

1.4 Use a word length of 16 bits and the two's-complement method to write the following numbers in the binary number system:

   a. 19
   b. −8.

1.5 Use the operator `<<` only once to print the following three lines:

```
One double quote: "
Two double quotes: ""
Backslash: \
```

1.6 Find the errors in the following program, and correct them:

```
include <iostream.h>
int main();
{   int i, j
      i = 'A';
      j = "B";
      i = 'C' + 1;
      cout >> "End of
              program";
      return 0
}
```

1.7 Use a hexadecimal constant to assign the following binary number to a variable i:

01010101 01010101

Print the value of i in the normal way, that is, as a decimal number.

1.8 What does the following statement print?

```
cout << "Single quote: \'\nDouble quote: \"\n"
        "Backslash: \\\nThe End.\n";
```

Expressions and Statements

To discuss the C++ language in an efficient way, we must be familiar with some more technical terms than those discussed in Chapter 1. For example, each of the following three forms is called an *expression*:

```
a + b
1
x = p + q * r
```

It may make sense for an expression, such as the last of these three, to be immediately followed by a semicolon (;). Then the result is no longer an expression but a *statement*. The characters +, *, and =, as used here, are called *operators*. In the first of the above three expressions the variables **a** and **b** are *operands*.

2.1 Arithmetic Operations

As we have seen in Chapter 1, we use the plus and minus operators + and − to add and subtract. In the expression

```
a - b
```

the minus operator has two operands (**a** and **b**). It is therefore called a *binary* operator. The situation is different with the minus sign in

```
(-b + D1)/(2 * a)
```

where we say we have a *unary* minus operator, because this operator has only one operand (**b**). In contrast to the original version of C, ANSI C and C++ also allow us to use + as a unary operator, so we can now write, for example,

```
neg = -epsilon;
pos = +epsilon;
```

which, for reasons of symmetry, looks nicer than without the plus sign.

With the binary operators +, −, and *, the result of the computation is integer if both operands are integer; if at least one of the operands has floating-point type, so has the result. There is no automatic detection of *integer overflow*. For example, suppose we have 16-bit integers with two's-complement representation. Then the largest **int** value that we can use is 32767, so the program fragment

```
int i=1000, j;
j = 100 * i;
```

will give the variable **j** some value in the range −32768, ..., 32767 instead of the expected value 100 000. There will be no error message. (In case you are interested in the value assigned to **j**, you should decrease the mathematically correct value 100 000 by 2^{16} as many times as is needed to obtain a result in the given range, that is, not less than −32768 and not greater than 32767. We therefore have $j = 100\,000 - 2 \times 2^{16} = -31072$.)

Except for integer overflow, the results of +, −, and * will be what anyone would expect. This may not be the case with the division operator /. As with the three previous operators, the result of

```
a / b
```

has integer type if both **a** and **b** have integer type, and floating type if **a** or **b** has floating type. This implies, for example, that

```
39 / 5    is equal to 7,
39. / 5   is equal to 7.8.
```

We see that there are in fact two essentially different division operators, one for integer and one for floating type. It depends on the operand types which one is taken. Beginners often make the mistake of writing, for example, **1/3** (which is equal to 0) instead of **1.0/3.0** with the intended value 0.333.... Instead of **1.0/3.0** you can also write **1.0/3** or **1/3.0**, and in each of these three expressions the zeros may be omitted.

When using integer division, we are sometimes interested not only in the *quotient* (obtained by /), but also in the *remainder*, which we obtain by using the operator %. For example:

`39 % 5`   is equal to 4.

The % operator must not be applied to floating types.

The three operators *, /, % have the same precedence, which is higher than that of + and −. If addition or subtraction should precede multiplication, we must use parentheses:

`(8 - 1) * 2`   is equal to 14,
`8 - 1 * 2`   is equal to 6.

Very often we want to increase a variable by some value. Instead of doing this by means of, for example,

`x = x + a`

we can write the following shorter and more efficient expression:

`x += a`

Once we are used to this new notation, we prefer the latter expression to the former also because it is more closely related to the way we think and speak: we say that we 'increase x by a', not that we 'assign the sum of x and a to x'.

Note that the above two forms are expressions. They would have been statements if they had been followed by a semicolon. Both expressions not only perform an assignment to x, but also yield a value, which is equal to the value assigned to x. For example, this whole line is an assignment statement, while x += a is an assignment expression with the value assigned to x as its value:

`y = 3 * (x += a) + 2;`

In this statement, the value of the expression preceding the semicolon is ignored.

Combining arithmetic operations with assignments is not confined to the addition operator. We can also use the following expressions, the meaning of which is obvious:

`x -= a`
`x *= a`
`x /= a`
`x %= a`

It often occurs that the value 1 is to be added to (or subtracted from) a variable. For these special cases there is an even more compact notation. Instead of, for example,

`i += 1`   and   `i -= 1`

we can write

```
++i   and   --i
```

The unary operators ++ and — are called *increment* and *decrement* operators, respectively. We can also write these operators *after* the operand, as in

```
i++   and   i--
```

Although the variable i is updated in this way as was done before, there is an important difference: the value of the whole expression is now equal to the old value of i. In other words, if we write such an operator before its operand, it is applied before its value is taken; if we write it at the end, it is applied only after its value has been taken. For example, after the execution of the statements

```
i = 0; j = (i++);
m = 0; n = (++m);
```

the four variables used have the same values as they would have if the following statements had been executed instead:

```
i = 1; j = 0;
m = 1; n = 1;
```

The parentheses in the above statements can be omitted. They were used here to illustrate the fact that those surrounding i++ do not cause i to be incremented before its value is taken, as is sometimes thought.

If we use i++ or ++i *only* to increment i, ignoring the values of these expressions, it does not matter which form is used: the statements i++; and ++i; (with semicolons!) are equivalent.

2.2 Types, Variables, and Assignments

In C and C++, the operator =, when used in an expression, indicates *assignment*: we use it to assign a value to a variable. If this variable has been assigned a value previously, that value is lost. Every variable has a fixed *size*, which is the number of bytes it occupies in memory. The size of a variable depends on its *type*. In Borland C++, for example, the elementary types have sizes as listed in the table below.

The types **char**, **short**, **int**, and **long** may be preceded by the keyword **unsigned**. Writing only **unsigned** is equivalent to writing **unsigned int**. We will discuss the keyword **unsigned** in more detail in Section 3.3.

Type	Size
char	1
short (or **short int**)	2
int	2
enum	2
long (or **long int**)	4
float	4
double	8
long double	10

We can inquire the size of a type by using **sizeof**. This is a unary operator, which can be applied either to a type name (written between parentheses) or to an expression. It is a good idea to use parentheses anyway, so that we need not bother about which case applies.

The following program shows how **sizeof** can be used, and many other things besides:

```
// TYPES: Types, variables, and assignments.

#include <stdio.h>

int main()
{   char ch = 'A';
    ch++;              // See Section 2.1 for ++
    float f = 5.0/3;
    double ff = 5.0/3;
    int i, j;
    j = 2 * (i = 5.0/3);           // i = 1
    printf("ch = %c    ASCII value: %d\n\n", ch, ch);
    printf("f = %20.17f    ff = %20.17f\n", f, ff);
    printf("i = %20d    j = %20d\n\n", i, j);
    printf("Type 'double' takes %d bytes.\n",
            sizeof(double));
    printf("Type 'long double' takes %d bytes.\n",
            sizeof(long double));
    return 0;
}
```

Although this is not a practical program, it demonstrates some important new points, including the use of the C library function **printf**, which we will discuss in a moment. First the five variables **ch, f, ff, i,** and **j** are declared. The variable **ch** is first given the value **'A'**, with value 65, and is then increased by 1, so its final value will be **'B'**, or 66. We want the value of **ch** to be printed both as **'B'** and as 66. Therefore **ch** occurs twice in the **printf** statement, with corresponding conversion specifications %c and %d, to be discussed shortly. It seems that the three variables **f, ff,** and **i** are assigned the same value, namely **5.0/3**. Yet these variables assume different values: because of their types the exact value of 5.0/3 is approximated reasonably by **f**, very well by **ff**, and very badly by **i**. This program also demonstrates that an *assignment expression*, such as **i = 5.0/3**, may occur in a more complicated expression. Since **i** has type **int**, the computed value 1.66... is truncated to the integer 1. With Borland C++, the output of this program is as follows:

```
ch = B   ASCII value: 66

f =   1.66666662693023682   ff =   1.66666666666666674
i =                     1   j  =                     2

Type 'double' takes 8 bytes.
Type 'long double' takes 10 bytes.
```

The C library functions printf and scanf; field width and precision

C++ programmers have access to the subroutine libraries of C. In C and C++, subroutines are called *functions*. We will discuss functions in detail in Chapter 4, but in the meantime we will already use some well-known standard functions, available in C standard libraries. Instead of the form **cout << ...**, we can use the function **printf** of the C library for 'standard input and output' (or *standard I/O*, for short). The header file to be used is *stdio.h* instead of *iostream.h*. The first argument of **printf** is a *format string*, which can contain both text to be printed literally and *conversion specifications*. Some simple conversion specifications are **%d** for decimal integers, **%c** for characters, **%f** for floating-point types, and **%s** for character strings. For each conversion specification, there is a corresponding argument that follows the format string. For example, if we want the **int** value **i** and the **char** value **ch** to be preceded by the text **Results:** and to be followed by the newline character **\n**, we can write

```
printf("Results: %d %c\n", i, ch);
```

Let us now revert to our program TYPES. We want the value of **ch** to be printed both as **'B'** and as 66. Therefore **ch** occurs twice in the **printf** statement, with corresponding conversion specifications **%c** and **%d**. The values of **f**, **ff**, **i**, and **j** in this program are printed in 20 positions, and the fractional parts of **f** and **ff** consist of 17 decimal digits. This is done by using **%20.17f** and **%20d** instead of simply **%f** and **%d**. In the following general forms, *m* and *k* are called the *field width* and the *precision*, respectively. They can only be integer constants, not variables:

%*m . k*f   Converts a value of type **float** (or **double**) to *m* decimal positions, with *k* digits after the period.

%*m*d   Converts an **int** value to *m* decimal positions.

If the field width *m* is larger than is needed, blank space is added at the left; if it is too small, as many positions are used as are needed.

Now that we have seen how to use **printf**, we may as well briefly discuss the corresponding input function **scanf**. Again, we use it in combination with the header file *stdio.h*. Suppose we want to read the integer **i**, the **float** value **f** and the **double** value **ff**. This can be done as follows:

```
#include <stdio.h>
...
scanf("%d %f %lf", &i, &f, &ff);
```

The ampersand character **&**, used three times here, is essential. It takes the address of the variable that follows, and it is addresses that **scanf** expects. Another thing **scanf** is very particular about is the letter **l** in %lf when the corresponding argument (**&ff**) is the address of a variable of type **double**. Finally, it is not wise to include additional text in **scanf** format strings, nor should we use extended conversion specifications such as %20.17f. If we do, that text and this field width (20) and precision (17) is required in the input data. Incidentally, the new, typical C++ facilities for input are to be recommended in this case; we would have

```
#include <iostream.h>
...
cin >> i >> f >> ff;
```

As for output, the easiest way of specifying a field width and a precision with stream I/O is by using the so-called *manipulators* **setw** and **setprecision**, for which the header file *iomanip.h* is necessary. For example, instead of

```
#include <stdio.h>
...
printf("%20.17f", x);
```

we can write

```
#include <iostream.h>
#include <iomanip.h>
...
cout << setw(20) << setprecision(17) << x;
```

Stream I/O vs. standard I/O

You may wonder what is the good of discussing both *stream I/O* (with *iostream.h*, **cin** and **cout**) and *standard I/O* (with *stdio.h*, **scanf** and **printf**). A book on C++ would be very incomplete if the typical C++ stream I/O facilities were omitted. These facilities are very elegant in that they are not restricted to standard types, such as **int, float** and so on, but can also be made applicable to user-defined types, as we will see in Section

7.9 and in Chapter 9. They are also 'safe' and therefore easy to use for beginners. The difference between stream I/O and standard I/O in this regard is illustrated by the above examples, in which values for **i**, **f**, and **ff** were read in. With **scanf**, any error made in the format string leads to very unpleasant results during execution time, while there are no such problems with stream I/O.

Standard I/O is also discussed in this book because it has the advantage of being standardized by ANSI. When using functions such as **printf**, we need not worry about compatibility problems with any present or future compilers. As for C++ stream I/O, it may be some years before all C++ compilers deal with these I/O facilities in exactly the same way. Especially when we are dealing with files (as discussed in Chapters 8 and 9), portability problems are more likely to occur with stream I/O than with standard I/O. It is very unlikely for this argument to remain valid in the long term, so hopefully we will gradually move from the old standard I/O to the new and more elegant stream I/O.

Enumeration types

The keyword **enum**, which occurs in the table of types at the beginning of this section, is normally used when we need some constants with names that say what they mean and with values that are irrelevant. For example, we can write

```
enum days
{  Sunday, Monday, Tuesday, Wednesday, Thursday,
   Friday, Saturday
}  yesterday, today, tomorrow;
```

After this declaration, we can use

-   The *enumeration type* **days**. We can declare some more variables with it, as, for example, in:

    ```
    days the_day_after_tomorrow, my_birthday;
    ```

-   The symbolic integer constants **Sunday, Monday, ..., Saturday**, which have the values 0, 1, ..., 6, respectively; these are the values of type **days**.

-   The variables **yesterday, today,** and **tomorrow**, which can be assigned values of type **days**.

Enumeration-type values can be converted to type **int**: such values can be assigned to **int** variables. By contrast, it is not correct to assign an **int** value to an enumeration-type variable. Each enumeration type is a unique type; we cannot convert one enumeration type to another. The comments in the following fragment, based on the above type **days**, illustrates all this:

```
int i;
enum color {black, white, red} pen = red;
i = yesterday;  // O.K.: conversion from days to int.
today = i + 1;  // Error: no conversion from int to days.
today = pen;    // Error: no conversion from color to days.
```

We can also specify numerical values ourselves for enumeration constants. The following example demonstrates this. It also shows that the declaration of variables (**great, greater, greatest**) can be separated from the declaration that specifies the enumeration type (**mathematician**) itself:

```
enum mathematician    // Numerical value = Year of birth
{ Cauchy=1789,
  Euler=1707,
  Fourier=1768,
  Gauss=1777,
  Hesse=1811,
  Hilbert=1862,
  Kronecker=1823,
  Laplace=1749
};
mathematician great, greater, greatest;
```

If we specify a value for a constant, and none for some that follow, that value is repeatedly incremented for these constants that follow. For example, after

```
enum example {aaa, bbb, ccc=48, ddd, eee, fff=1, ggg};
```

we have

```
aaa = 0, bbb = 1, ccc = 48, ddd = 49, eee = 50,
fff= 1, ggg = 2
```

This example also shows that two constants of an enumeration type may have the same value, as is the case here with **bbb** and **fff**. However, all constant names must be distinct, even if they belong to different enumeration types, for it would otherwise not be possible to tell the value and the type of a given constant name.

As we will see in the next section, the C++ has no built-in *logical* or *Boolean* type. However, we can easily define such a type ourselves, writing, for example

```
enum Boolean {FALSE, TRUE};
```

After this declaration, we can write **FALSE** instead of **0** and **TRUE** instead of **1**, and we can declare variables of type **Boolean**.

A *tag*, written in the previous examples between the keyword **enum** and {, is optional. In our last example, we might as well write

```
enum {FALSE, TRUE};
```

if we only want to use the constants **FALSE** and **TRUE**. The enumeration type defined in this way has no name, so we cannot refer to it later to declare variables.

Register variables

As mentioned in Section 1.2, computers usually have some *registers* and can work faster with registers than with memory locations. It may therefore be advantageous for some variables, which are used very frequently, to be kept only in registers, not in memory. We can ask the compiler to do this by using the keyword **register** when we declare the variables in question, as, for example, in

```
register int i;
```

The compiler will then use a register instead of a memory word for **i**, if this is possible. If not, the keyword **register** is ignored. You may wonder why not always use this keyword. The first reason is that the number of registers is normally very small, and they are also used for all kinds of other work, which we do not want to be slowed down because of too few free registers being available. Second, only memory locations have addresses, registers have not. Therefore the 'address of' operator **&** must not be used for register variables. This implies that after the above declaration of **i** the call **scanf("%d", &i)** is illegal. Incidentally, there are compilers that try to keep variables in registers anyway, so when we omit the **register** keyword, the generated code may still be very efficient.

The const and volatile keywords

We can use the *type qualifier* **const** to define constants. (If we use **const** in ANSI C, the objects defined in this way are technically still variables and must therefore not be used in certain contexts, known as *constant expressions*. This is different in C++: here the defined objects are really constants, not variables.) Here is an example of how we can use the keyword **const**:

```
const int weeklength=7;
```

On this line, **=7** denotes *initialization*, not assignment. It must not be omitted here. We cannot assign values to constants, so

```
weeklength = 7; // Error
```

would not be a valid assignment statement. For constants such as **weeklength**, initialization is therefore required. At the end of Section 5.5, we will see that we can use **const** also when specifying formal parameters of functions.

Another new keyword is **volatile**. It is used syntactically in the same way as **const**, but, in a sense, it has the opposite meaning. In principle, it is possible for **volatile** variables to be changed not only by ourselves but also by hardware or by system software. Another point is that **volatile** variables are not kept in registers, as may be the case with normal variables.

2.3 Comparison and Logical Operators

When programming decisions and repetitions, we often need the following operators:

Operator	Meaning	
<	<	(less than)
>	>	(greater than)
<=	≤	(less than or equal to)
>=	≥	(greater than or equal to)
==	=	(equal to)
!=	≠	(not equal to)
&&	AND	(logical *and*)
||	OR	(logical *or*)
!	NOT	(logical *not*)

The operators <, >, <=, >= are known as *relational* operators, while == and != are called *equality operators*. The former have higher precedence than the latter. We may collectively use the term *comparison operators* for these two operator classes. A comparison, such as **a < b**, is an expression with two possible values, which we would intuitively identify with *true* and *false*. In C++ the integers 1 and 0 are used for this purpose:

    1   means *true*,
    0   means *false*.

Comparisons (and logical expressions in general) have type **int**: there is no such thing as a 'Boolean' or 'logical' type in C++, as there is in some other languages. As a result of this,

    (3 < 4) + (7 < 9)

is a valid integer expression, and its value is 2. A very funny example is

```
5 < 4 < 3
```

This is interpreted as

```
(5 < 4) < 3
```

or as

```
0 < 3
```

so that its value is 1.

The unary operator ! is normally used to turn *true* into *false*, and vice versa. For example, the values of the following two expressions are equal for any **x** and **y**:

```
x < y
! (x >= y)
```

We can express the effect of ! more technically as follows. The value of !i is 1 if **i** is equal to 0, and it is 0 if **i** is unequal to 0. Not only 1 but any nonzero value can be used as *true*. For example, the value 2 (like 1) denotes *true*, so !2 should denote *false* and is therefore equal to 0. Note that we can write

```
i = !!i;
```

if we (only) want to overwrite any nonzero value of **i** with 1.

We can combine comparisons (and other logical expressions) by using the logical operators && and | |, as is done, for example, in the test

```
x > a  &&  x < b
```

to check that **x** lies between **a** and **b**. (The example 5 < 4 < 3 above shows why we cannot write **a** < **x** < **b** here.) With the two forms

*operand*1 && *operand*2
*operand*1 | | *operand*2

it is guaranteed that the *operand*2 will not be evaluated if the value of the result is already known after the evaluation of *operand*1. After all, for any value of *operand*2,

0 && *operand*2   is equal to 0, and
1 | | *operand*2   is equal to 1.

This behavior of && and | | is important, not only because (with complicated *operand*2) it may save computing time, but also because it may prevent undesirable actions, such as division by zero. For example, in the following expressions the division by **n** will not take place if **n** happens to be zero:

```
n != 0  &&  q < 1.0/n
!(n == 0  ||  q >= 1.0/n)
```

(Note that these two expressions are equivalent!)

Beginning C++ programmers often make the mistake of writing one equal sign instead of two. Doing this in the last example would *cause* dividing by zero instead of preventing it! Remember that **n = 0** is an expression, which, after assigning 0 to **n**, also yields a value. As this value, 0, means *false*, the second operator in

```
n = 0  ||  q >= 1.0/n
```

will be evaluated, which will cause a division by zero.

If you are familiar with Pascal, the following table may be useful:

C++-*operator*	*Pascal notation*
=	:=
==	=
!=	<>

2.4 Compound and Conditional Statements

Compound statements

It will by now be clear that *statements* describe actions. In contrast to expressions, they do not yield values. Many statements, such as those below, consist of an expression followed by a semicolon:

```
cin >> n;
x = a + b;
cout << "The End.\n";
```

We can use *braces* { } to build complex statements from simpler ones, just as we can use parentheses ( ) to build complex expressions. For example, the line

```
{x = a + b; y = c + d; z = e + f;}
```

contains a *compound statement*, built from three simpler statements. We often use compound statements in syntactic positions that allow only one statement, but in which we want to write more than one. We will apply this idea shortly.

Compound statements are also called *blocks*, especially if we declare variables in them. A declaration in a block is valid from this declaration until the closing brace of that block. This portion of the program is called the *scope* of the variables declared by that declaration. Variables are said to be *visible* in their scope, except for any other scopes in enclosed blocks in which other variables with the same names are declared, as the following program illustrates:

```
// SCOPE: Illustration of 'scope' and 'visibility'.
#include <iostream.h>

int main()
{  float x = 3.4;
   {  cout << "x = " << x << endl;
      // Output: x = 3.4 (because float x is visible).
      int x = 7;
      {  cout << "x = " << x << endl;
         // Output: x = 7 (because int x is visible).
         // float x still in scope but hidden.
         char x = 'A';
         cout << "x = " << x << endl;
         // Output: x = A (because char x is visible).
         // float x and int x still in scope but hidden.
      }
      cout << "x = " << x << endl;
      // Output: x = 7 (because int x is visible).
      // float x still in scope but hidden.
      // char x out of scope.
   }
   cout << "x = " << x << endl;
   // Output: x = 3.4 (because float x is visible).
   // int x and char x out of scope.
   return 0;
}
```

Note that a variable declared in an outer block can be hidden in an inner block only if its name is the same as that of another variable. For example, if we had declared **float y=3.4** instead of **float x=3.4**, variable y would have been visible in the inner blocks. The output of program SCOPE is:

```
x = 3.4
x = 7
x = A
x = 7
x = 3.4
```

Conditional statements

We often want the execution of a statement to depend on a condition. In C++ we use the term *expression* rather than *condition*, and we want the given statement to be executed if that expression is nonzero. This is achieved by a *conditional statement* (also called *if-statement*) of the following form:

if (*expression*) *statement*1

We can also use this extended form of the conditional statement:

if (*expression*) *statement*1 **else** *statement*2

Figures 2.1(a) and (b) show how these conditional statements work.

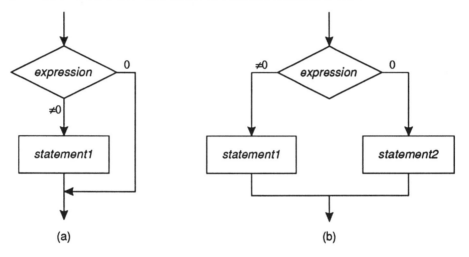

(a)   (b)

*Figure 2.1. Conditional statements: (a) without **else**; (b) with **else***

If *expression* has a nonzero value (which means *true*), *statement*1 is executed and *statement*2, if present, is ignored. In the opposite case, with *expression* equal to 0, *statement*1 is ignored and *statement*2, if present, is executed. The following examples should be studied carefully.

Example 1

In this example, *statement*1 is a compound statement and there is no *statement*2. It swaps the values of **a** and **b** if **a** is greater than **b**:

```
if (a > b)
{   w = a;
    a = b;
    b = w;
}               // Now a <= b
```

Example 2

The statements in a conditional statement can again be conditional statements, as is the case here with *statement2*:

```
if (x > 0) cout << "Positive"; else
if (x < 0) cout << "Negative"; else cout << "Zero";
```

A pair of (superfluous) braces clarifies this example:

```
if (x > 0) cout << "Positive"; else
{ if (x < 0) cout << "Negative"; else cout << "Zero";
}
```

Example 3

We can also take a conditional statement for *statement1*, as in

```
if (x <= 0)
   if (x < 0) cout << "Negative"; else cout << "Zero";
```

In this example we have two **if** keywords, and at first sight it may not be clear to which of these the **else** keyword belongs. This ambiguity is resolved by the rule that, in case of doubt, the **else** belongs to the most recent **if**. Therefore the above line should be read as

```
if (x <= 0)
{ if (x < 0) cout << "Negative"); else cout << "Zero";
}
```

not as

```
if (x <= 0)
{ if (x < 0) cout << "Negative";
} else cout << "Zero";
```

Note that the only essential difference between the last two versions consists of the position of the closing brace }. The difference in layout, however important it may be for us humans, is ignored by the compiler.

Example 4

This example shows that even in complicated situations we can make a program readable by paying attention to the layout and, in particular, to the way indentation is used:

```
if (a >= b)
{   x = 0;
    if (a >= b+1)
    {   xx = 0;
        yy = -1;
    } else
    {   xx = 100;
        yy = 200;
    }
} else
{   x = 1;
    xx = -100;
    yy = 0;
}
```

The indentation method used in this book, with each brace pair in the same column, is based on the way Algol programs were written as early as 1960 (with **begin** and **end** instead of { and }). This style is also frequently applied to Pascal programs, which are generally regarded as very readable.

Example 5

When developing large programs, we normally want to see a good many statements on one screen of, say, 25 lines, or on one printed page. It may therefore be good practice to write a rather short conditional statement on one line, as is done in:

```
if (a < b) {w = a; a = b; b = w;}
```

This form is as readable as the equivalent form in Example 1, which was written on five lines. Let us use this example for a brief discussion about where to insert semicolons. If you are familiar with Pascal, you will know that in that language statements are separated by semicolons. The **end** keyword of a Pascal compound statement is therefore followed by a semicolon if another statement follows, and it need not be preceded by a semicolon. In C++, a semicolon at the end of a statement is part of that statement. Not every statement ends with a semicolon: its final character may also be a closing brace (}). This explains why a closing brace of a statement is never followed by a semicolon but may be preceded by one.

Example 6

```
if (i) i = 1;
```

Not only 1, but any nonzero value means *true*. This if-statement is therefore equivalent to the following one, which is slightly less efficient:

```
if (i != 0) i = 1;
```

In both cases i is assigned the value 1, unless it is equal to 0, in which case its value is not altered. As we have seen in Section 2.3, there is an essentially different way of obtaining the same effect:

```
i = !!i;
```

The null statement

If somewhere a statement is required but we feel no need to write one, it is permissible to write only a semicolon, which is then called a *null statement*. For example, the first semicolon in the following conditional statement represents a null statement:

```
if (a < b) ; else x = 123;
```

We must not omit this semicolon, because the keyword **else** must be preceded by a statement. It goes without saying that the following conditional statement has the same effect as the previous one but is much clearer:

```
if (a >= b) x = 123;
```

A more interesting application of the null statement follows in the next section.

2.5 Iteration Statements

There are three types of *iteration statements*, also called *repetition statements*, or, more briefly, *loops*:

while-statement:
> **while** (*expression*) *statement*

do-statement:
> **do** *statement* **while** (*expression*);

for-statement:
> **for** (*statement1   expression2; expression3*) *statement2*

To see how they work, let us use all three of them for the same purpose, namely to compute the sum

$$s = 1 + 2 + ... + n$$

without using the equality $s = \frac{1}{2} n(n + 1)$. Supposing that **s**, **n**, and **i** have been declared as integer variables, we can compute **s** as follows:

With a *while-statement*:

```
s = 0; i = 1;
while (i <= n)
{  s += i;  i++;
}
```

With a *do-statement* (to be used here only if **n** > 0):

```
s = 0; i = 1;
do
{  s += i;
   i++;
}  while (i <= n);
```

With a *for-statement*:

```
s = 0;
for (i=1; i<=n; i++) s += i;
```

Figure 2.2(a) illustrates both the first and the third solutions (with **while** and **for**, respectively), while Figure 2.2(b) shows how the second solution (with **do ... while**) works.

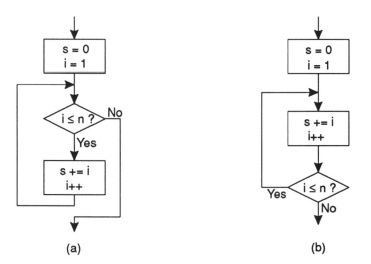

Figure 2.2. Loops: (a) while-statement and for-statement; (b) do-statement

In all three solutions, the process of repeatedly increasing both **s** by **i** and **i** by 1 continues as long as the test **i <= n** succeeds. In the while-statement this test is done at the beginning of the loop, before **s** is increased. This is an important point, because **n** may be 0 (or negative). In that case the eventual value of **s** will be equal to 0.

In the do-statement, on the other hand, that test takes place after the inner part of the loop has been executed. The first time, **s** is increased by **i** regardless of the value of **n**. So if **n** is zero, **s** will be equal to 1, which is undesirable. We should therefore use the do-statement (also called *do-while-loop*) only if we know **n** to be positive. The inner part of a do-while-loop is always executed at least once, but the inner part of a while-statement may not be executed at all.

The given solution with the *for*-statement works exactly like that with the while-statement. We can describe the effect of

for (*statement*1   *expression*2; *expression*3) *statement*2

by means of the following, equivalent form with **while**:

```
statement1
while (expression2)
{   statement2
    expression3;
}
```

(Actually there is an exception to this equivalence, as we will see when discussing the continue-statement in the next section.) It may look strange that we should write *statement*1, instead of *expression*1 followed by a semicolon. We do this because it enables us to use an initialized declaration, such as **int i = 0;**, which in C++, as we know, is a statement. (Note that **int i = 0** is not an expression.) Remember, **for(** is not the beginning of a new scope, so it may be followed by **int i=0;** only if there is no other identifier **i** in scope. The scope of **i** declared in the for-statement terminates at the closing brace (}) of the smallest surrounding compound statement. Consequently, the following is incorrect:

```
for (int i=0; i<n; i++) s += i;
for (int i=0; i<m; i++) t += i*i;   // Error
```

On the second line, the **i** of the first line is still in scope, so another variable **i** cannot be declared here.

As we have seen in the previous section, a statement may consist of only a semicolon, which we then call a null statement. This also applies to *statement*1 in the for-statement. It is less obvious that we may omit *expression*2 and *expression*3. If we do, the semicolon must be present. For example, *statement*1 is the null statement and *expression*3 is omitted in

```
a = b = 1; x = 0;
for ( ; x < 1000; ) x += (a += b++);
```

We can replace the second of these two lines with the following, equivalent while-statement:

```
while (x < 1000) x += (a += b++);
```

(As we will see in Section 3.5, the parentheses surrounding **a += b++** are superfluous in these fragments.) In the above for-statement, *statement*1 and *expression*3 are omitted, while **x < 1000** is used for *expression*2. There would be an endless loop if we also omitted *expression*2. With the break-statement, to be discussed in the next section, it will be possible to write a for-statement that terminates normally even though *expression*2 is omitted.

It is by no means necessary for a for-statement to use a 'running variable' which is initialized by *statement*1, tested in *expression*2, and updated in *expression*3, as is **i** in the following (frequently occurring) form:

```
for (i=1; i<=n; i++) ...
```

For example, we might replace our last example of a for-statement with the following, possibly confusing but equivalent fragment:

```
b = 1; x = 0;
for (a = 1; x < 1000; b++) x += (a += b);
```

Let us now turn to a complete program. It will produce a table with two columns x and $f(x)$, where

$$f(x) = x^2 + x + 1/x$$

We want x to run from 2.0 to 4.0, with step 0.2. The following program, TABLE, is based on I/O facilities that are also available in C. An equivalent version, using *iostream.h* instead of *stdio.h*, will be discussed in Section 9.2. The way function **printf** is used here was already demonstrated in Section 2.2, but this program shows more clearly that specifying detailed formatting information can be essential:

```
// TABLE: This program produces a table by means of printf.

#include <stdio.h>

int main()
{ printf(" x          f(x)\n\n");
  for (int i=20; i<=40; i+=2)
  { double x = i/10.0;
    printf("%3.1f %15.10f\n", x, x*x + x + 1/x);
  }
  return 0;
}
```

Note the use of the conversion specifications **%3.1f** and **%15.10f**, each with a field width and a precision, as discussed in Section 2.2. They are particularly useful in programs that produce tables: with so many numbers in the output, it is very important that we can specify exactly how they are to be printed. The output of this program is as follows:

```
  x          f(x)

 2.0     6.5000000000
 2.2     7.4945454545
 2.4     8.5766666667
 2.6     9.7446153846
 2.8    10.9971428571
 3.0    12.3333333333
 3.2    13.7525000000
 3.4    15.2541176471
 3.6    16.8377777778
 3.8    18.5031578947
 4.0    20.2500000000
```

The C++ language does not require the 'running variable' in a for-statement to have integer type, so it seems more natural to use a floating-point variable instead of the **int** variable **i** for this purpose, as is done in

```
#include <stdio.h>

int main()
{  printf("  x          f(x)\n\n");
   for (double x = 2.0; x <= 4.0; x += 0.2)
      printf("%3.1f %15.10f\n", x, x*x+x+1/x);
   return 0;
}
```

However, this version is not correct. Floating-point values are only approximated: the values actually stored in memory may slightly differ from the theoretically correct values. In this example, this may not really affect the final digits in the above table, but yet there may be something wrong. The condition **x <= 4.0** in the for-statement says that this statement is to terminate as soon as x is greater than 4. Now the problem here with the floating-point variable x is that this variable may be slightly greater than 4 at the moment that it should be exactly equal to 4. If this happens, the last line of the above table is omitted. In our original program, TABLE, there is no such problem, because rounding errors do not apply to the integer running variable **i**. It is true that the problem in the last program can easily be remedied by writing, for example, **4.1** instead of **4.0** in the for-loop, but it is wise always to use integer running variables. In this way we avoid *cumulating* rounding errors. This example shows that besides knowledge of the C++ language itself we should also have some idea about how numbers are stored inside the computer.

2.6 Break, Continue, Goto, Switch

The break-statement

The execution of a loop terminates immediately if in its inner part the following statement is executed:

```
break;
```

If this *break-statement* occurs inside some nested loops, only the innermost enclosing loop is terminated. Here is a program which demonstrates this statement:

```cpp
// BREAK: Demonstration of the break-statement.
#include <iostream.h>

int main()
{   double s=0, x;
    cout << "Enter numbers, separated by blanks.\n";
    cout <<
    "They are added up as long as they are positive.\n\n";
    for ( ; ; )
    {   cin >> x;
        if (x <= 0) break;
        s += x;
    }
    cout << "Sum of the positive numbers that have "
            "been read: " << s << endl;
    return 0;
}
```

The interesting point about this program is that the test for loop termination is placed neither at the beginning nor at the end but in the middle of the loop. This is a very natural thing to do: we can test a number only after reading it, so inside the loop reading x should precede the test. On the other hand, if the loop is not terminated, s is to be increased by x, so it is logical to write s += x; after the test. In Section 3.2 we will discuss loops with the test in the middle once again. Instead of

```
for ( ; ; )
```

we might have written

```
while(1)
```

But for the break-statement, we would have endless loops in both cases.

The continue-statement

The *continue-statement* looks similar to the break-statement, but it works essentially differently. We write it (inside a loop) as

```
continue;
```

Normally the continue-statement is executed conditionally, as in

```
while (...)
{   xxx
    if (condition) continue;
    yyy
}
```

where ..., *xxx*, *yyy* stand for valid program text. The meaning of this loop is given by the following, equivalent form:

```
while (...)
{   xxx
    if (!(condition))
    {   yyy
    }
}
```

The continue-statement causes an immediate jump to the test for continuation of the (smallest enclosing) loop. Note that in the former fragment we have only one brace pair, whereas there are two in the latter. This shows that continue-statements can reduce the number of nested compound statements.

With **continue** in the for-statement, the 'running variable is updated' before the test for continuation is performed. More precisely, we can replace the form

```
for (statement1 expression2; expression3)
{   xxx
    if (condition) continue;
    yyy
}
```

with the following while-construction, which is equivalent to it. Note that *expression3* is evaluated even if the *yyy* fragment is skipped:

```
    statement1
    while (expression2)
    {   xxx
        if (!(condition))
        {   yyy
        }
        expression3;
    }
```

The goto-statement

As we have seen, continue-statements can sometimes be used to reduce the number of
nested compound statements: with many nested brace pairs it is not always easy to see
which closing brace belongs to a given opening brace, especially if (in large programs)
they are very far apart. However, in most cases it is the other way round: properly
indented nested compound statements make a program considerably more readable
than programs written in the style of 'unstructured' languages, such as assembly
languages, where 'jump' or 'branch' instructions are frequently used. C++ programmers
can use something similar, namely the *goto-statement*. Its use is not recommended.

Let us consider two programs, EVEN1 and EVEN2, one without and one with
goto-statements. They solve the same problem: integers are to be read from the
keyboard, and the sum of those which are even is to be computed. Odd integers are
ignored; the integer −1 signals the end of the input data. These two programs are
equivalent, but the style of EVEN2 is old-fashioned. Its readability is not as good as
that of EVEN1, because we cannot immediately see its loop structure. Program EVEN2
may not be a striking example, because it is very short and simple. Generally,
programs with goto-statements become far less readable if they grow larger and more
complicated. Curiously enough, the trouble with the goto-statement is that we can do
too much with it: we can use it to jump to positions where we should not jump to. The
higher-level control constructs for loops and conditional execution are more restricted
and therefore safer.

```
    // EVEN1: Solution without goto-statements.
    #include <iostream.h>
    int main()
    {   int x, s=0;
        cout << "Enter positive integers, followed by -1:\n";
        for ( ; ; )
        {   cin >> x;                   // Read x.
            if (x == -1) break;         // Exit if x is -1.
            if (x % 2 == 0) s += x;     // Use x only if it is even.
        }
        cout << "Sum of even integers: " << s << endl;
        return 0;
    }
```

```
// EVEN2: Solution with goto-statements.
#include <iostream.h>
int main()
{   int x, s=0;
    cout << "Enter positive integers, followed by -1:\n";
l1: cin >> x;                          // Read x.
    if (x == -1) goto l2;              // Exit if x is -1.
    if (x % 2 == 0) s += x;            // Use x only if it is even.
    goto l1;                           // Back to start of loop.
l2: cout << "Sum of even integers: " << s << endl;
    return 0;
}
```

The switch-statement

The *switch-statement* can be regarded as a (very restricted and therefore innocent) kind of goto-statement. The place we jump to depends on the value of an integer expression. Its general form is

switch (*expression*) *statement*

with one or more so-called *case-labels* in the statement. The *expression* must be of type **int** or of a related type, such as **char** or an enumeration type, which is then converted to **int**; floating-point types are not allowed.

In the following example, the variable y is increased by 1 if x is equal to one of the integers that occur in the case-labels, and left unchanged otherwise:

```
switch (x) case 100: case 150: case 170: case 195: y++;
```

The switch-statement is more often used in a somewhat different way, as the following example demonstrates. It shows another application of the break-statement, which may be used not only in loops but also in switch-statements:

```
switch (letter)
{ case 'N': case 'n': cout << "New York\n"; break;
  case 'L': case 'l': cout << "London\n"; break;
  case 'A': case 'a': cout << "Amsterdam\n"; break;
  default: cout << "Somewhere else\n"; break;
}
```

For example, let us assume **letter** to be equal to **'L'** (or **'l'**). Then a jump to the statement that prints **London** takes place. The break-statement that follows causes immediate exit from the switch-statement. Without it, **Amsterdam** would also have been printed. If **letter** is not equal to one of the letters in the case-labels, a jump to the default-label takes place, so that **Somewhere else** is printed. If the line starting with **default** had been omitted, nothing would have been printed in that case. Only one default-label is allowed. The values in the case-labels must be constant expressions of type **int** (or of some related type) and they must all be different. Note that the colon after case-labels may be followed by any number of statements, which need not be enclosed in braces. Beginning C++ programmers who use switch-statements often forget to insert break-statements, and are then surprised that the computer does more than they expect.

Exercises

2.1 Write a program to read a sequence of positive integers and to print the greatest of these. Use a negative integer to signal the end of the input data.

2.2 Write a program that reads a sequence of positive real numbers and computes their average. A negative number signals the end of the input data.

2.3 Write a program that reads an integer (into a variable of type **int**) and computes the sum of its final two decimal digits.

2.4 Write a program that reads 20 integers and counts how often a larger integer is immediately followed by a smaller one.

2.5 Write a program to read 10 integers and to find the second smallest of them.

2.6 Write a program that reads a decimal digit d and prints a table with two columns: one for positive integers x, less than 100, and one for their squares x^2. Only those lines in which the digit d occurs both in x and in x^2 are to be printed. For example, if d is equal to 2, the table will contain the line

     82   6724

since $82^2 = 6724$ and 2 occurs both in 82 and in 6724.

2.7 With a positive integer s read from the keyboard, find all sequences of two or more consecutive integers whose sum is equal to s. For example, if s is 15, there are exactly three solutions:

     1   2   3   4   5
     4   5   6
     7   8

2.8 Write a program that reads the (small) positive integers n and k, and uses these to print a board of $n \times n$ squares, similar to a chessboard. The white squares are blank and the black ones consist of $k \times k$ asterisks (*). As with a chessboard, there must be a black square in the lower-left corner.

3

More Operators

3.1 Conditional Expressions

Besides the conditional *statement* (beginning with **if**) there is also the *conditional expression*, in which the two characters **?** and **:** are used instead of the keywords **if** and **else**. It has the following form:

*expression*1 **?** *expression*2 **:** *expression*3

Actually, these three expressions are subject to certain restrictions, to be discussed at the end of Section 3.6. To determine the value of the conditional expression, *expression*1 is evaluated first. Its purpose is similar to that of the parenthesized expression after **if** in a conditional statement. If its value is nonzero, *expression*2, and otherwise *expression*3, is evaluated. In other words, on the basis of *expression*1 a choice is made between *expression*2 and *expression*3, and the value of the chosen expression is taken as the value of the whole conditional expression. The conditional statement and the conditional expression are different not only in their appearance but also in the way they are used, that is, they are used in different contexts. A conditional expression, possibly surrounded by parentheses, can occur in any expression; a conditional statement cannot. Here is an example in which a conditional expression is used in this way:

```
z = 3 * (a < b ? a + 1 : b - 1) + 2;
```

With a conditional statement we would have to write

```
if (a < b) z = 3 * (a + 1) + 2; else z = 3 * (b - 1) + 2;
```

or, using the temporary variable **t**,

```
if (a < b) t = a + 1; else t = b - 1;
z = 3 * t + 2;
```

The form with the conditional expression is more efficient than these two program fragments with conditional statements. Conditional expressions are also useful as arguments of functions. We will not discuss functions in more detail until Chapter 4, but we already know some standard functions, such as **printf**. We can, for example, write

```
printf("The greater of a and b is %d", a > b ? a : b);
```

Again, an equivalent program fragment without a conditional expression is longer and less efficient:

```
printf("The greater of a and b is ");
if (a > b) printf("%d", a); else printf("%d", b);
```

Besides, the former solution corresponds more closely to the way we think and speak, since we normally say: 'we print the greater of *a* and *b*', using the word *print* only once. We therefore also prefer using the name **printf** only once for this purpose in our program.

With the typical C++ stream I/O, we can write the short form

```
cout << "The greater of a and b is " << (a > b ? a : b);
```

instead of

```
cout << "The greater of a and b is ";
if (a > b) cout << a; else cout << b;
```

As we will see in Section 3.6, the parentheses enclosing the conditional expression are necessary in this example. Here is a third example of using a conditional expression:

```
printf(u == v ? "Equal" : "Unequal");
```

Although the first argument of **printf** must be a string, it need not be a string *constant*, but it may be any expression the value of which is a string. (In Section 5.4 we will see that something more can be said about this subject.)

Now that we have seen so many cases in which a conditional expression is to be preferred to a conditional statement, you may wonder if there are also cases in which we need or prefer the latter. This is indeed the case. First, we should bear in mind that in a conditional statement the 'else part' may be absent, whereas in a conditional expression there must always be a colon, followed by an expression. For example, the effect of the conditional statement

```
if (a < b) c = 0;
```

cannot be obtained with a conditional expression, unless we write something that is
both contrived and inefficient, such as

```
c = (a < b ? 0 : c);
```

or

```
a < b ? (c = 0) : 0;
```

Second, the statements that are part of a conditional statement can be quite complex;
for example, they can be compound statements in which loops occur. In such cases we
cannot use conditional expressions. The conditional statement is therefore by no means
a superfluous element in the C++ language.

3.2 The Comma-operator

Two expressions, separated by a *comma-operator*, as indicated in

    *expression*1, *expression*2

form a new expression. The two expressions are evaluated in the given order, and the
value of the whole expression is equal to that of *expression*2. This language construct
is useful only if *expression*1 does something more than just yielding a value (since that
value is ignored). Here is an example in which this is the case:

```
// SUM1: Solution based on comma-operator.
s = 0;
while (cin >> i, i > 0) s += i;
```

This program fragment computes the sum of positive integers entered on the keyboard
and followed by an integer that is zero or negative. It uses the expression

```
cin >> i, i > 0
```

Alternatively, we can use the older way of reading integers, replacing this expression
with

```
scanf("%d", &i), i > 0
```

The call to the standard function **scanf**, preceding the comma-operator, is an *expression*. We will discuss the value returned by **scanf** shortly; we ignore it if we write the *statement*

```
scanf("%d", &i);
```

(which is really a statement, not an expression, because of the semicolon at the end). Instead of **scanf**, program fragment SUM1 uses typical C++ input with the operator **>>**.

The interesting point about SUM1 is that the expression **cin >> i** occurs between the parentheses that follow the **while** keyword, although its purpose is not to test for loop continuation. The comma-operator is needed here, because we want another expression, **i > 0**, for this test. Note that the test is done between two actions that are also in the loop, as Figure 3.1 shows. This is also the case if we use the **scanf** function in combination with the comma-operator as shown above.

Figure 3.1 also applies to program fragment SUM2, which is another way of writing a loop with the test in the middle; it is based on the break-statement (see Section 2.6).

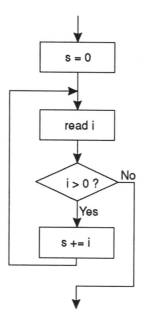

Figure 3.1. Loop with test in the middle

```
// SUM2: Solution based on the break-statement.
s = 0;
for ( ; ; )
{  cin >> i;
   if (i <= 0) break;
   s += i;
}
```

We now see that in C++ (and in C) we have at least two ways of programming a loop with the test in the middle. If we had none, which is the case in Pascal (supposing that we do not want to use the goto-statement), we would probably have used the following solution to the same problem:

```
// SUM3: Solution in the spirit of Pascal.
s = 0;
cin >> i;
while (i > 0)
{   s += i;
    cin >> i);
}
```

Version SUM3 does not correspond to Figure 3.1. A flow diagram for it would have two boxes with *read i*, one outside and one inside the loop. As a solution to our summation problem, SUM3 is less natural than SUM1 and SUM2.

Signaling the end of numerical input data

In our last example, the integer sequence read from the keyboard was terminated by a nonpositive integer. We often want to use some other means to signal the end of the input data, such as, for example, entering the word END. Let us first solve this problem in the traditional way, that is, using the header file *stdio.h* and the function **scanf**. We do this by using the value returned by **scanf**. This value is an integer equal to the number of data items (such as numbers) that are read. For example, we can write the following assignment statement:

```
n = scanf("%f %f %f", &x, &y, &z);
```

If this call to **scanf** is successful, that is, if three numbers can be read, the returned value is 3, so this is the value assigned to **n**. If only two can be read because of some nonnumerical character following the second number in the input, **n** will be given the value 2, and so on. If we now modify our summation problem in that the word END (or some other nonnumerical characters) signals the end of the input data, a solution to this new problem is

```
// SUM4: Input data terminated by the word END, for example.
s = 0;
while (scanf("%d", &i) == 1) s += i;
```

If **scanf** has to read an integer, as is the case in SUM4, it begins by skipping any leading white-space characters. If then an integer follows, its characters are read until a character is encountered that does not belong to the integer. That character is not regarded as being read. The same applies when the above call to **scanf** is unsuccessful because, say, the **E** of **END** is encountered instead of the first character of an integer.

It is important to know this, because after SUM4 some more calls to **scanf** may follow; we then have to skip the nonnumerical characters in the input stream before we can read another number. If we know that there is only one such character, we can use a **char** variable **ch** and write either

```
ch = getchar();
```

or, equivalently,

```
scanf("%c", &ch);
```

Now that we have used **getchar**, to read one character, we may as well mention the analogous way of writing one character. For the latter purpose we can write

```
putchar(ch);
```

which is equivalent to

```
printf("%c", ch);
```

So much for the traditional way of reading numerical input data, terminated by nonnumeric characters. As for the typical C++ facilities for input (with the header file *iostream.h*), we must bear in mind that, like a call to **scanf**, an expression such as

```
cin >> i
```

yields a value, which normally is again the input stream **cin**; hence the possibility of writing, for example,

```
cin >> i >> j
```

However, the value of **cin >> i** (where i has a numeric type, such as **int**) is zero if the read attempt fails. (In Section 9.4, we will see that the value of the expression **cin >> i** can be converted to a *pointer*. Pointers can be zero or nonzero and may therefore occur as truth values in constructions such as **while(...)**, as we will discuss in Section 5.6.)

```
// SUM5: Input data terminated by the word END, for example.
#include <iostream.h>

int main()
{ int s=0, i;
  cout <<
  "\nEnter some integers, terminated by the word END, "
  "for example:\n";
  while (cin >> i) s += i;
  cout << "Sum: " << s << endl;
  return 0;
}
```

This distinction between possible zero and nonzero results enables us to test for the end of numerical input data in a very simple and elegant way, as program SUM5 shows. If we were to read some more numbers after the while-loop in this program, it would be necessary to skip all nonnumeric characters used to terminate the first number sequence. Assuming that after those characters (such as, for example, the three letters of the word END) have been entered, the Enter key is pressed, we could try to do this as follows:

```
char ch;
do cin >> ch; while (ch != '\n');     // Incorrect!
```

However, this does not work, because each time **cin >> ch** is executed all leading white-space characters are skipped. When we are reading numbers, this is normally what we want, but this time we want to read only one character at a time, even if the character read is a white-space character, such as '\n'. Fortunately, this more literal way of reading one character is also possible. All we have to do is replace **cin >> ch** with **cin.get(ch)**. Thus our program fragment that skips all characters until a newline character has been read should read

```
do cin.get(ch); while (ch != '\n'); // Correct.
```

The curious form **cin.get(ch)** will be discussed in detail in Chapters 6 and 9. This type of function call is introduced here so that we can already use it as a typical C++ alternative to the older form **ch = getchar( )** (which would require the header file *stdio.h* instead of *iostream.h*).

More complicated use of commas

Reverting to the original subject of this section, we must deal with two questions. First, can we have three or more expressions, separated by comma-operators? This is indeed the case. The comma-operator behaves like some other operators in this regard. For example,

```
x = a + b, y = x + 1, z = x + y
```

means

```
(x = a + b, y = x + 1), z = x + y
```

so here we have again one expression, followed by a comma-operator, followed by another expression. This is similar to $u + v + w$, meaning $(u + v) + w$.

The second question is how the compiler can tell a comma-operator from a comma that is used for a different purpose. Consider, for example, the following call to **printf**:

```
printf("%d", ++i, 3 * i);  // ???
```

This must be an error because there is only one **%d** conversion specification (see Section 2.2) and there are two values to be 'printed'. (Incidentally, if the format string had been **"%d %d"**, the **printf** statement would still have been suspicious, since the order in which the arguments **++i** and **3 * i** are evaluated is undefined.) But why is the comma in

```
++i, 3 * i
```

not regarded as a comma-operator? If it were, the above call to **printf** would be equivalent to

```
printf("%d", (++i, 3 * i));
```

which is a perfectly correct statement, giving the value of **3 * i**, evaluated after **++i**, as output. The answer to this question is that function arguments cannot be expressions built by using comma-operators (unless such expressions are surrounded by parentheses). Using a simpler example, the comma used in the call

```
f(x, y)
```

is an argument separator, not a comma-operator. We will discuss function calls in more detail in Chapter 4. Expressions that must not be built by using comma-operators but may otherwise be as simple or as complex as we like are technically known as *assignment-expressions*. This name indicates that (even) assignment-operators, such as = and +=, can be used to build such expression, but comma-operators cannot. Any function argument is an *assignment-expression*, even if there is no assignment at all in it. This rather strange and formal terminology, used by language designers and compiler writers, will be discussed in more detail at the end of Section 3.6.

3.3 Bit Manipulation

We can apply the following bit-manipulation operators to integer operands:

    &   Bitwise AND
    | Bitwise OR
    ^   Bitwise XOR (exclusive OR)
    ~   Inversion of all bits
    <<   Shift left
    >>   Shift right

(Note that we have already used the operators << and >> for other purposes, namely for stream input and output. Likewise, the single ampersand (&), used here for 'bitwise AND' is also used as the unary 'address of' operator. This is quite normal in C++: the meaning of an operator token is clear only if we know the number and the types of the operands.)

The term *bitwise*, used above, means that the operation in question applies to all pairs of bits in the same positions. This will be clear from the examples that follow. Let us assume **sizeof(int)** to be 2, so that type **int** takes 16 bits. The operator & gives a 1 in a bit position of the result only if the two bits of the operands in the same position are also 1. For example, we can find the value of **0x3A6B & 0x00F0** as follows:

```
0x3A6B             = 0011 1010 0110 1011
0x00F0             = 0000 0000 1111 0000
―――――――――――――――――――――――――――――――――――――― &
0x3A6B & 0x00F0 = 0000 0000 0110 0000 = 0x0060
```

As this example shows, we can use the operator & to extract some bits from a word of 16 bits. Counting the bits from right to left, starting at 0, we have extracted the bits 4, 5, 6, 7 in this example. In the result they have the same values as these bits in the first operand, **0x3A6B**, have; this is so because the bits 4, 5, 6, 7 in the second operand (called a *mask*) are 1 and all others are 0. For example, by writing

```
int i = 0x3A6B, j;
j = i & 0xF0;
```

we select the bits (0110) in the positions 4, 5, 6,7 of variable **i** and copy them into variable **j**, where they will occur in the same positions. All other bits of **j** will be zero.

We have an analogous situation with |. This operator gives 0 for all positions in which the two corresponding operand bits are 0, as the following example shows:

```
0x3A6B             = 0011 1010 0110 1011
0x00F0             = 0000 0000 1111 0000
―――――――――――――――――――――――――――――――――――――― |
0x3A6B | 0x00F0 = 0011 1010 1111 1011 = 0x3AFB
```

This illustrates that we can use the operator | to set some bits (that is, to make them equal to 1) and leave the others unaltered.

The operator ^ gives 1 for all positions in which the two corresponding operand bits are different, and it gives 0 if they are equal:

```
0x3A6B             = 0011 1010 0110 1011
0x00F0             = 0000 0000 1111 0000
―――――――――――――――――――――――――――――――――――――― ^
0x3A6B ^ 0x00F0 = 0011 1010 1001 1011 = 0x3A9B
```

We can see that ^ inverts the selected bits and leaves the others unaltered.

With the operator ~ each bit in the result is the inverse of the corresponding bit of its operand. It has only one operand, that is, it is a unary operator. Here is an example:

```
0x3A6B  = 0011 1010 0110 1011
~0x3A6B = 1100 0101 1001 0100 = 0xC594
```

We can use both operators & and ~ if we want to *reset* some bits, that is, if we want to copy all bits, except for some selected positions which are to be set to zero. For example, after the execution of

```
int i = 0x3A6B, j;
j = i & ~0xF0;
```

the bits of **j** will be equal to those of **i**, except for those in the positions 4, 5, 6, 7, which will be zero. Remember, the mask ~0xF0 is equal to 0xFF...F0F, where the numbers of leading hexadecimal digits **F** is determined by the word length. In other words, we write ~0xF0 instead of 0xFF0F if **sizeof(int)** = 2, and instead of 0xFFFFFF0F if **sizeof(int)** = 4. The expression ~0xF0 is clearly to be preferred for reasons of portability.

With << the result is obtained by shifting the first operand as many positions to the left as the second operand specifies. We lose bits on the left, and zero bits are inserted on the right, as the following example shows:

```
0x63B7      = 0110 0011 1011 0111
0x63B7 << 4 = 0011 1011 0111 0000 = 0x3B70
```

We can shift to the right in a similar way by using >>:

```
0x63B7      = 0110 0011 1011 0111
0x63B7 >> 4 = 0000 0110 0011 1011 = 0x063B
```

Here the leftmost bit of the first operand is 0. Unfortunately, things are not so easy if that bit happens to be 1. As we have seen in the Sections 1.3 and 1.6, we can distinguish between the types

unsigned int	(or **unsigned**, for short), and
signed int	(or, briefly, **int**).

With an **unsigned** first operand, it is guaranteed that zeros will be shifted into the word on the left-hand side. This is also the case if the first operand has type **int** and its leftmost bit is 0, as is the case in the above example. In the remaining case, with an **int** operand the leftmost bit of which is 1, the result is system dependent: with most computers, the leftmost bit, regarded as a 'sign bit', will shift into the word on the left-hand side, but zeros may be used instead. If the first operand is a hexadecimal constant, as in the above example, we are certain that zeros are inserted on the left, because such a constant is taken as **unsigned**. In practice, however, we normally use variables rather than constants; if we want zeros to be inserted on the left, we should declare such variables as **unsigned**, not as **int**.

Bit operations combined with assignments

Not only the arithmetic operators +, −, *, /, and %, but also the bit operators &, |, ^, <<, and >> can be combined with assignment, which gives the following new operators:

&= |=   ^=   <<=   >>=

For example, we can shift the contents of the **int** variable **i** one bit to the left by writing

```
i <<= 1;
```

instead of

```
i = i << 1;
```

(As we will see in Section 3.6, << has higher precedence than =.)

Output and input of hexadecimal numbers

Now that we are frequently using hexadecimal constants, it is useful to know that the format string for **scanf** and **printf** accepts hexadecimal conversion specifications. We use these by writing %...**X** instead of %...**d**. For example, the statement

```
printf("%04X", 255);
```

gives the output

```
00FF
```

The **0** in %04X causes padding on the left with zeros instead of with spaces. We can also use this principle with decimal conversion specifications, but that is normally not desirable. If we had written %04x, with lower case **x**, the output would have been

```
00ff
```

If we want to *read* hexadecimal numbers we can simply use %**X** (or %x) with **scanf**. This gives us complete freedom in the way the hexadecimal numbers are spelled in the input data. For example, the forms **0xFF, 0Xff, FF, 00ff** will all be accepted. The following program may be useful if you are given a hexadecimal constant and want to know its value (written, as usual, in the decimal number system):

```
#include <stdio.h>

int main()
{   int i;
    printf("Enter a hexadecimal integer: ");
    scanf("%X", &i);
    printf("This is written in the decimal number system"
            " as: %d.\n", i);
    return 0;
}
```

3.4 Simple Arrays

Each variable used so far corresponds to only one number (or one character). With many programming problems we want to use sequences of numbers (or other objects), the elements of which have the same name and are distinguished by an integer 0, 1, 2, 3, ... We can do this by using *arrays*. Here we will only deal with the most elementary aspects of arrays; they will be discussed in more detail in Chapter 5. The array declaration

```
int a[100];
```

enables us to use the following variables:

```
a[0], a[1], ..., a[99]
```

The constant 100 in the declaration says that there are a hundred array elements, but the final element is **a[99]**, not **a[100]**. In this example the elements of the array have type **int**, as indicated in the declaration. This may be any other type instead. When using array elements, we can write any integer expression between the square brackets, as is done, for example, in the statement

```
k = 50 * a[3 * i + j/2] - 1;
```

provided that the expression **3 * i + j/2** has a value that is less than 100 and not negative. The value denoted between brackets is called a *subscript*. It must have type **int** (or **unsigned**), no matter what the array-element type is. This example also illustrates that array elements can be used in the same way as the simple variables we have been using so far.

In the declaration, the *dimension* 100 is only given as an example, but we must always write array dimensions as constants, or, in general, as *constant expressions*. For example, if **n** is a variable, **int a[n]** is incorrect, but **int a[3 * 75 + 1]** is correct. It is possible to denote constants by symbolic names (that is, by identifiers). If we write, for example,

```
#define LENGTH 100
```

at the top of the program, the symbolic constant **LENGTH** can be used instead of 100. As it is a constant, we cannot assign other values to **LENGTH** later, but we *can* write

```
int a[LENGTH];
```

which would not have been allowed if **LENGTH** had been a variable. With this new way of declaring **a**, we would consistently use **LENGTH** instead of 100, writing, for example,

```
for (i=0; i<LENGTH; i++) a[i] = 0;
```

if all elements of **a** are to be set to zero. If later we want to replace 100 with some other value, only the above **#define** line needs to be modified. Another advantage of symbolic constants is that we can use names that tell something about the meaning of these constants. Such a style of programming, with emphasis on readability and documentation, is highly recommended. We will discuss other interesting possibilities with **#define** lines in Section 4.10. For this moment, remember that, like **#include** lines, they should really be separate lines (not ending with semicolons).

In C++ we can define the constant **LENGTH** also in another way, as program LIFO shows:

```
// LIFO: This program reads 30 integers and prints them
//       in the reverse order (Last In, First Out).
#include <iostream.h>
#include <iomanip.h>

int main()
{  const int LENGTH=30;
   int i, a[LENGTH];
   cout << "Enter " << LENGTH << " integers:\n";
   for (i=0; i<LENGTH; i++) cin >> a[i];
   cout << "\nThe same integers, in reverse order:\n";
   for (i=0; i<LENGTH; i++)
   cout << setw(6) << a[LENGTH-i-1]
        << (i % 10 == 9 ? '\n' : ' ');
   return 0;
}
```

Actually, we can define **LENGTH** in the same way in ANSI C, but only in C++ can we use **LENGTH**, defined in this way, in the following declaration of array **a**:

```
int a[LENGTH];
```

Program LIFO reads 30 integers from the keyboard and prints them in reverse order, that is, we use the principle 'last in, first out'.

As for **setw**, occurring in this program, recall that we have also used this in Section 2.2. Notice the conditional expression

```
i % 10 == 9 ? '\n' : ' '
```

whose value is a blank in most cases but is a newline character when i is equal to 9, 19, or 29. In this way, the output will show three lines of ten integers each. (In the input the integers may be distributed over several lines any way the user likes.)

In Section 5.6 we will discuss a way of using certain variables as arrays, except that their dimensions need not be constants but may depend on variables.

Initializing an array

We can initialize an array by writing a list of constant expressions, separated by commas, surrounded by braces and preceded by =, as the following example shows:

```
int a[4] = {34, 22};   // All four elements initialized.
int b[4];              // No elements initialized.
```

Any trailing elements for which we do not specify values are set to zero, so the values of **a[0]**, **a[1]**, **a[2]** and **a[3]** are 34, 22, 0 and 0, respectively. This applies only if we initialize at least one element: array **b** is not initialized. There is a special, very convenient facility for initializing character arrays:

```
char name[20] = "Tim"; // "Tim" instead of {'T','i','m','\0'}
```

We will discuss the initialization of arrays in more detail in Sections 4.5 and 5.4.

3.5 Associativity

It is obvious that the expression

```
a - b + c - d
```

is equivalent to the first of the following two expressions:

```
((a - b) + c) - d                    a - (b + (c - d))
```

This is expressed in a technical way by saying that the operators + and – (which have the same precedence) are *left associative*. We see that this phrase means that the expression in question is equivalent to one in which pairs of parentheses, *starting on the left*, have been inserted. Each operator always associates in the same way: it is either left associative or right associative. This characteristic of an operator is called its *associativity*. Note that the concept of associativity is relevant if the same operator occurs more than once in an expression or if several operators with the same precedence occur in it.

Since most operators, like + and –, are left associative, the most efficient way of discussing associativity is to focus on the exceptions. Only the following operators associate are *right associative*:

(i)   All unary operators (with only one operand).
(ii)   The operator ?:, used in conditional expressions.
(iii)   The assignment operators =, +=, –=, *=, /=, %=, &=, |=, ^=, <<=, >>=

All other operators are left associative. Here is a (not very practical) example of (i):

```
- ! 0
```

Since – and ! are used here as unary operators, they are right associative, so when inserting imaginary parentheses we must start on the right, which gives –(!0). This means that –!0 is equal to –1.

Let us also consider a more interesting example of (i). Unlike mathematics, the C language has some unary operators that follow their operands. This is the case with ++ in

```
-n++
```

Since both operators – and ++ in this expression are unary, they are right associative, which means that we have to read this expression as –(n++), not as (–n)++. Again, we should think of inserting parentheses, starting on the right. Incidentally, (–n)++ would not have been a valid expression, because –n is not a variable and cannot be incremented. This is, however, not the proper way of explaining the meaning of –n++; we should really use rule (i) for this purpose.

As for (ii), here is an example, which without any explanation may not be clear:

```
a < b ? x : c == d ? y : z
```

Since the operator ?: is right associative (and because this operator has lower precedence than the others in this expression, as we will see in the next section), we should read this as

```
a < b ? x : (c == d ? y : z)
```

Let us illustrate rule (iii) by means of a complete program:

```
// ASSIGN: Assignment operators.
#include <iostream.h>

int main()
{   int i=20, j=10, k, l, m;
    k = l = i += j += m = 1;
    cout << "m=" << m << "  j=" << j << "  i=" << i
         << "  l=" << l << "  k=" << k << endl;
    return 0;
}
```

Since all operators in **k = l = i += j += m = 1;** are right associative, imaginary parentheses should start on the right, which gives

```
k = (l = (i += (j += (m = 1))));
```

We may really write this statement instead of the corresponding statement without parentheses. Whether or not we do this, the output is as follows:

```
m=1   j=11   i=31   l=31   k=31
```

(Because we have assignment *expressions*, with operators that associate from right to left, there is no need for a special language concept called 'multiple assignments', as there is in some other languages.)

An operator's associativity does not determine the order in which its operands are evaluated. It is particularly important to be aware of this if we are tempted to write something like

```
k = (++i) * (5 + i);   // Wrong
```

Which operand of this multiplication is evaluated first is undefined. For example, if **i** is initially zero, **k** may be assigned the value $1 \times 5 = 5$ or $1 \times 6 = 6$. Here is a more complicated example:

```
a[i+=3] = (b[i+=4] = (c[i+=5] = (i+=6)));  // Wrong
```

We must not assume that **i += 6** is performed first and **i += 3** last. If we omit all parentheses ( ) here, its meaning is exactly the same. In either form the effect of this statement is undefined. In general, if any assignment occurs in an expression, the variable which is given a value should not occur once again in that expression. If it does, the effect is undefined.

The only operators for which the order of evaluation is defined are **&&**, **||**, **?:** and the comma-operator (**,**).

3.6 Precedence of Operators

In the following table, all operators are listed in order of decreasing precedence, including those which we have not yet discussed. The operators on the first line have the highest precedence, those on the second line the second highest, and so on; operators on the same line have the same precedence.

Operators in decreasing order of precedence (see Section 3.5 for associativity):

```
()    []    .    ->    ::
!    ~   ++   --   +   -   (type)   *   &   sizeof   new   delete  (all unary)
.*    ->*
*    /    %
+    -
<<    >>
<    <=   >   >=
==    !=
&
^
|
&&
||
?:
=    +=   -=   *=   /=   %=   &=   |=   ^=   <<=   >>=
,
```

Each operator occurs in the following list once again, along with a brief indication of its meaning and a section in this book where you can find more about it. Note that the characters *, &, +, and − occur twice: each of them is used both for a binary and a unary operator:

Operator	Meaning
::	Scope resolution (Sections 4.2 and 6.5)
()	Function calls (Section 4.1)
[]	Subscripting (Sections 3.4 and 5.1)
.	Selecting a component of a structure (Section 6.1)
->	Selecting a component of a structure or class by means of a pointer (Section 6.2)
.*	Pointers to class members (Section 7.6)
->*	Pointers to class members (Section 7.6)
!	*NOT*, unary operator (Section 2.3)
~	Inversion of all bits, unary operator (Section 3.3)

++	Increment, unary operator (Section 2.1)
--	Decrement, unary operator (Section 2.1)
+	Plus, unary operator (Section 2.1)
+	Addition, binary operator (Section 2.1)
-	Minus, unary operator (Section 2.1)
-	Subtraction, binary operator (Section 2.1)
(*type*)	Cast, unary operator (Section 3.7)
new	Create (allocate memory) (Section 5.6)
delete	Delete (free memory) (Section 5.6)
*	'Contents of address', unary operator (Sections 4.3 and 5.1)
*	Multiplication, binary operator (Section 2.1)
&	Bitwise *AND*, binary operator (Section 3.3)
&	'Address of', unary operator (Section 5.1)
sizeof	Number of bytes in memory, unary operator (Section 2.2)
/	Division, either floating point or integer (Section 2.1)
%	Remainder with integer division (Section 2.1)
<<	Shift left (Section 3.3); stream output (Sections 1.1 and 9.2)
>>	Shift right (Section 3.3); stream input (Sections 1.1 and 9.3)
<	Less than (Section 2.3)
>	Greater than (Section 2.3)
<=	Less than or equal to (Section 2.3)
>=	Greater than or equal to (Section 2.3)
==	Equal to (Section 2.3)
!=	Not equal to (Section 2.3)
^	Bitwise *Exclusive OR* (*XOR*) (Section 3.3)
|	Bitwise *OR* (Section 3.3)
&&	Logical *AND* (Section 2.3)
||	Logical *OR* (Section 2.3)
?:	Conditional expression (Section 3.1)
=	Assignment (Section 2.2)
+=	Addition combined with assignment. The following operators have similar meanings: -=, *=, /=, %=, <<=, >>=, &=, |=, ^= (Sections 2.1 and 3.3)

A hierarchy of expressions

Instead of using a list of operators in decreasing order of precedence, as we did at the beginning of this section, we can define precedence rules by introducing a hierarchy of expressions. The term *expression* is at the top of the hierarchy because it is the most general one. Starting with this most general term, we gradually move to the bottom, each time imposing restrictions on more specialized forms of expressions, which act as building blocks for the more general ones. From top to bottom, the choice of operators that we can use to build the expressions in question is increasingly restricted to those of higher precedence. This hierarchy is based on a great many rather technical terms, sometimes called *syntactical categories*, which might at first be confusing. In accordance with *The C++ Programming Language* by Stroustrup, we will use here a hyphen in a term such as *assignment-expression* and print it in italic to indicate that we are using the term in its special, technical sense. Curiously enough, an *assignment-expression* need not contain any assignment at all; the name only indicates that it *may* contain an assignment. This principle also applies to other terms. For example, a *conditional-expression* need not contain ?: but it *may* do so. So far, we informally used the term 'conditional expression' (without a hyphen) only for expressions that really contain the ?: operator. If you are aware of this distinction between formal and informal terminology, you will understand the following list of formal terms. A rigorous treatment can be found in the book just mentioned. Each term is characterized by the operators of lowest precedence that *may* be used to build it, but need not really occur in it.

Formal term	Built from	And possibly from
expression	*assignment-expression*	,
assignment-expression	*conditional-expression*	=, +=, etc.,
		unary-expression
conditional-expression	*logical-or-expression*	?:,
		expression
logical-or-expression	*logical-and-expression*	||
logical-and-expression	*inclusive-or-expression*	&&
inclusive-or-expression	*exclusive-or-expression*	|
exclusive-or-expression	*and-expression*	^
and-expression	*equality-expression*	&
equality-expression	*relational-expression*	==, !=
relational-expression	*shift-expression*	<, >, <=, >=
shift-expression	*additive-expression*	<<, >>
additive-expression	*multiplicative-expression*	+, −
multiplicative-expression	*pm-expression*	*, /, %
pm-expression	*cast-expression*	.*, −>*
cast-expression	*unary-expression*	(*type*)
unary-expression	*postfix-expression*, ...	++, −− (before operand)
postfix-expression	*primary-expression*, ...	++, −− (after operand)

Notes

1. The first line of this table indicates that an *expression* consists of one or more *assignment-expressions* separated by comma-operators. Note that there may be only one *assignment-expression* in the expression, in which case no comma-operator is used to build the *expression*.

2. An *assignment-expression* consists of a *conditional-expression*, possibly preceded by several occurrences of a *unary-expression* followed by an assignment operator. Here are some examples of *assignment-expressions*:

```
a[2*i] -= x += i < j ? i : j
i = j = k = 0
a + b
```

3. A *conditional-expression* can consist of a single *logical-or-expression*. If a given *conditional-expression* is preceded by

> *logical-or-expression* **?** *expression* **:**

the result is again a conditional expression, and so on. Since the very general term *expression* is used here for the form between **?** and **:**, we may apparently use commas here, as is done in the first of the following examples, which are all *conditional-expressions*:

```
a > 100 ? i = 1, j = 2 : k
a > 1000 ? 3 : a > 100 ? 2 : 1
1
a > 1000
```

The form after **:** must be a *logical-or-expression*, which is rather a specialized expression. We can therefore not write **k = 3**, let alone **k = 3, l = 4**, instead of **k** in the first example.

4. A complete, syntactical definition of the terms *unary-expression*, *postfix-expression* and *primary-expression* would be beyond the scope of this book and would also be hard to understand at this moment. Of these three, *unary-expression* is the most general and *primary-expression* is the most specialized term: every *primary-expression* is also a *postfix-expression*, which in turn is a *unary-expression*. Starting at the bottom of the hierarchy, we first look at some typical *primary-expressions*:

```
123
(i++, j+i)
k
```

They are at the same time examples of the slightly more general notion of *postfix-expression*. By contrast, the following examples are no *primary-expressions*, but they are still *postfix-expressions*:

```
k++
a[i]
scanf("%d", &i)
float(i)
```

Finally, the notion of *unary-expression*, being the most general of the three, includes all of the seven above examples, but also the following more typical *unary-expressions*:

```
++i
-i
-i++
++ ++i
sizeof(int)
sizeof(i)
```

Although this discussion has been a bit technical, it has practical consequences. For example, in note 3 we have seen a rather strange *conditional-expression* with a comma-operator in the middle of it even though there are no surrounding parentheses. Tricky constructs such as this one are best analyzed by using the formal syntactical notions we have just been discussing.

3.7 Arithmetic Conversions and the Cast-operator

In Section 2.1 we have dealt with the arithmetic operators +, −, *, /, and %. We will now discuss in more detail how the type of the expression

   operand1   operator   operand2

(in which *operator* is one of the five operators just mentioned) depends on the types of *operand1* and *operand2*. Now that we are familiar with associativity and precedence of operators, it will be clear that this general form applies not only to very simple expressions, such as **a** + **b**, but also to more complicated ones, such as

```
a * b - c * d - e * f
```

According to Sections 3.5 and 3.6 we should read this as

```
((a * b) - (c * d)) - (e * f)
```

This has indeed the general form just shown, with **((a * b) − (c * d))** as *operand1*, and **(e * f)** as *operand2*.

   The precise rules to find the type of an expression may seem rather complicated, but fortunately we will seldom need them, because they have been devised in such a way that the type in question is just what we intuitively expect. If you think the following discussion tedious, don't worry. It is included here because it is important to know that every arithmetic expression has a type that can be derived from those of its operands, and this book might be considered incomplete if it did not show how this can be done. Yet we will discuss one example, program BEWARE below, where some familiarity with these rules will be useful.

First, *integral promotion* may take place: any operands that have type **char**, **short** (both in their signed and unsigned varieties) or an enumerator type are 'promoted' to type **int** if this type can represent all the values of the original type. If not, the original type is converted to **unsigned int**.

Type conversion (to be discussed below) is now applied to the operands to ensure that their types will be the same. The common type thus obtained is then used as the type of the result. This operand type conversion is done by applying at most one of the seven rules listed below. These rules are to be considered *in the given order*, and only one of them is to be applied; as soon as the two operands have the same type, any remaining rules are ignored. For brevity, the phrase 'an operand is converted to a given type' will include the case that this operand already has that type. For example, rule 1 includes the case that both operands are **long double**:

1. If either operand is **long double**, the other is converted to this type.
2. If either operand is **double**, the other is converted to this type.
3. If either operand is **float**, the other is converted to this type.
4. If either operand is **unsigned long**, the other is converted to this type.
5. If either operand is **long** and the other is **unsigned**, the unsigned operand is converted to **long**, provided that **long** can represent all the values of **unsigned**. If that is not the case, both operands are converted to **unsigned long**.
6. If either operand is **long**, the other is converted to this type.
7. If either operand is **unsigned**, the other is converted to this type.

Note that very often none of these rules apply because both operands have type **int** (possibly due to integral promotion, discussed earlier in this section).

The types signed char and unsigned char

Besides type **char**, we have the types **signed char** and **unsigned char**. In C++, these are three distinct types. If we use **char** variables only to store 'real' characters, the distinction is not important, because these use only seven bits so that the 'sign bit' is zero; in other words, the normal characters have positive values between 0 and 127. Things are different if we assign other values, such as, for example, '\xFF' to a **char** variable. In this case we had better write **signed char** or **unsigned char**, instead of just **char**, to avoid machine dependence. The implementation must specify whether the high-order bit of a plain **char** object is treated as a sign bit. Although formally **char** is distinct from both **signed char** and **unsigned char**, it behaves as one of these two types in the following program, the output of which is system dependent:

```
/* SIGNEDCH: This program finds out whether the leftmost bit
             of type char is a sign bit.
*/
#include <iostream.h>
```

```
int main()
{   signed char s_ch='\xFF';
    unsigned char u_ch='\xFF';
    char ch='\xFF';  // Binary: s_ch = u_ch = ch = 11111111
    int s, u, i;
    s = s_ch;  // From signed char to int
    u = u_ch;  // From unsigned char to int
    i = ch;    // From char to int (system dependent)
    cout << "For this C++ implementation, type char has " <<
    (  i == s ? "a sign bit.\n" :
       i == u ? "no sign bit.\n" :
       "not been implemented correctly.\n"
    );
    return 0;
}
```

We can write the binary representations of **s** and **u**, along with their values, as follows in two's complement and in 16 bits:

```
s = 11111111 11111111 = -1    (= s_ch)
u = 00000000 11111111 = 255   (= u_ch)
```

The value of **i**, on the other hand, is system dependent. It is equal to either **s** or **u**. Note that the values of **s_ch**, **u_ch**, and **ch** are a matter of interpretation: they have the same internal representation, namely 11111111. The difference between signed and unsigned character types becomes apparent only after converting these types to type **int**. In program SIGNEDCH this is done by using assignment statements. As discussed in this section, conversion to type **int** (that is, *integral promotion*) also takes place in expressions, such as in **s_ch + 1** and **u_ch + 1**; the values of these expressions are 0 and 256, respectively, despite the fact that **s_ch** and **u_ch** are represented by identical bit strings.

You may think this discussion about signed and unsigned characters rather theoretical and perhaps even useless. However, character variables are in practice used not only for normal characters but also for any byte values and for 'very short' integers. Especially in the latter case it is very important for the keyword **char** to be preceded by either **signed** or **unsigned**.

Signed and unsigned int

Program BEWARE shows that we should be very careful with comparing **int** and **unsigned int** values. Before we look at such comparisons, note that we can use the expression ~0x1 (or ~1) to obtain a word with all 1-bits except for the bit at the extreme right, which is 0. With 16-bit words, we could write 0xFFFE, but then we would have to write 0xFFFFFFFE with 32-bit words. The ~ operator provides a convenient and portable way of padding with 1-bits at the left.

```
// BEWARE: Can a negative value be equal to a positive one?
#include <iostream.h>

int main()
{   unsigned u = ~0x1; // u = 0xF...FE
    int i = u;             // i = -2 (same bit pattern as u)
    if (i == u) cout << "i == u\n";
    if (i < 0) cout << "i < 0\n";
    if (u > 0) cout << "u > 0\n";
    return 0;
}
```

This program has the following curious output:

```
i == u
i < 0
u > 0
```

Although i and u have the same internal representation, they are of different types. In the comparison i == u, conversion of i from int to unsigned takes place, according to point 7 at the beginning of this section. Such a conversion does not alter the bit pattern of i so both operands now have the same large positive value ($2^n - 2$). Since i is equal to −2, the test i < 0 clearly gives a positive answer. To evaluate u > 0, we have an unsigned and an int value again, so point 7, just mentioned, is applied here to the second operand, 0. This does not alter the value of 0, so the test u > 0 also succeeds.

The cast-operator

Forced type conversion, also known as *coercion*, can be achieved by means of a special operator, the *cast*. Both in C and in C++ we can write the desired type between parentheses, in front of the expression to be converted, as, for example, in

```
(float)n
```

In C++, there is a new, alternative way of writing a cast, with the same effect, namely

```
float(n)
```

We will see in Section 6.9 that this new notation fits very nicely in the C++ language in connection with so-called 'constructors' for user-defined types. For this reason we prefer this new notation to the old one.

Casts are useful for many purposes; one is to convert a signed type to the corresponding unsigned type or vice versa. Let us use our example about signed and unsigned characters once again. If we write

```
signed char s_ch='\0xFF';
int i;
i = unsigned char(s_ch);
```

the value of **i** will be 255, while it would be –1 if the cast had been omitted.

A very useful application of the cast is a division operation that, although applied to integers, is to yield a real quotient. For example, in

```
int i=14, j=3;
float x, y;
x = i/j;
y = float(i)/float(j);
```

we have x = 4.0 and y = 4.666.... According to the conversion rules discussed in this section, we could have omitted one of the two casts in the last statement. For example,

```
y = float(i)/j;    // y = 4.666...
```

would also have been correct. By contrast, the following statement performs integer division (with integer 4 as its result!) before the cast is applied:

```
y = float(i/j);   // y = 4.0
```

In the last example, the result would have been the same if we had omitted the cast, since conversion is performed automatically if an integer value (4) is assigned to a floating-point variable (**y**).

A conversion can really alter a value, as is the case in

```
int i;
float x = -6.9;
i = x;
```

Here **i** is given the value –6. Using a cast is highly recommended here, not to make the computer do some additional work for us, but rather for the sake of documentation. Using a cast by writing

```
i = int(x);
```

instead of the above assignment **i = x**; we can see more clearly that **i** is obtained by truncating **x**. The presence of this cast does not make any difference in regard to the code generated by the compiler.

3.8 Lvalues

Let us consider assignment expressions of the following form

```
E1 = E2
```

In most cases **E1** will be the name of a variable, but it can also be a quite complex expression, as we will see in a moment. An expression that may occur as a left operand of an assignment is called a *modifiable lvalue*. To simplify our discussion, we will simply use the term *lvalue* when we actually mean *modifiable lvalue*. It will be clear that none of the following expressions is an lvalue:

```
3 * 5
i + 1
printf("%d", a)
"ABC"
```

The most obvious kinds of lvalues are names of simple variables and array elements. We may use surrounding parentheses. For example, after

```
int i, j, a[100], b[100];
```

the following three expressions are lvalues:

```
i
a[3 * i + j]
(i)
```

In Chapter 5 we will see why the name of an array is not an lvalue; with the above declaration of **a** and **b** we cannot write

```
a = b;   // Error
```

Again using the above declaration, the following is a valid assignment statement, which assigns zero to the smaller of the variables **i** and **j** and leaves the other unchanged:

```
(i < j ? i : j) = 0;
```

According to Section 3.6, ?: has higher precedence than =, so we may write this as

```
i < j ? i : j = 0;
```

The conditional expression **E1 ? E2 : E3** is an lvalue only if **E2** and **E3** are of the same type and are both lvalues. Incidentally, this applies only to C++; conditional expressions cannot be lvalues in the C language.

Except for reference types, to be discussed in Section 4.3, the result of a cast is not an lvalue, so this example is not correct:

```
float(x) = 3.14;    // Error
```

A comma expression is an lvalue if its right operand is:

```
(i = 1, j) = 2;     // Equivalent to i = 1; j = 2;
```

Each of the assignment operators =, +=, -=, *=, /=, %=, &=, |=, ^=, <<=, >>= requires an lvalue as its left operand. The resulting expression is an lvalue. However, using such lvalues as is done in the following example is unwise:

```
int i;
(i = 2) = 3;        // '= 2' makes no sense.
(i += 5) = -i;      // Result undefined.
```

Assigning the value 2 to i makes no sense here because this value is immediately overwritten by 3. On the third line, there are two possible results. Either i += 5 or the second operand, -i, is evaluated first. In the former case, the final value of i will be -(3 + 5) = -8, in the latter it will be -3. In general, the order of evaluation of subexpressions in an expression is undefined. Exceptions are the operators &&, || and the comma operator (,), for which left-to-right evaluation is guaranteed.

The expressions E1 and E2 must be lvalues in ++E1 and E2++. Curiously enough, ++E1 is an lvalue but E2++ is not. (Remember, ++E is equivalent to E+=1, which, as we have seen, is also an lvalue.) This is illustrated by the following example:

```
int i, j;
i = 0; j = ++ ++i;   // j = i = 2
i = 0; j = i++ ++;   // Error.
```

It is strongly recommended to use a blank space in expressions such as ++ ++i, but if we do not, the meaning is the same. Sequences of more than two successive plus signs, not separated by blank space are sometimes very difficult to interpret. For example, if we write i+++j, it is not easy to choose between i++ + j and i + ++j. The former happens to be the right choice, as the following example illustrates:

```
int i, j, k;
i = j = 0; k = i++ + j;    // i = 1, j = 0, k = 0
i = j = 0; k = i+++j;      // Same as preceding line
i = j = 0; k = i + ++j;    // i = 0, j = 1, k = 1
i = 0; j = ++++i;          // j = i = 2, as in j = ++ ++i;
i = 0; j = + + + +i;       // j = i = 0, as in j = +(+(+(+i)));
```

The last line shows that we cannot write a blank space between the two plus signs of a ++ operator. The same applies to other operators consisting of more than one characters, such as <=, <<, and so on.

The decrement operators in −−i and i−− behave like the corresponding increment operators ++ with regard to lvalues and association.

Exercises

In Exercises 3.1, 3.2, 3.3 a sequence of integers is to be read from the keyboard, followed by some nonnumeric code to signal the end of the sequence. The sequence may have any length, so you cannot store all integers that are read into an array.

3.1 Read in a sequence of integers. Find out what is the largest of these and how many times this largest integer occurs in the sequence.

3.2 Read in a sequence of integers (some of which may be equal). Count how many distinct integers are given. You may assume that there will be no more than 100 (although the sequence length is unlimited).

3.3 Read in a sequence of integers. From each integer, its least significant six bits are taken, which form a small integer (less than 64). The program is to produce a table with all small integers obtained in this way, along with their frequencies.

3.4 Write a program which reads a date given as three positive integers (day, month, year), as, for example,

```
31 12 1990
```

Your program is to compute the day number of this date, counted from January 1st of that year. So in the given example, that day number would be 365. Take into account that the year may be a leap year. This is the case if the given year number is a multiple of 4 but not a multiple of 100. There is one exception: it is also a leap year if it is a multiple of 400.

3.5 Show that by means of bit operations you can store four nonnegative integers, each less than 16, into an **int** variable **x**. Write a program which first reads four such integers, a_0, a_1, a_2, a_3, and stores them into the variable **x**. Then the user is asked to enter an integer i ($0 \leq i \leq 3$) to find a_i (in **x**) and to print its value.

3.6 Show how you can efficiently multiply an integer that is read from the keyboard (and that is not too large) by 100, without using the operator *. Use the operator << several times.

3.7 Read a hexadecimal integer from the keyboard (using the conversion specification %x). In its binary representation we count the bits 0, 1, ..., starting on the right. Swap the following bits, and print the result as a hexadecimal integer:

> bit 0 and bit 7,
> bit 1 and bit 6,
> bit 2 and bit 5,
> bit 3 and bit 4.

3.8 As Exercise 3.7, but now the bits 0 to 7 are to be rotated one position to the left (instead of being swapped):

> bit 0 moves to bit 1;
> the original bit 1 moves to bit 2;
>
> ...
>
> the original bit 6 moves to bit 7;
> the original of bit 7 moves to bit 0.

3.9 Read in the number sequence

$$n, x, a_n, a_{n-1}, ..., a_1, a_0$$

to compute

$$y = a_n x^n + a_{n-1} x^{n-1} + ... + a_1 x + a_0$$

by means of *Horner's method*. This means that, for example, with $n = 3$, the following identity is used

$$a_3 x^3 + a_2 x^2 + a_1 x + a_0 = \{(a_3 x + a_2) x + a_1\} x + a_0$$

With values of n other than 3 the method works analogously. Use type **double** for all numbers except for n, which is an integer.

4

Functions and Program Structure

4.1 Definition and Declaration of Functions

In mathematics functions are abstract notions. By contrast, they consist of concrete program text in C and C++. In some other languages a distinction is made between functions on the one hand and procedures or subroutines on the other. In C++ we use the term *function* for both purposes.

Let us begin by considering a function **fun** with four parameters, **x**, **y**, **i**, and **j**, where **x** and **y** have type **float**, and **i** and **j** have type **int**. We will define this function in such a way that **fun(x, y, i, j)** is equal to

$$\frac{x - y}{i - j}$$

if $i \neq j$. If $i = j$, we cannot compute this quotient because in a division the denominator must not be zero. In that case, **fun** is to return the value 10^{20}, preceded by the sign of the numerator **x − y**, unless this is also zero: if that happens, **fun** is to return the value 0. Program FDEMO1 shows how this can be done. It consists of two functions, **main** and **fun**. As you can see in this program, the following occurs twice:

```
float fun(float x, float y, int i, int j)
```

We say that **fun** is *declared* inside the **main** function and *defined* after it. The function *definition* is the function itself, whereas the function *declaration* is only an announcement of it.

```
// FDEMO1: Demonstration program with a function.
#include <iostream.h>

int main()
{  float fun(float x, float y, int i, int j), xx, yy;
   int ii, jj;
   cout <<
   "Enter two real numbers followed by two integers:\n";
   cin >> xx >> yy >> ii >> jj;
   cout << "Value returned by function: "
        << fun(xx, yy, ii, jj) << endl;
   return 0;
}

float fun(float x, float y, int i, int j)
{  float a = x - y;
   int b = i - j;
   return b != 0 ? a/b :
          a > 0 ? +1e20 :
          a < 0 ? -1e20 : 0.0;
}
```

The technical term for an expression such as

```
fun(xx, yy, ii, jj)
```

is a (function) *call*; **xx**, **yy**, **ii**, and **jj** are called *arguments*. A function call implies the execution of the actions described by the function, after which the program is resumed at the position immediately after the call. The *parameters* (**x**, **y**, **i**, **j**) are used as local variables in the function, with the values of the corresponding arguments (**xx**, **yy**, **ii**, **jj**) as their initial values. The term *local variables* is more often used for variables such as **a** and **b** in our example. They do not exist outside the function.

A *return-statement* of the form

```
return expression;
```

causes a jump back to the calling function (**main** in our example), with the evaluated *expression* as the *return value*. In FDEMO1 we have used a rather complicated conditional expression in the return-statement.

Here is a demonstration of program FDEMO1, which computes 80.0/16 = 5.0:

```
Enter two real numbers followed by two integers:
100.5 20.5
20 4
Value returned by function: 5
```

In the same way as we can split up a combined declaration, such as

```
int m, n, k;
```

into several separate declarations, we can replace the line

```
float fun(float x, float y, int i, int j), xx, yy;
```

in program FDEMO1 with

```
float fun(float x, float y, int i, int j);
float xx, yy;
```

We have to specify the type of each parameter, even if it is the same as that of the previous one. For example, the following is not allowed:

```
float fun(float x, y, int i, j)    // Error
```

A function declaration is often called a *function prototype*. It is identical with the first line of the function definition, except for the semicolon at the end, which is written in the declaration but must be absent in the definition. We may omit the parameter names in a function declaration, as, for example, in

```
float fun(float, float, int, int);
```

However, we prefer including such names: first, they may be useful for documentation purposes, and, second, the compiler may use them in error messages for any incorrect function calls. For each function definition we can obtain the corresponding function prototype in a very simple way, namely by copying its first line and writing a semicolon at its end.

A function (such as **fun** in our example) may be declared either inside a function (such as **main**) that contains a call to it, or before it, at the global level. The latter is the case in

```
...
float fun(float x, float y, int i, int j);

int main()
{  ...
}
```

When declared at the global level, the declaration is valid until the end of the program module, that is, until the end of the file. A declaration inside a function is valid only in that function. A function may be defined only once, but may be declared as often as we like. Suppose that besides **main**, there is another function, **f**, that also calls **fun**. Then if we declare **fun** inside **main** we also have to declare it inside **f**; we need not do this if **fun** is declared globally, before **main** and **f**. Remember, the *definition* of one function cannot occur inside another.

So far, we have discussed function definitions and function declarations as if they were always distinct entities. However, this need not be the case. Remember, a function definition also counts as a function declaration. This is interesting because we can write functions in any order. In our example, defining **fun** before **main** means that **fun** is defined before it is called, so that no separate declaration is needed. (Note, however, that if we have two functions **f** and **g**, which, under certain conditions, call each other, we need a special declaration for one of them.) The following program, FDEMO2, is completely equivalent to FDEMO1:

```
/* FDEMO2: Demonstration program with a function.
           Function definition acts also as a
           function declaration.
*/
#include <iostream.h>

float fun(float x, float y, int i, int j)
{   float a = x - y;
    int b = i - j;
    return b != 0 ? a/b :
           a > 0 ? +1e20 :
           a < 0 ? -1e20 : 0.0;
}

int main()
{   float xx, yy;
    int ii, jj;
    cout <<
    "Enter two real numbers followed by two integers:\n";
    cin >> xx >> yy >> ii >> jj;
    cout << "Value returned by function: "
         << fun(xx, yy, ii, jj) << endl;
    return 0;
}
```

As you can see, **fun** is not declared on the second line of the function **main**, as it was in FDEMO1; such a declaration is not needed here because of the order of the functions **fun** and **main**.

Function arguments need not be simple variables but they can also be more complex expressions. For example, we can write

```
float result = fun(xx + 1, 2 * yy, ii + 2, jj - 1);
```

In this case the parameters x, y, i and j will be assigned the values of xx + 1, 2 * yy, ii + 2 and jj − 1, respectively. The order in which the arguments are evaluated is undefined. In the above example that order is irrelevant, but the following example is different in this regard:

```
float result = fun(xx, yy, ++i, i + 3);   // Wrong
```

Here the value of i is changed when the third argument is evaluated, and i is also used in the fourth argument. The order in which the third and the fourth arguments are evaluated is undefined, which means that in evaluating i + 3 either the increased or the original value of i is used. Consequently, the value assigned to **result** will depend on the C++ compiler we are using, which is clearly undesirable. Another example of such bad program code is the following call to **printf**:

```
printf("%d %d", a[i], i++);      // Wrong
```

If, for example, i is zero before this call, either a[0] or a[1] (followed by 0) is written.

4.2 The **void** Keyword; Global Variables

Functions not returning a value

The function **fun** of Section 4.1 returns a **float** value, as the keyword **float** at the beginning of both its declaration and its definition shows. Instead, functions may return values of other types, or no value at all. Functions that do not return values are similar to what we call *procedures* in Pascal and *subroutines* in Fortran or assembly language. Instead of a normal type keyword, such as **float**, we write **void** at the beginning of such functions, as the following program illustrates:

```
// MAX3: A function that prints the maximum of three integers.
#include <iostream.h>

int main()
{  int i, j, k;
   void max3(int x, int y, int z);
   cout << "Enter three integers: ";
   cin >> i >> j >> k;
   max3(i, j, k);
   return 0;
}

void max3(int x, int y, int z)
{  if (y > x) x = y;
   if (z > x) x = z;
   cout << "The maximum of these three is: " << x << endl;
}
```

Note that **max3** does not contain a return-statement; we may write

```
    return;
```

at the end of this function, but this would be superfluous and very unusual, since a function, when its end is reached, returns to its caller anyway. Yet this simple form of the return-statement may be useful if it is executed conditionally and is followed by other statements, as in

```
void test(int x)
{ if (x < 0) return;
  ...
}
```

As for function **max3**, its parameter **x** is really used as a local variable: its value is altered. This will not affect the corresponding argument **i**. (If we wanted to alter **i** in this way, a different approach would be required, as we will see in Section 4.3.)

Functions without parameters

The keyword **void** can also be used to indicate that a function has no parameters. Program NOPAR contains such a function, which reads in a real number. As mentioned in Section 3.2, we can use the value returned by either **cin >> ...** or **scanf(...)** to check whether or not a read attempt has succeeded. So far, we have usually omitted such checks about the correctness of the input data, but in practice it is wise to include them in our programs. In a large program, we may want to read input data at a great many places; it would then be rather tedious if we had to include such a check each time we wanted to read a number. Instead, we can write a function of our own to perform the two tasks of reading and checking. Program NOPAR shows how this can be done:

```
// NOPAR: Using a function without parameters.
#include <stdio.h>

double readreal(void);

int main()
{   double xx;
    float x;
    printf("\nEnter a real number: ");
    xx = readreal();
    printf("Another one, please:  ");
    x = readreal();
    printf("The following numbers have been read: %f %f",
    xx, x);
    return 0;
}
```

```
double readreal(void)
{   double x;
    char ch;
    while (scanf("%lf", &x) != 1)
    {   do ch = getchar(); while (ch != '\n');
        // Rest of incorrect line has now been skipped,
        // see also Section 3.2.
        printf("\nIncorrect. Enter a number:\n");
    }
    return x;
}
```

The word **void** is used both in the declaration and in the definition of **readreal**. It denotes that this function has no parameters. You may wonder if, in both places, the word **void** could have been omitted. This is not the case in the C language, in which a declaration of **readreal** without **void** would mean that this function could have any number of parameters. In C++, however, the old C practice of omitting any information about parameters in function declarations is no longer allowed: if, in the declaration or the definition of a function, the list of parameters is empty and the word **void** is absent as well, then that function has no parameters. Unlike C, the language C++ therefore regards the following two forms as equivalent:

```
double readreal(void)
double readreal()
```

Consequently, the two occurrences of the keyword **void** in program NOPAR are superfluous.

As we have already seen, a function that returns a value may also be called as one that does not. For example, if we want to skip three numbers in the input, ignoring their values, we can use our function **readreal** as follows:

```
readreal(); readreal(); readreal();
```

The main function

In the past, most C programmers wrote the first line of a **main** function as

```
main()
```

Omitting a return type implies type **int**, not **void**. This short form is equivalent to

```
int main()
```

Writing **int** here is more logical, especially since we also write this return-statement, usually at the end of the **main** function:

```
return 0;
```

For example, with MS-DOS, the return value, such as 0 here, can be used in a batch file as an *error level*. We therefore replace 0 with a different value, such as 1, if we want to terminate program execution in the case of a run-time error. If we omit the return-statement in the **main** function, some compilers will give this error message:

```
Function should return a value.
```

To avoid this error message, some programmers define **main** as a **void** rather than an **int** function by replacing the above first line of the **main** function with

```
void main()
```

However, this might cause an operating system to use some undefined value returned by **main**. We therefore prefer using **int** instead of **void** here, in accordance with examples in books by Stroustrup and by Kernighan and Ritchie. The return-statements that we must provide as a consequence may seem a nuisance in small example programs but they are only a negligible proportion of the amount of program text in real applications.

Global variables

The variables that we use in a function can be either *local* or *global*. We call them *local* if they are declared and used only in that function. As a rule, we use local variables, unless this has serious drawbacks. The alternative, *global* variables, are declared (or, more specifically, *defined*) outside functions, at the same level as functions are defined. Here is a very simple (and therefore unrealistic) example:

```
#include <iostream.h>
int i;

void print_i()
{  cout << i << endl;
}

int main()
{  i = 123;
   print_i();
   return 0;
}
```

Because we have defined i prior to **print_i** and **main**, we can use this variable in both functions. Note that function **print_i** does not have parameters, nor does it return a value. Although, in principle, functions like this can do all kinds of useful work, this programming style is not recommended. We should be very careful with functions that have *side effects*, that is, functions that change the values of global variables. For example, if we had assigned a new value to **i** in function **print_i**, the call **print_i( )** would have been confusing, because the function name does not suggest any side effects: we expect **i** to have still the value 123 after the call.

The scope-resolution-operator ::

C++ enables us to use a global variable even in a function in which another variable with the same name is defined. We can indicate that the global variable is meant by writing the *scope-resolution-operator* :: in front of the variable name, as the following program illustrates:

```
#include <iostream.h>
int i=1;

int main()
{  int i=2;
   cout << ::i << endl;   // Output: 1 (global variable)
   cout << i << endl;     // Output: 2 (local variable)
   return 0;
}
```

The colon pair :: is also used in connection with structures and classes, as we will see in Section 6.5.

4.3 Altering Variables via Parameters

So far, function parameters could be regarded as local variables, which obtain their initial values from the corresponding arguments. This principle does not enable us, for example, to write a function that exchanges the values of two variables, passed to it as arguments. If we try to do this as follows:

```
void swap0(int x, int y)  // Error
{  int temp=x;
   x = y; y = temp;
}
```

then, with two **int** variables **i** and **j**, the call

```
swap0(i, j)
```

will not have the desired effect. Although, inside **swap**, the values of **x** and **y** are exchanged, the arguments **i** and **j** are used only once, namely to give the parameters x and y their initial values. After exchanging these, the new values of x and y are not passed back to i and j. The principle of parameter passing used here is technically known as 'call by value'.

Still, we can achieve our goal, and in C++ this can even be done in two ways. The first is specific to C++ and is based on 'call by reference' parameter passing. The second is the one C programmers are familiar with; it is based on using addresses and pointers. We will now discuss these two methods.

Reference parameters and reference variables

Here is a solution to our swapping problem; it is based on using the *reference parameters* x and y, and the parameter-passing method used is known as 'call by reference':

```
void swap1(int &x, int &y)
{   int temp=x;
    x = y; y = temp;
}
```

Note the use of the ampersand &. When used for parameters as above, it indicates that not only the *value* of the arguments but also their *addresses* are passed to the function. The variables x and y are no longer local variables but rather alternative notations for the arguments, such as i and j in the call

```
swap1(i, j);
```

It will be clear that the arguments of **swap1** must be lvalues (see Section 3.8), so i + 1 instead of i would not be allowed.

The idea of reference parameters, as used in **swap1**, will be easier to understand if we also discuss *reference variables* in general, outside the context of function calls. In the following program, x is a *reference variable*; it is not really an independent, new variable but rather an alternative way of accessing i:

```
// REFVAR: Demonstration of a reference variable.
#include <iostream.h>

int main()
{   int i, &x=i;
    i = 2; x *= 100;
    cout << "The value of i is now " << i << ".\n";
    cout << "Using x, we also find i = " << x << ".\n";
    return 0;
}
```

The most remarkable point of this program is that x *= 100 actually multiplies i by 100. Then the new value of i is printed. The output is

```
The value of i is now 200.
Using x, we also find i = 200.
```

In contrast to other variables, reference variables *must* be initialized so we cannot write

```
int &x;   // Error.
```

After the initialized declaration of x in program REFVAR, any assignment to x means an assignment to i. It is not possible to link x with another variable, say, j instead of i, later.

In function swap1, when called with i as its first argument, the relationship between x and i is the same as it is in program REFVAR. There is only a difference in notation: the formal parameters x and y are related to the arguments i and j by the call swap1(i, j) as would be the case after

```
int &x=i, &y=j;
```

Addresses

The C language does not offer the 'call by reference' parameter-passing facility we have been discussing for C++. Yet we can write a function in C to swap the values of two variables (as well as other functions that alter the values of variables via their parameters). This method is also available in C++, and it is certainly worthwhile to be familiar with it. It is based on supplying *addresses* as arguments and on two unary operators, each with an operand that follows the operator:

Operator	Meaning
&	The address of the object given by the operand
*	The object that has the address given by the operand

An *address* is a number permanently associated with a memory location. As * is the inverse operator of &, the expression *&i is just a complicated way of writing i. We are normally interested only in the *value* of a variable, not in its *address*, that is, we are not interested in where a variable is located in memory. Yet we often use the operator &, as we have already done in calls such as

```
scanf("%d", &n);
```

Since scanf is given the address of n, it can place a value into this variable. Similarly, the function swap that we need will be called as follows:

```
swap(&i, &j);
```

From this call and from the fact that arguments supply the corresponding parameters with initial values, it follows that the parameters of **swap** must be variables whose values are addresses. If these parameters are **p** and **q**, the values of **p** and **q** are addresses of certain locations, and we must write ***p** and ***q** to denote the contents of these locations. As we are dealing with addresses of **int** variables, ***p** and ***q** have type **int**, which explains why **p** and **q** are declared as

```
int *p, int *q
```

in the following function definition, which is the solution to our swapping problem:

```
void swap(int *p, int *q)
{   int temp=*p;
    *p = *q; *q = temp;
}
```

Remember, in each call to **swap** we must not forget to supply addresses as arguments, as we have done in the call **swap(&i, &j)**. This function **swap** can interchange the values of any two **int** objects. Let us, for example, consider the case that these are elements of array **a**, declared as

```
int a[100];
```

If we want to interchange the values of the first and the final elements, we can write

```
swap(&a[0], &a[99]);
```

Pointers

We have seen that in the function **swap** the expression ***p** has type **int**. However, the first parameter itself is **p** (not ***p**). We know that inside a function a parameter is in fact a local variable, so we may wonder what type this variable has. Variables that have addresses as their values are called *pointers*, so **p** is a *pointer*, and its type is *pointer-to-int*. We will discuss pointers in more detail in Section 5.3.

4.4 Types of Arguments and Return Values

Argument types

Function arguments are automatically converted to the required parameter types, if this is possible. If it is not, an error message is given. For example, the call **f(5)** in the following program is correct, even though **5** has type **int** and **f** has a **float** parameter. This call is in fact equivalent to **f(5.0)**, and the output of this program is 26.

```
#include <iostream.h>

float f(float x)
{   return x * x + 1;
}

int main()
{   cout << f(5);
    return 0;
}
```

The conversion from **5** to **float**, the type of parameter **x**, is possible because such a conversion is also possible in the assignment statement

```
x = 5;
```

This is a general rule: any conversions from argument types to parameter types are similar to analogous conversions that may take place in assignments; if the latter is possible, so is the former, and vice versa. With the above function **f**, the call to **f** in the following **main** function is incorrect:

```
int main()
{   float t=5;
    cout << f(&t);    // Error
    return 0;
}
```

The address argument **&t** is incompatible with the float parameter **x**. The error made here is analogous to the one in the assignment statement

```
x = &t;    // Error
```

where both x and t have type **float**. The compiler will not accept these constructions.

Types of return values

The conversion rules for assignments also apply to return-statements. An example is

```
int g(double x, double y)
{   return x * x - y * y + 1;
}
```

Although the keyword **int** at the beginning of this function says that **g** will return an integer, the expression in the return-statement has type **double**. The compiler will accept this, and perform the same conversion as it does when compiling the following assignment statement, where **i** has type **int**:

```
i = x * x - y * y + 1;
```

In either case truncation takes place, so 7.9, for example, is converted to 7. As discussed in Section 3.7, a cast is to be recommended in this assignment statement, so that we may see more clearly what actually happens. The same applies to the return-statement: although not required by the compiler, the cast in the following version of the return-statement is very welcome as a reminder that, because of conversion from **double** to **int**, the values before and after conversion may be different:

```
return int(x * x - y * y + 1);
```

4.5 Initialization

It is often convenient to *initialize* variables, that is, to give values to them as we are declaring them. We have already done this several times, but we have not yet discussed all aspects of this subject. When initializing variables, we should bear in mind the following rules:

(i) Variables can be initialized only when memory locations are assigned to them.
(ii) In the absence of explicit initialization, the initial value 0 is assigned to all variables that are global or static.

As we already know, the term *global* in (ii) refers to variables that are declared outside functions. The new term *static* is used for all variables in the declaration of which the keyword **static** is used. Global and static variables have in common that their memory locations are *permanent*, whereas nonstatic, local variables are assigned memory locations temporarily, on a 'stack'. As the latter variables are *automatically* assigned memory locations when the functions in which they are declared are entered, they are called *automatic* variables, and we may use the keyword **auto** for them. Memory for automatic variables is released when the functions in which they are declared are left. According to rule (i), static variables local to a function are initialized only the first time this function is called.

For example, in the following program the variable **i** is set to 1 only once. The first call prints that value and increments **i**. The second call is more interesting in that **i** is not initialized once again: it still has its last value, 2, because the keyword **static** causes its memory space to be permanent. Consequently, this program prints the values 1 and 2:

```
#include <iostream.h>

void f()
{  static int i=1;
   cout << i++ << endl;
}
```

```
int main()
{   f(); f();
    return 0;
}
```

If we had separated the declaration and the assignment (by writing **static int i; i=1;** instead of **static int i=1;**) the value 1 would have printed twice, as it would have been if we had simply omitted the keyword **static**.

According to rule (ii), the declaration

```
static int i;
```

is equivalent to

```
static int i=0;
```

where i can be either a global or a local variable. If we omit the keyword **static** in these two lines, the resulting declarations are equivalent only if i is a global variable.

We have not yet discussed why static variables might be useful. As for *global* static variables, they are useful for programs that consist of more than one file, as we will see in the next section. A simple, but interesting application of a *local* static variable is its use as a 'flag' that indicates whether a function is called for the first time. Sometimes we want some special action to take place during the first call. Here is a very simple example, which you can easily replace with a more practical one yourself:

```
void f()
{   static int firsttime=1;
    if (firsttime)
    {   cout <<
        "This is printed only the first time f is called.\n";
        firsttime = 0;
    }
    cout << "This is printed each time f is called.\n";
}
```

We can also initialize *arrays*, by writing their initial values within a pair of braces. Again, the rules (i) and (ii) apply. There must not be more initial values between the braces than there are array elements. If there are fewer (but at least one!), the trailing elements are initialized to 0. For example, with

```
float a[100] = {23, 41.5};
```

we have

```
a[0] = 23; a[1] = 41.5; a[2] = ... = a[99] = 0.
```

If, for an initialized array, we omit the array length, the number of initial values is taken as that length, as, for example, in

```
int b[] = {95, 34, 72};
```

which is equivalent to

```
int b[3] = {95, 34, 72};
```

So far, we have been writing (numerical) initial values as *constants*, which is allowed for any variable that is initialized. We can generalize this as follows. First, we may write *constant expressions* (such as **123 * 4 – 3 * 30**) whenever constants are allowed. For simple automatic variables, we can go further than that and initialize them with any expression of a suitable type. But remember, global and static variables (with permanent memory) and arrays may only be initialized with constant expressions. These rules are easy to remember if we bear in mind that initialization can take place only when memory space is allocated. For variables with permanent memory space, this is before the program is executed, so values computed at run time cannot be used for the initialization of such variables.

If we want to initialize arrays of characters, we can write a list of character constants between braces, as is done in

```
char str[16] = {'C', 'h', 'a', 'r', 'l', 'e', 's', ' ',
                'D', 'i', 'c', 'k', 'e', 'n', 's'};
```

Although the initialization list consist of only 15 character constants, we give array **str** the value 16 to accommodate a trailing null character ('\0'). We need not write this null character at the end of the list because in a partially initialized array all remaining elements are set to zero, and for character constants 'zero' means the null character.

However, the above way of initializing is very tedious for long strings, as in this example. Fortunately, a much more convenient way is available; we can abbreviate the declaration just given by

```
char str[16] = "Charles Dickens";
```

If we had omitted **16** here, array **str** would still have had length 16 because that is the number of bytes used for the given string literal (including the null character). If, instead of 16, we specify a larger number, all trailing unused elements of **str** would contain the null character '\0'. We cannot replace 16 with a smaller value in this example because there must be room for a trailing null character, which will automatically be added. We will discuss arrays of characters, or *strings*, in Section 5.4.

Default arguments

A simple but nice facility in C++ is the possibility of supplying a function with fewer arguments than there are parameters. All we have to do is supply the parameters with default argument values, which we write in the same way as when initializing normal variables. Once a parameter is initialized, any subsequent parameters must also be initialized. For example, with function **f** of the form

```
void f(int i, float x=0, char ch='A')
{ ...
}
```

the following calls are allowed:

```
f(5, 1.23, 'E');
f(5, 1.23);           // Equivalent to f(5, 1.23, 'A');
f(5);                 // Equivalent to f(5, 0, 'A');
```

If function **f** is not only *defined*, but also separately *declared*, any default argument values may be specified only once, either in the declaration or in the definition, but not in both. For example, we may write

```
void f(int i, float x=0, char ch='A'); // Declaration
...
void f(int i, float x, char ch)          // Definition
{ ...
}
```

We must not insert =0 and ='A' in this definition because default values were already given in the declaration.

4.6 Separate Compilation

Large C++ programs are preferably split up into several program files, also called *modules*. This is important in view of maintenance: any future program changes should preferably affect only a few modules of limited size. The modules of a program are compiled separately and linked together later by a so-called *linker*. We will not discuss commands for compiling and linking, because these subjects are system dependent and do not belong to the C++ language. Instead, we will focus on these program modules themselves. Although the following two modules, separated here by a horizontal line, form one program, they are two distinct files; we can compile them one by one, and link them together afterwards:

```
// MODULE1

#include <iostream.h>

int main()
{   void f(int i), g(void);
    extern int n;
            // Declaration of n (not a definition)
    f(8);
    n++;
    g();
    cout << "End of program.\n";
    return 0;
}
```

```
// MODULE2

#include <iostream.h>

int n=100;
            // Definition of n (also a declaration)
static int m=7;

void f(int i)
{   n += i+m;
}

void g(void)
{   cout << "n = " << n << endl;
}
```

An interesting point about variable **n** is that it is used in both modules. We say that the variable **n**, like the functions **f** and **g**, is *defined* in module 2 and *declared* in module 1. If a variable declaration begins with the keyword **extern**, as is the case with **n** in module 1, it is not at the same time a variable definition. Without this keyword, it is a definition. Every variable definition is at the same time a variable declaration; as the latter term is more common than the former we have often used it for declarations that were, more specifically, definitions. We may use a variable only after it has been declared (in the same file). Only variable definitions allocate memory and may therefore contain initializations. We define a variable only once but we may declare it as often as we like. A variable declaration at the global level (outside functions) is valid from that declaration until the end of the file; a declaration (such as that of **n** in module 1) inside a function is valid only in that function. In this regard, definitions and declarations of global variables are similar to those of functions; the main difference is that we may omit the keyword **extern** in function declarations.

Another interesting variable is **m**, defined in module 2 as

```
static int m=7;
```

As we know, *local* static variables have permanent memory, as have global variables. Since **m** is a global variable, its memory location is already permanent, so the keyword **static** seems superfluous here. However, **static**, when used for a global variable, makes this variable the 'private property' of the module in which it occurs, that is, other modules do not have access to it. Note that this is somewhat similar to *local* static variables, which, although having permanent memory, are the 'private property' of the functions to which they are local. If we had written

```
extern int m;
```

in module 1, the linker would have given an error message because the static variable **m** of module 2 is not published to the linker.

Figure 4.1 shows that the linker can build an executable program, using object modules each of which is obtained by compiling a source module. You can easily verify the following output of the program consisting of modules 1 and 2:

```
n = 116
End of program.
```

Although not demonstrated in this program, the keyword **static** can also be applied to *function* definitions. We then write it at the very beginning, before the type of the return value. Such functions will not be published to the linker, so that other modules have no access to them. The keyword **static**, both for global variables and for functions, is useful to avoid conflicts of names and to prevent accidental use of them. Imagine a very large program, consisting of a great many modules, in which we have to look for an error caused by a global variable that at some moment obtains a value that we did not anticipate. If that variable is static, we can restrict ourselves to the module in which it is defined; if not, we have to extend our investigation to all other modules in which it is declared (with the keyword **extern**).

As a rule, we prefer local variables to global ones. If it is really necessary or desirable for some variables to be global, we preferably make them static, which means that they are 'local with regard to the file in which they are defined'. As we know, all C++ functions are global: we cannot define a function inside another function. However, by using the keyword **static** for them, their scope is restricted to the file in which they occur, which makes them 'less global' than nonstatic functions. When you are writing a module of a large program, you are strongly recommended to use the keyword **static** for the definition of every function and of every global variable that is used only in that module. Ignoring this advice leads to what is called 'name-space pollution'.

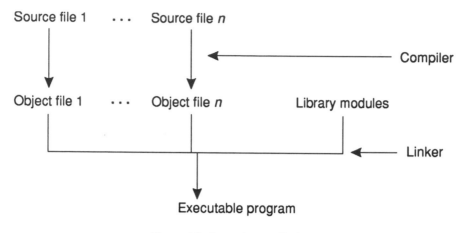

Figure 4.1. Separate compilation

4.7 Some Mathematical Standard Functions

We can successfully use the C++ language in a great variety of applications fields, including science and engineering. For these purposes we often need to use some well-known mathematical functions, available in a standard library. We include their declarations in our program by writing

```
#include <math.h>
```

Except for some rather technical functions (to be discussed in Section 10.6), these declarations are listed below, along with some information about these functions, which will probably be sufficient for those who want to use them. Remember, thanks to our including *math.h*, we need not actually write these declarations in our programs:

```
double cos(double x);              cos x  (x in radians)
double sin(double x);              sin x
double tan(double x);              tan x
double exp(double x);              exp x
double log(double x);              ln x
double log10(double x);            log x (base 10)
double pow(double x, double y);    x^y
double sqrt(double x);             √x
double floor(double x);            floor(4.9) = 4.0 etc.
double ceil(double x);             ceil(8.1) = 9.0 etc.
double fabs(double x);             |x|
double acos(double x);             arccos x
double asin(double x);             arcsin x
```

```
double atan(double x);              arctan x, range (–π/2, π/2)
double atan2(double y, double x);   see explanation below
double cosh(double x);              cosh x
double sinh(double x);              sinh x
double tanh(double x);              tanh x
```

Besides the function **fabs**, to be used for floating-point expressions, there are also the functions **abs** for type **int** and **labs** for type **long**. These are declared in the header file *stdlib.h* (see Section 10.12). These three functions should not be confused. The function **fabs** is too slow for **int** values, and, more seriously, **abs** converts floating values to **int**:

```
float x = abs(-4.56);     // x = 4.0
float y = fabs(-4.56);    // y = 4.56
```

The function **atan2** comes in very handy if, in the *xy*-plane, a point P(*x*, *y*), not coinciding with the origin O, is given and we want to know the (positive or negative) angle φ between OP and the positive *x*-axis, as shown in Figure 4.2. This angle φ is equal to **atan**(*y*/*x*) if *x* is positive. However, the latter expression is undefined for zero *x* and is different from φ for negative *x*. For any *x* and *y* (not both zero), φ = **atan2**(*y*, *x*) is defined, satisfying

$$\cos \varphi = x/\sqrt{(x^2 + y^2)} \qquad \sin \varphi = y/\sqrt{(x^2 + y^2)} \qquad -\pi < \varphi \le \pi$$

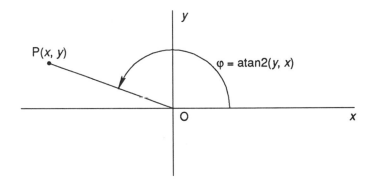

Figure 4.2. The **atan2** *function*

4.8 Function Overloading

Unlike C, the C++ language allows us to define two or more functions with the same name, provided that their numbers of parameters or their parameter types differ. For example, we can write the following two output functions for numbers:

```
void writenum(int i)       // Function 1
{  printf("%10d", i);
}

void writenum(float x)     // Function 2
{  printf("%10.4f", x);
}
```

After these function definitions, a call of the form

```
writenum(expression);
```

will call function 1 if *expression* has type **int** and function 2 if it has floating-point type. These two functions **writenum** are distinguished by their parameter types. Here is an example in which the distinction is made on the basis of the number of parameters:

```
double f(float x)
{  ...
}

double f(float x, float y)
{  ...
}
```

It is not required for both functions **f** to return values of the same type, as is the case here. Note, however, that functions with the same name but different return types must also be different in the number or types of their parameters. For example, the following would be incorrect:

```
int g(int n)
{ ...
}

float g(int n)  // Error: again only one int parameter.
{ ...
}
```

Defining several functions with the same name is technically known as *overloading*. (In Section 6.8 we will see that not only functions but also operators can be overloaded.)

Besides functions of our own, *standard library functions* can also be overloaded. Take, for example, the mathematical standard function **sqrt**, declared in *math.h* as

```
double sqrt(double a);
```

Suppose that we want to apply this function very often to an integer a and that we want an integer result, namely the greatest integer the square of which is not greater than a. On the other hand, the standard function **sqrt** must remain available because we will use it for floating-point arguments. We will therefore overload the standard function **sqrt** with a integer function **sqrt** of our own, so that we have

```
sqrt(200)    =  14
sqrt(200.)   =  14.1421...
```

Since our own **sqrt** function uses only integer arithmetic, it may be faster than the standard function on your machine. (Actually, on a 486 PC with a mathematical coprocessor, there is no significant difference in speed, but on a 386 without a co-processor the difference is enormous.) The method to be used is based on the Newton–Raphson algorithm, which is well known in numerical analysis. For those not familiar with it, our computation can also be explained as follows. Suppose that we already have some approximation x $(1 \leq x \leq a)$ of $\sqrt{a}$. We then compute $q = a/x$. In the ideal case we have $a = x^2$ and $q = x$. Otherwise, q is another approximation of $\sqrt{a}$. If x is less than $\sqrt{a}$, then q is greater than $\sqrt{a}$ and vice versa, and the arithmetic mean $(x + q)/2$ will be a better approximation. We therefore use this as a new value for x and repeat this process. When working with integers, we can terminate as soon as x and q differ by at most 1; the smaller of x and q is then the desired answer. For example, with $a = 8$ and $x = 2$ we have $q = 4$; by executing **x = (x + q)/2** and **q = a/x** we find x = 3 and q = 2. We must now be careful to prevent an endless loop: the next values would be $x = 2$ and $q = 4$, which we have had already. We should therefore end the loop as soon as $|x - q| \leq 1$. With $x = 3$ and $q = 2$, we then use the smaller, 2, of these two values. We could start this iterative process with $x = 1$. However, we can do much better by shifting a to the right by about half its length. This clearly makes sense if a is an even power of 2. For example, if $a = 64$, we can immediately find $x = \sqrt{a}$ by deleting half of its trailing zeros:

$$a = (1000000)_{\text{bin}} = 64$$
$$x = (1000)_{\text{bin}} = 8$$

In this case we need not perform our iterative process at all. This is different if a is not an even power of 2, but then we can easily find a reasonable initial value for x by shifting a to the right by about half its bit length. Using 200 instead of 64, for example, we can use

$$a = (11001000)_{\text{bin}} = 200$$
$$x = (1100)_{\text{bin}} = 12$$

In the iterative process we then find $q = 200/12 = 16$, followed by $x = (12 + 16)/2 = 14$, $q = 200/14 = 14$. Comparing these two examples, with a shifted to the right by 3 positions, we can now be more precise with regard to how many positions we should shift a to the right to find our initial x value: with a consisting of m significant bits, we shift a to the right by $m/2$ bits if m is even and by $(m - 1)/2$ bits if m is odd. Note that this recipe gives immediately the final values $x = 1$ for $a = 1$, 2 and 3 and $x = 2$ for a = 4 and 5. Although all this may sound rather complicated, the program text for this is very compact, as function **sqrt** in the program SQROOT shows. This program calls both our own function and the standard function **sqrt**. Either function is called *n* times, where *n* is read from the keyboard. Depending on the machine we are using, we may be able to demonstrate that our integer function **sqrt** is faster than the standard function with the same name by taking a large value for *n*:

```
// SQROOT: Overloading sqrt with a fast integer version.
#include <iostream.h>
#include <math.h>

int sqrt(int a)
{   unsigned x = a, b = a<<1, q;
    while (b >>= 2) x >>= 1;
    while (x > (q = a/x) + 1 || x < q - 1) x = (x + q) >> 1;
    return x < q ? x : q;
}

int main()
{   cout <<
    "Both the (truncated) integer square root and the\n" <<
    "real square root of a will be computed n times.\n" <<
    "Enter the positive integers a and n: ";
    int a, iroot;
    long n, i;
    cin >> a >> n;
    for (i=0; i<n; i++) iroot = sqrt(a);   // Our own sqrt.
    cout << "Integer square root: " << iroot << endl;
    float froot, fa=float(a);
    for (i=0; i<n; i++) froot = sqrt(fa);
                                    // Standard function sqrt.
    cout << "Real square root: " << froot << endl;
    return 0;
}
```

Note that after the introduction of our function **sqrt**, with an **int** parameter, the argument 200 in the call **sqrt(200)** is not converted to type **double**, as would have been the case otherwise.

If we think of using overloading in cases where only the number of parameters differ, we should seriously consider the possibility of using default arguments instead, as discussed at the end of Section 4.5. Recall that there we had an example of a function **f** called as follows, without using overloading:

```
f(5, 1.23, 'E');
f(5, 1.23);
f(5);
```

In this example, overloading would lead to duplicated code, which is avoided if we write only one function **f** with default arguments.

Type-safe linkage

You may wonder how the linker can distinguish between several functions with the same name, differing only in the types of their parameters. After all, with separate compilation, it is possible for one module to call a function, say, **f**, with an **int** argument, while there are two definitions of **f** in other modules, one with an **int** and one with a **float** parameter. This problem is solved by *name mangling*: the function name **f** is appended with coded information about its parameters, and this information is supplied to the linker. This convention provides a very safe way of linking program modules together, hence its name *type-safe linkage*. We can benefit from it even if we do not apply function overloading at all. Suppose that in one module we use a function **f**, which we declare in this module as follows:

```
void f(int i);
```

Suppose also that there is only function **f**, which has the following form:

```
void f(float x)
{  ...
}
```

This definition happens to be in a module other than the declaration just shown. If we had been programming in C, we would have had a serious problem, not detected by the compiler and the linker. In C++, however, the linker will detect this error.

4.9 References as Return Values

In Section 4.3 we have discussed reference parameters. The return value can also be a reference, as is the case with the function **smaller** in the following program:

```
//REFFUN: Reference as return value.
#include <iostream.h>

int &smaller(int &x, int &y)
{  return (x < y ? x : y);
}

int main()
{  int a=23, b=15;
   cout << "a = " << a << "  b = " << b << endl;
   cout << "The smaller of these is " << smaller(a, b)
        << endl;
   smaller(a, b) = 0;  // A function call as left-hand side!
   cout <<
   "The smaller of a and b is set to 0. Thus we now have \n";
   cout << "a = " << a << "  b = " << b << endl;
   return 0;
}
```

This program shows two calls of the function **smaller**. The first is only to compute the smaller of **a** and **b**, which could also have been done if the three occurrences of the ampersand **&** in the first line of **smaller** had been omitted. The second call in the statement

```
smaller(a, b) = 0;
```

is much more interesting. In most languages we cannot write a function call as the left-hand side of an assignment statement. In C++ this is possible because of the reference concept in this language. Function **smaller** does not return (only) the value of one of its arguments, but rather this argument itself. It is essential here that the arguments are variables and that we use **&** in the declaration of the parameters **x** and **y**.

The output of demonstration program REFFUN is as follows:

```
a = 23  b = 15
The smaller of these is 15
The smaller of a and b is set to 0. Thus we now have
a = 23  b = 0
```

Warning

If a function returns a reference, it is essential for the variable in question to exist after the function call. We must therefore not try to return a local variable of a function as a reference. The following function is therefore not correct:

```
int &incorrect()
{ int x=123;
   return x;      // Error due to & in the first line.
}
```

Most compilers will not compile this text but rather give an error message.

4.10 Inline Functions and Macros

Calling a (normal) function causes a jump to the function code to be executed; later, a jump back to the calling function (such as, for example, **main**) will take place. Also, any arguments have to be passed to the function and a return value has to be passed back to the calling function. If the function contains very little code and is to be called very frequently, it may make sense to use the keyword **inline** at the beginning of its declaration (and its definition). By doing this, we ask the compiler to implement the function in question by inline code, that is, as if we had actually written the code to be executed, instead of writing a call to a function that contains such code. For example, suppose that we often want to compute

$$1 + 2 + ... + n = \tfrac{1}{2}n(n + 1)$$

as a function of n, and that, for aesthetic reasons, we want to write this each time as a function call, although we would rather not call a real function for reasons of efficiency. We then write

```
inline int sum(int n) {return n * (n + 1) / 2;}
```

We can later call it as a normal function, although the compiler will try to implement it as inline code. For example, writing

```
y = 1.0 / sum(k+1);
```

is then equivalent to something like

```
{int t; y = 1.0 / (t = k + 1, t * (t + 1) / 2);}
```

Note that the argument value $k + 1$ is computed only once.

Macros

Inline functions are new in C++. In C we can use macros for the same purpose. As these are also available in C++ and are widely used, we will pay some attention to them as well, even though in C++ inline functions are to be preferred. In our example, we could write

```
#define sum(n) ((n) * ((n) + 1) / 2)
```

This is a *macro definition*. Macro calls have the same form as function calls, so this macro, too, can be used as follows:

```
y = 1.0 / sum(k+1);
```

Macro calls are *expanded* before the actual compilation process takes place. In this example, the resulting expanded statement will be

```
y = 1.0 / ((k + 1) * ((k + 1) + 1) / 2);
```

Between the first slash and the semicolon, we find the macro expansion. It consists of the form **((n) * ((n) + 1) / 2)**, found in the macro definition, in which all occurrences of parameter **n** have been replaced with the argument **k + 1**. It will now be clear why there are so many parentheses in the above macro definition. If we had written

```
#define sum(n) n * (n + 1) / 2
```

then **y = 1.0 / sum(k + 1);** would have been expanded as

```
y = 1.0 / k + 1 * (k + 1 + 1) / 2;
```

which is seriously wrong. Note that the above macro is less efficient than the inline function, because in our example it computes $k + 1$ twice.

Macros can have any number of parameters. Here is a very simple macro, which has no parameters at all:

```
#define LENGTH 100
```

After this, we can write the symbolic constant **LENGTH** instead of 100. This macro definition is of the form

```
#define identifier text
```

Each occurrence of *identifier* is replaced with *text*. This text need not be a constant, such as 100, but it may also be a longer and more complicated sequence of characters. At the end of the line we may use the backslash for continuation on the next line, as in

```
#define TITLE Windows Wisdom \
for C and C++ Programmers
```

The replacement of each occurrence of *identifier* with *text* takes place only if the identifier is a *token*, that is, if it is not part of another identifier: our last example does not apply to the identifier **TITLE1**, although **TITLE** occurs in this longer identifier. The term *token* is used for small basic units: identifiers, keywords, constants, operators and other separators. Between two successive tokens, at least one white-space character is required if they would otherwise form one new token.

Now that we have seen macros with and without parameters, we can understand that the following version of our previous example is incorrect:

```
#define sum (n) ((n) * ((n) + 1) / 2)
```

Because of the blank following **sum**, this macro has the form

```
#define sum   xxx
```

It is therefore regarded as one without parameters: the token **sum** is expanded into

```
(n) ((n) * ((n) + 1) / 2)
```

which is not what we want.

Problematic error messages

Since macro calls are expanded by the preprocessor, they no longer exist during syntax checking later. Therefore any messages about syntax errors apply to the expanded text, not to the macro definitions in which they occur. For example, if by mistake we write a semicolon at the end in

```
#define f(x) ((x)*(x)+(x)+1);
```

then the apparently correct line

```
y = f(a) * f(b);
```

will produce the following expansion:

```
y = ((a)*(a)+(a)+1); * ((b)*(b)+(b)+1);;
```

The compiler will not display this expansion but give an error message that refers to the shorter, correct line with the two macro calls. To make things worse, the compiler will not recognize * in the middle of the expanded expression as a multiplication operator, but rather regard this character as the 'indirection operator', to be discussed in detail in the next chapter. This explains a possibly confusing error message, such as *Invalid indirection*, produced by the compiler.

Special situations

If in a macro definition we use the names of earlier defined macros, these will be expanded as well; in other words, a macro may call other macros. However, unlike functions, macros cannot call themselves: if, in a macro definition, its own name is used, the latter is not expanded. For example, after

```
#define cos(x) cos((x) * PI/180)
```

the macro call **cos(phi + a)** is expanded to **cos((phi + a) * PI/180)**, and the identifier **cos** in this expansion is not expanded once again.

Another special situation arises if a macro is defined more than once. This is allowed provided the replacement text is identical in all these definitions. For example, the following two lines are contradictory and must therefore not occur in this combination:

```
#define LENGTH 100
#define LENGTH 1000
```

If in the latter line we replace 1000 with 100, these two identical lines may both be used. Curiously enough, this is a useful facility, since the same macro can now be defined in more than one header file, provided that such macro definitions are identical. It is then allowed to include several such header files in the same program file.

The string-generating character

If, in a macro definition, a parameter is immediately preceded by the character #, that parameter is surrounded by double quotes in the macro expansion. For example, with

```
#define printtext(x) printf("%s\n", #x)
```

the macro call **printtext(Example)** will be expanded to

```
printf("%s\n", "Example")
```

The interesting point of this is that we can use the parameter in question several times, both with and without #, as this example shows:

```
#define printvalue(x) printf(#x " = %f\n", x)
```

Thanks to this slightly more complicated macro definition, we can simply use the macro call **printvalue(Temperature)** to obtain the following expansion:

```
printf("Temperature" " = %f\n", Temperature)
```

which in turn is equivalent to

```
printf("Temperature = %f\n", Temperature)
```

as we have discussed in Section 1.5.

The token-concatenation operator

In most programming languages there is no way of concatenating tokens to form new ones. In C and C++ this can be done with macros. For example, suppose we want to abbreviate these three lines:

```
table_entry[0] = table_entry0;
element[5] = element5;
article[9] = article9;
```

As you can see, a name and a number occur twice on each line, but the second time they are no longer individual tokens (such as **table_entry** and 0), but rather combined into one token (**table_entry0**). Here is a macro definition that we can use for this purpose:

```
#define set(x, i) x[i] = x##i
```

The 'operator' ## (to be used only in macro definitions!) concatenates x and i, or, rather, the corresponding arguments, used in macro calls such as

```
set(table_entry, 0);
set(element, 5);
set(article, 9);
```

These macro calls expand to the three above assignment statements.

4.11 Other Preprocessor Facilities

Besides macros, there are other program lines that begin with the character #, and that are processed by the preprocessor before the actual compilation takes place. We will discuss these in this section.

Header files

The preprocessor also expands **#include**-lines, such as

```
#include <stdio.h>
#include "myfile.h"
```

These two lines are logically replaced with the contents of the header files *stdio.h* and *myfile.h*. We say that in this way we *include* these files. Notice the difference in notation between **<stdio.h>** and **"myfile.h"**, which is to indicate where the header file is to be found:

<...>   The header file is searched for (only) in the general include directories.
"..."   The header file is successively searched for
              1.   in the current directory, and, if not found there,
              2.   in the general include directories.

In practice, header files are frequently used to declare functions and to define macros and (only) inline functions. In particular with programs that consist of many modules, header files provide a convenient way of reducing the amount of source code: we often want to write calls to the same functions (and macros) in different modules, and we can now simply include the header files in which these functions are declared (and in which these macros are defined). Without the facility of using header files, it would be necessary to duplicate program text, which, in case of program modifications, would be a potential source of errors. It is possible to write #include lines in header files: if the header file *a.h* contains the line **#include "aa.h"**, including *a.h* implies including *aa.h*.

    Suppose that we have written two header files, say, *a.h* and *b.h*, which are used in several program modules. Sometimes we use only *a.h*, sometimes only *b.h*, and occasionally we include them both. It may then be desirable to write the definition of some macro in both *a.h* and *b.h*. This implies that, if we include both *a.h* and *b.h*, that macro will occur twice after the inclusion of *a.h* and *b.h*. Fortunately, such a duplication is allowed, provided the macro definitions are identical.

We should not write function *definitions* (other than inline functions) in header files because that might cause problems for the linker. The following example illustrates this. Note that there are three files, two of which are program modules to be compiled and linked together:

```
// TEST.H
inline int f(int x){return x * x;}
int g(int x);
```

```
// MOD1: First program module
#include <iostream.h>
#include "test.h"

int main()
{   int j=f(3);
    int k=g(4);
    cout << j << " " << k << endl;
    return 0;
}
```

```
// MOD2: Second program module
#include "test.h"
int g(int x){return f(x);}
```

Since **f** is an inline function, we can define it in the header file *test.h*. If we omit the keyword **inline**, the linker would find the compiled version of this function twice and would then produce an error message. Function **g**, not being an inline function, is *defined* in module MOD2 and (only) *declared* in *test.h*. Incidentally, any global variables may be declared in a header file but should not be defined there for the same reason.

Conditional compilation

We can instruct the preprocessor to compile a program fragment (A) only if a certain condition is met; if not, there can be another fragment (B) that is to be compiled instead. This can be done as follows:

```
#if constant expression
  Program fragment A
#else
  Program fragment B
#endif
```

Note that this is a *preprocessor statement*, not a normal conditional statement: it is executed during compilation time, not during execution time. We always write **#if** at its beginning and **#endif** at its end. The line **#else** (and program fragment B) is optional. The condition after **#if** must be a constant expression so that it can be evaluated by the compiler. If its value is nonzero, the compiler compiles program fragment A; otherwise it compiles program fragment B, if present.

Conditional compilation is interesting especially in combination with the use of header files. For example, if **MAX** is a symbolic constant defined (as a macro without parameters) in header file *a.h*, we can write

```
#include "a.h"
#define LENGTH 100

#if LENGTH < MAX
...    // Program fragment A
#endif
```

Whether or not program fragment A is compiled depends on how **MAX** is defined in the header file *a.h*.

Preprocessor statements for conditional compilation may be nested. However, instead of doing this, we can often use a special construction with **#elif**, as, for example,

```
#if LENGTH < 100
... // Fragment A
#elif LENGTH < 1000
... // Fragment B
#else
... // Fragment C
#endif
```

As its name suggests, **#elif** is a combination of **#else** and **#if**, but it does not require an **#endif** (as would **#if**). This example is equivalent to the following, with two **#ifs** and therefore also with two **#endifs**:

```
#if LENGTH < 100
... // Fragment A
#else
#if LENGTH < 1000
... // Fragment B
#else
... // Fragment C
#endif
#endif
```

With conditional compilation we can make the compiler temporarily ignore a portion of our program. We sometimes want to do this during program development. Most people would insert the comment tokens (/* and */) for this purpose, but this will cause a problem if the program fragment that is to be ignored already contains comment, because comments must not be nested. In that case we can simply use a line with **#if 0** at the beginning and one with **#endif** at the end (instead of /* and */). For example, the second and the third of the following lines are ignored by the compiler, and the comment on the second line causes no problems:

```
#if 0
  i = 123;  /* Some comment */
  j = i + 1;
#endif
```

Tests about names being known

The preprocessor can check whether or not a name has been defined, as the following example shows:

```
#if !defined(PI)
#define PI 3.14159265358979
#endif
```

Only if **PI** has not been defined will the second line be processed; if **PI** has already been defined, this line is ignored. This prevents any problems with conflicting definitions of **PI**: we may define symbolic constants more than once, but such multiple definitions must be identical. Therefore the above conditional definition of the constant **PI** is useful if (a) we do not know whether this constant has been defined in a header file that we are using and (b) we do not know the precision used in such a definition, if any.

In combination with **defined(...)**, we can use the logical operators !, ||, and &&. These operators cannot be used in combination with the older alternative forms **#ifdef** and **#ifndef**:

`#ifdef` *name*	is equivalent to	`#if defined(`*name*`)`
`#ifndef` *name*	is equivalent to	`#if !defined(`*name*`)`

If we want to cancel the effect of

```
#define name text
```

we can 'undefine' *name* by writing

```
#undef name
```

Thus, to be complete, we should say that the operator **defined** and the preprocessor directives **#ifdef** and **#ifndef** apply to names defined with **#define**, *in so far as these names have not been undefined by means of* **#undef**.

It is not an error to use **#undef** for a name that has not been defined at all, so we may use it to cancel any previous definition of a name without being sure that there is one.

Numbering of program lines

Error messages from the compiler normally refer to line numbers (1, 2, ...). If for some reason or other we want the lines to be numbered, for example, 1001, 1002, ..., from some position in the program, we can write

```
#line 1001
```

in that position. If the compiler also mentions the name of the program file, we can instead supply a different name to be used. For example, if the desired new name is *aaa.cpp* and it is to be used after the new line number 1001, we can write

```
#line 1001 "aaa.cpp"
```

Making the compiler print error messages

We can use a line starting with **#error** to make the compiler display an error message. This is useful especially in connection with conditional compilation and with special information in header files. For example, suppose that we have various versions of a certain header file (say, *myfile.h*), and we want to check that its correct version (say, version B) is included. If in that header file the version number is defined as

```
#define V_B
```

(in which the replacement text is allowed to be absent) we can perform this check as follows:

```
#include "myfile.h"
#if !defined(V_B)
#error You should use Version B of myfile.h!
#endif
```

If we use a version of *myfile.h* that does not contain the definition of **V_B**, the compiler will display the error message given on the **#error** line, after which compilation terminates.

Instead of testing identifiers of our own header files, we can test one of a standard header file, say, *dos.h*. If that identifier is unique for the compiler we are using, we can check in this way whether the required compiler is being used, and generate a clear error message if this check fails. This is very useful if compiler-dependent source text is distributed among programmers who may try to use the wrong compiler.

Pragmas

Although we prefer to restrict ourselves to language elements accepted by any C++ compiler, it may sometimes be necessary or desirable to deviate from this principle and to use facilities that depend on a particular compiler and on a particular machine. For such system-dependent facilities, lines of the form

```
#pragma ...
```

can be used. The three dots in this line denote some piece of text that causes the compiler, if it recognizes that text, to perform certain actions. Most applications of **#pragma** are rather technical. For example, it may be possible to write **#pragma inline** to insert inline assembly code in our programs. For further details, please refer to the reference manual for your C++ compiler.

Predefined names

There are also some names that are immediately available and that can be used in 'constant expressions':

    __LINE__   An integer indicating the current line number. (Note that the term *constant* is dubious here: if it is used on different program lines its value will not be the same throughout the program but rather will depend on its position. (In total, there are four underscores in **__LINE__**).

    __FILE__   A string indicating the name of the file that is being compiled.

    __DATE__   A string of the form "M*mm dd jjjj*", indicating the date of compilation (for example, "**M12 31 1999**" for December 31st, 1999).

    __TIME__   A string of the form "*hh:mm:ss*", indicating the time of compilation (for example, "**15:00:00**" for 3 o'clock in the afternoon).

    __cplusplus   A constant defined only if we are using a C++ compiler. (Most C++ implementations for the PC actually consist of both a C and a C++ compiler, and the C++ compiler is used only if we use the *.cpp* file-name extension.)

Remember, the values of these names are fixed at the moment of compilation. Therefore, if you write

```
printf(__DATE__);
```

and your program is compiled at December 31st, 1999, this statement is equivalent to

```
printf("M12 31 1999");
```

which means that the same date will be printed whenever you run the program. If you want to use the date of program execution (rather than that of program compilation) you need to use a different method, which will be discussed in Section 10.14.

Exercises

In the following exercises, whenever you are asked to write a function (or macro), this should be a general one; you should also demonstrate this function by a program (or, rather, a 'main module') that need not be general. In at least one of these exercises, use distinct modules for the main module and the function to practise the principle of separate compilation (or 'modular programming').

4.1 Write the function **rectangle(w, h)**, to print an open rectangle of asterisks (*). The parameters **w** and **h** are the width and the height of the rectangle, expressed in numbers of asterisks.

4.2 Write the function **digitsum(n)**, which computes and returns the sum of the decimal digits of the integer parameter **n**.

4.3 Write the function **sort4**, which has four parameters. If the integer variables **a**, **b**, **c**, and **d** are available and have been assigned values, we want to write

```
sort4(&a, &b, &c, &d);
```

to sort these four variables, so that, after this call, we have

$$a \leq b \leq c \leq d$$

4.4 In the following program, function f contains a call to itself, and is therefore said to be *recursive*. This program reads the integer k from the keyboard. With the values $k = 0, 1, 2, ..., 5$, investigate (first without and then with the computer) what the output of this program will be.

```
#include <iostream.h>

void f(int n)
{ if (n > 0)
   { f(n-2); cout << n << " "; f(n-1);
   }
}

int main()
{ int k;
  cout << "Enter k: "; cin >> k;
  cout << "Output:\n";
  f(k);
  return 0;
}
```

4.5 Write the function **gcd(x, y)** which computes the greatest common divisor of the integers x and y. These two integers are nonnegative and not both equal to zero. Use *Euclid's algorithm*, according to which we can write (using the C operator %):

$$gcd(x, y) = \begin{cases} x & \text{if } y = 0 \\ gcd(y, x \% y) & \text{if } y \neq 0 \end{cases}$$

Write a C function **gcd** that is recursive and therefore closely related to this formulation of Euclid's algorithm. (A function is said to be *recursive* if it calls itself; see also Exercise 4.4.) Write also a nonrecursive version, **gcd1**.

4.6 Write the macro **max2(x, y)**; its value (that is, the value of its expansion) is equal to the greater of **x** and **y**. Use **max2** to write another macro, **max3(x, y, z)**, the value of which is the greatest of **x, y**, and **z**. Solve this problem also by means of inline functions. Which solution do you prefer and why?

4.7 Write a function which can be declared as follows:

```
unsigned int datecode(int day, int month, int year);
```

The task of **datecode** is to encode a given date in the (rightmost) 16 bits of an **unsigned int** value, and to return that value. From left to right we use

7 bits for the final two digits of the year (≤ 99).
4 bits for the month number (≤ 12),
5 bits for the day number (≤ 31),

Take care that both the long and the short notations (for example, 1992 and 92) are allowed as the third argument of **datecode**.

4.8 Write a function declared as

```
unsigned char bcd(int n);
```

This function has the task to build a byte (of eight bits) containing the least significant two decimal digits of the argument, n, in 'binary coded decimal' format, and to return this byte. For example, if n is equal to 12345, the rightmost decimal digits, 4 and 5, are written 0100 and 0101 in four bits, so in this case the byte to be returned is represented by the bit sequence 0100 0101.

5

Arrays, Pointers, and Strings

5.1 Address Arithmetic

This section is more important than it may seem at first sight. Although its title might suggest it to be about some technical subject that 'normal' users could safely ignore, the rest of this chapter, and in fact a considerable portion of the C++ language, is based upon it.

In Section 4.3 we discussed expressions such as **&x**, the values of which are addresses. There are other kinds of expressions, which when evaluated also yield addresses. One of these is the name of arrays, written without brackets; the address obtained in this way is that of the first element of the array in question. For example, after the declaration

```
char s[50];
```

we can use **s**, not followed by **[...]**, as shorthand for **&(s[0])**, which, incidentally, we may write as **&s[0]**.

Another expression whose value is an address is **s + i**, where **i** is an integer. In this case the address is that of **s[i]**, so we have the following equivalences (with ≡ meaning 'is equivalent to').

$$s \qquad \equiv \qquad \&s[0]$$
$$s + i \qquad \equiv \qquad \&s[i]$$

This notation may look a bit complicated, but it is simply based on the following situation:

```
  s      s + 1    s + 2              . . .              s + 49
+------+------+------+-------------------------------+------+
| s[0] | s[1] | s[2] |            . . .              | s[49]|
+------+------+------+-------------------------------+------+
```

If you wrote a program in assembly language and you wanted to use an array of 50 bytes, you would use a name, such as **s**, for its start address. The addresses of the allocated bytes would be **s, s + 1, ..., s + 49**; it would then be very natural to denote these bytes themselves as **s[0], s[1], ..., s[49]**, and that is what we are doing in C and C++.

In our example, the addresses (yielded by the expressions) **s** and **s + i** lie **i** bytes apart. A byte is used here as a unit only because **s** is a **char** array, that is, because each element takes one byte. In general, address arithmetic takes into account the size of the object the address of which is given, and uses that size as a unit of memory space. This makes address arithmetic more convenient and more useful than it would otherwise have been. (It also illustrates that, unlike assembly language, C and C++ are high-level languages.) For example, let us use **int** array **a**, declared as

```
int a[10];
```

In this case the addresses **a** and **a + i** lie **i** integers (not **i** bytes) apart. Therefore the equivalence

```
a + i      ≡      &a[i]
```

also holds for **int** array **a** (and, in fact, for *any* array). The following two lines are therefore equivalent:

```
for (i=0; i<10; i++) scanf("%d", &a[i]);
for (i=0; i<10; i++) scanf("%d", a + i);
```

Besides the *address of* operator **&**, there is also the *indirection* operator *****, as we have seen in Section 4.3. We use it to denote an object the address of which is given. Now that we know which addresses are represented by **a** and **a + i**, the following equivalences will be clear:

```
*a        ≡      a[0]
*(a + i)  ≡      a[i]
```

The following two lines are therefore equivalent:

```
for (i=0; i<10; i++) printf("%7d", a[i]);
for (i=0; i<10; i++) printf("%7d", *(a + i));
```

It is also possible to subtract an integer from an address, as is done in

```
&a[9] - 3
```

Recalling that **&a[9]** can be written as **a + 9**, we see that this subtraction gives **a + 6**, which can be written as **&a[6]**. We can also subtract an address from another address, as in

```
&a[9] - &a[6]
```

Rewriting this as

```
(a+9) - (a+6)
```

makes it evident that the result is 3. Other arithmetic operations on addresses are not allowed. For example, we cannot compute the sum of two addresses.

Suppose that **p** and **q** denote the addresses of two elements of the same array. We now want to find some address between **p** and **q**, preferably the one in the middle. If **p** and **q** were subscript values, we could write **(p + q)/2**, but we cannot use this expression now, because that would involve two illegal address operations (addition and division). The way to obtain the desired value is by using either of the following two expressions:

```
p + (q - p)/2
p + ((q - p) >> 1)
```

Here all operations are legal, for **q − p** has integer type, and so has **(q − p)/2**, which may therefore be added to **p**. Instead of **/2**, we can write **>>1** if we like: for signed integers, shift right means division by 2 and the compiler may generate faster code for such a shift than for the equivalent division.

5.2 Function Arguments and Arrays

It follows from the previous section that we have access to all elements of an array if we are given its start address. There is therefore no need in C++ (and in C) for any special parameter-passing mechanism for arrays. Instead of the array itself, we use the address of its first element as an argument; in the function that is called we can compute the addresses of the other elements by means of address arithmetic. This principle is very convenient: the fact that the name of an array denotes its begin address makes array arguments very simple. The following program demonstrates a function that finds the smallest element of a given integer array:

```
// MINIMUM: Finding the smallest element of an integer array.
#include <iostream.h>

int main()
{   int table[10], minimum(int *a, int n);
    cout << "Enter 10 integers: \n";
    for (int i=0; i<10; i++) cin >> table[i];
    cout << "\nThe minimum of these values is "
         << minimum(table, 10) << endl;
    return 0;
}

int minimum(int *a, int n)
{   int small = *a;
    for (int i=1; i<n; i++)
        if (*(a+i) < small) small = *(a+i);
    return small;
}
```

Recalling Section 4.3, we know that

```
int *a, ...
```

in the first line of function **minimum** means that **a** denotes the address of an integer. The corresponding argument, **table**, is the address of **table[0]**, so the following two calls are equivalent:

```
minimum(&table[0], 10)
minimum(table, 10)
```

The above version of function **minimum** makes it very clear that address arithmetic is applied. As an alternative, we can write a version that does not do this to the same extent but may, on the other hand, be considered more readable because it uses conventional array notation. In the last section we have seen that we may replace **a[i]** with ***(a + i)**. These two expressions are really equivalent: we can also replace the latter with the former, which leads to

```
int minimum(int *a, int n)
{   int small = a[0];
    for (int i=1; i<n; i++)
        if (a[i] < small) small = a[i];
    return small;
}
```

We can emphasize the array nature of **a** even more by replacing the first line of this function with

```
int minimum(int a[], int n)
```

Note that the array length is omitted in **a[ ]**; if we had written it, then it would necessarily have been a constant, which would have made the function less general and elegant.

Although not demonstrated here, it is also possible to alter the array elements in question instead of only using their values. Any assignment to **a[i]** or to ***(a + i)** implies the modification of array **table** in the **main** function.

5.3 Pointers

If we declare

```
int *p, n=5, k;
```

then **p** is a *pointer variable*, or *pointer*, for short. We use pointers to store addresses, like we use arithmetic variables to store numbers. For example, we can place the address of **n** in **p** by writing

```
p = &n;
```

In this example, ***p** denotes an object (of type **int**) in memory. Immediately after this assignment statement, this object happens to be the **int** variable **n**. After storing the address of **n** in **p** in this way, and as long as we do not assign another address to **p**, we can regard ***p** as just another expression for **n**. If we proceed with

```
k = *p;
```

the value of **k** will therefore be 5, as if we had written **k = n;**. The process of obtaining this value 5 using **p** is known as *dereferencing*, and the unary operator ***** in ***p** is sometimes called a *dereferencing operator*. You should be very careful in distinguishing between the expressions **p** and ***p**. Since **p** is of type 'pointer-to-**int**', we can assign *addresses* of **int** objects to it; by contrast, we can assign **int** *values* to ***p** because this expression has type **int**.

In Sections 4.3 and 5.2, we have already been using pointers, since a parameter, such as **a** in

```
int minimum(int *a, int n)
```

can be used as a local variable. In this section, we are also using pointers as normal variables, not parameters. For example, we can use such a variable **p** in yet another version of **minimum**:

```
int minimum(int *a, int n)
{   int small = *a;
    for (int* p=a+1; p<a+n; p++)
       if (*p < small) small = *p;
    return small;
}
```

Initially, **p** is assigned the value **a + 1**, that is, the address of **a[1]**. This is shown in Figure 5.1, where it is assumed that **minimum** has again been invoked by the following call

```
minimum(table, 10)
```

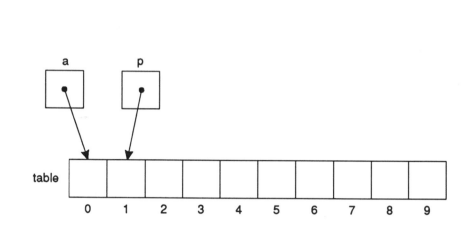

Figure 5.1. Situation immediately after **p = a + 1**

By repeatedly incrementing **p**, we move each time to the next element, until **p** is equal to **a + n**. Then **p** is equal to the address of the memory location that follows the final element, **table[n–1]**. Incidentally, this example shows that the 'less than' operator < can be applied to addresses. (The latter also holds for the operators >, <=, >=, ==, and !=.)

Our last version of **minimum** is not intended to be an improvement on the version in Section 5.2, but it only illustrates the use of pointers. Our next example has the same purpose. It differs from our previous example in that it is not related to arrays, and it shows that pointers can lead to very compact code. Suppose that we know that **i** is equal to 1, 2, or 3. Depending on this, it is required to assign a number, read from the keyboard, to **x**, **y**, or **z**, respectively. Then that variable is to be divided by 5, and, finally, the resulting value must be printed. It is required that the other two variables remain unaltered. The use of a pointer enables us to decide only once which of the variables **x**, **y**, or **z** is to be used:

```
float x, y, z, *p;
int i;
...
p = i == 1 ? &x : i == 2 ? &y : &z;
                                    // Assign &x, &y, or &z to p
scanf("%f", p);                     // Read x, y, or z
*p /= 5;                            // Divide x, y, or z by 5
printf("New value: %f", *p);        // Print x, y, or z
```

Since the value of **p** is already an address, we must not use the 'address of' operator **&** in the above call to **scanf**. Conversely, the second argument of **printf** must have type **float**, not pointer-to-**float**, hence the use of the indirection operator * in the call to this function.

The importance of assigning values to pointers

After declaring a pointer, say **p**, we must not use *p before assigning a value to **p**. If we do, we make a mistake similar to using, for example, –i immediately after declaring the **int** variable **i** without initializing it. The following program illustrates this error:

```
int main()
{ char *p, ch;
  *p = 'A';     // Error
  return 0;
}
```

This error is very serious: the undefined value of **p** is used and interpreted as an address; then the contents of this address are altered. This may destroy some important piece of information in memory. What makes things worse, you may get away with it on one machine and run into all kinds of trouble on another. In this example, it is very easy to correct it by inserting the statement

```
p = &ch;
```

before

```
*p = 'A';
```

After this correction, the latter statement has the effect of assigning the value **'A'** to the variable **ch**.

We can use a pointer as an array, but, again, this is possible only after we have given it a suitable value. If it is a function parameter, such an initial value is automatically provided for by the corresponding argument, but for other pointer variables we have to take care of this ourselves, as is done in the following program:

```
int main()
{   char s[10], *p;
    p = s;
    p[9] = 'A';
    return 0;
}
```

In this program, the declaration of s allocates a block of ten bytes for it. By contrast, only one location (for an address) is allocated by declaring p, and its initial value is undefined. By executing the statement p = s;, the address of s[0] is assigned to p, after which we can use p[0], p[1], ..., p[9] in the same way as s[0], s[1], ..., s[9]: the variables p[i] and s[i] denote the same memory location. If the statement p = s; had been omitted, the statement p[9] = 'A'; would have been incorrect and as dangerous as the statement *p = 'A'; discussed in our previous example.

Although we can use p[i] and s[i] in the same way in this example, there are differences between p and s. First, we can assign values to p, not to s. This is logical because p is a variable, while the array name s has a fixed value, the start address of the array. Second, the **sizeof** operator gives different values for p and s:

sizeof(p)   =   number of bytes for an address (2 or 4 for most machines);
sizeof(s)   =   **10 * sizeof(int)**, if s has 10 **int** elements.

Pointer conversion and void-pointers

We sometimes feel a need for a general kind of pointer, to which we can assign the address of any object, irrespective of its type. Suppose we declare i and **p_char** as follows:

```
int i;
char *p_char;
```

Since the address of an integer has the same internal format as the address of a character, you may wonder if the following statement is allowed:

```
p_char = &i;          // Error
```

This is not the case. The expression &i has type pointer-to-**int**, while **p_char** is of type pointer-to-**char**. In an assignment statement such as this one, these two types are incompatible, which means that this statement is invalid. However, we can easily correct it by using a cast:

```
p_char = (char *)&i;   // O.K.
```

Note the asterisk in **(char *)**. It says that &i is to be converted to type pointer-to-**char**, not to type **char**.

In the original version of C this type pointer-to-**char**, combined with casts from one pointer type to another, was normally used as a substitute for a general pointer type. In C++ (and ANSI C), we can instead use *void-pointers*, also known as *generic pointers*. We can write, for example,

```
void *p_void;
```

We do not need a cast to assign the address of an object of any type to **p_void**. For the opposite conversion, that is, from a void-pointer to a normal pointer, C++ (unlike ANSI C) requires a cast. On the basis of our previous declarations, the following statements are therefore correct and the cast in the second cannot be omitted:

```
p_void = &i;        // From pointer-to-int to pointer-to-void
p_char = (char *)p_void;
                    // From pointer-to-void to pointer-to-char
```

Generic pointers may also be used in comparisons. For example, here is a valid and an invalid comparison:

```
int *p_int;
char *p_char;
void *p_void;
...
if (p_char == p_int) ... // Error
if (p_void == p_int) ... // O.K.
```

Address arithmetic must not be applied to void-pointers. After all, the value of **p_void** can be the address of any type, so, if **p_void + 1** were to yield an address, it would not be clear how many bytes this address should lie apart from the address stored in **p_void**. Therefore **p_void + 1** is not a valid expression. In Section 5.6 we will see that the new, general pointer type applies to the standard function **malloc**.

Typedef declarations

For any type, no matter how complicated, there is a way to introduce a new identifier denoting this type. We do this by writing the keyword **typedef**, followed by a normal declaration. Here is a very simple example:

```
typedef double real;
```

If we had omitted the word **typedef**, the identifier **real** would have been a variable of type **double**. By writing **typedef** here, we make this identifier **real** denote the *type* of that variable instead of the variable itself. In other words, the above line makes the name **real** synonymous with **double**, so we can now write, for example,

```
real x, y;
```

instead of

```
double x, y;
```

Here is a more interesting example:

```
typedef int *ptr;
```

To know what this means, we compare it with the form obtained by omitting the word **typedef**: the name **ptr** would then be a variable of type pointer-to-**int**. Consequently, the above line makes **ptr** denote this type, pointer-to-**int**. It therefore enables us to write

```
ptr p;
```

with the same meaning as

```
int *p;
```


A slightly different notation

Since we must be able to read programs written by others, it is worthwhile to consider also a slightly different way of writing pointer declarations. White-space characters are in most cases not significant, so instead of our last declaration we can also write

```
int* p;
```

Having the blank after the asterisk instead of before it seems to be an improvement, because this blank clearly separates the pointer type **int*** (to be read as pointer-to-**int**) from the pointer variable **p**. Unfortunately, regarding the notation **int*** as a pointer type is confusing if we declare more than one variable, as in

```
int* p, q;
```

If **int*** were really equivalent to a single type identifier such as **ptr**, both **p** and **q** would be pointers. However, this is not the case. Instead of being a pointer, **q** is an **int** variable: the asterisk applies only to **p**, not to **q**. This is expressed more clearly by the equivalent declaration

```
int *p, q;
```

We will therefore not follow some other authors in writing **int* p**, but rather use the notation **int *p**, as we have done so far.

Initialization of pointers

The way we initialize pointers deserves our special attention. For example, we can write

```
int i, a[10], *p = &i, *q = a;
```

You should be aware that **&i** is the initial value of **p**, not of ***p**. Similarly, the start address of array **a**, that is, the address of **a[0]** is the initial value of **q**, not of ***q**.

5.4 Strings

We are already familiar with the idea that an *address* can appear in the following three forms:

(i)   An expression that begins with the operator **&**, such as **&table[0]**.
(ii) The name of an array, such as **table**.
(iii) A pointer, such as **p**.

There is another important form, which also yields an address:

(iv)   A string (also called a *string constant* or *string literal*), such as **"ABC"**.

If the string **"ABC"** occurs in a program, the three characters **'A'**, **'B'**, and **'C'**, extended with the null character, **'\0'**, are stored somewhere in memory, similar to the way a character array with the same four elements would be stored. We may therefore regard **"ABC"** as an array of four **char** elements. The actual value of this string is the address of its first character, and its type is pointer-to-**char**. Applying the operator ***** to an object of this type yields the character that forms its contents; it is also possible to use address arithmetic with strings:

```
*"ABC"              is equal to          'A'
*("ABC" + 1)        is equal to          'B'
*("ABC" + 2)        is equal to          'C'
*("ABC" + 3)        is equal to          '\0'
```

As we have seen, not only array names but also pointers may be *subscripted* (that is, they may be followed by an integer expression in brackets). Array names and pointers have in common that they have type pointer-to-... (where ... can be any type) or, in other words, that their values are addresses. This can be generalized to all other expressions with these characteristics. A string is an example of such an expression, so the above left column can be written in array notation, which gives

`"ABC"[0]`	is equal to	`'A'`
`"ABC"[1]`	is equal to	`'B'`
`"ABC"[2]`	is equal to	`'C'`
`"ABC"[3]`	is equal to	`'\0'`

Only if we know that **"ABC"** yields an address can we understand how the following program works:

```
// POINTER
#include <stdio.h>

int main()
{  char *p;
   p = "ABC";
   printf(p);
   return 0;
}
```

First, it would be wrong to imagine that the assignment statement in this program should copy characters. Instead, only the start address of the character sequence **ABC**, stored somewhere in memory, is assigned to **p**. So much for this assignment statement. As for the next statement, we see that pointer **p** is used as an argument in the call to **printf**, which seems to be essentially different from more usual calls, such as

```
printf("ABC");
```

However, these two calls are in fact very similar. In both cases, **printf** is supplied with an address as its argument, which is exactly what it expects. After all, both **p** and **"ABC"** are expressions the values of which are addresses and with type pointer-to-**char**. As expected, the output of program POINTER is

```
ABC
```

You can now easily verify that the output would have been

```
BC
```

if the call to **printf** had been replaced with either of the following calls:

```
printf(p + 1);
printf("ABC" + 1);
```

All this also applies to the typical C++ way of writing output statement, so instead of the above program POINTER, we could have written

```
// POINTER
#include <iostream.h>

int main()
{   char *p;
    p = "ABC";
    cout << p;
    return 0;
}
```

and so on.

'String variables'

Instead of a special type of variable to store strings, we simply use arrays of characters for this purpose. With such arrays we have to distinguish between what we may call their physical and their logical lengths. The former is simply the length of the array; for example, it is 11 in array s, declared as

```
char s[11];
```

By convention, the sequence of characters stored in s is extended with a null character ('\0'). For example, we can say that the four assignment statements

```
s[0] = 'A'; s[1] = 'B'; s[2] = 'C'; s[3] = '\0';
```

store "ABC" in s. The logical length of this string is 3. Note that actually four elements of s are used in this case. We see that the logical length is always less than the physical length and is therefore at most 10 in our example. After the execution of these four assignment statements, the following call to **printf** will again print ABC:

```
printf(s);
```

Initialization of character arrays and character pointers

We have seen in Sections 3.4 and 4.5 that arrays of characters can be initialized. It is instructive to compare the following five definitions, which are equivalent:

```
char s[4] = {'A', 'B', 'C', '\0'}; // (1)
char s[4] = {'A', 'B', 'C'};        // (2)
char s[]  = {'A', 'B', 'C', '\0'}; // (3)
char s[4] = "ABC";                  // (4)
char s[]  = "ABC";                  // (5)
```

In each case, array **s** will have four elements. In (3) this follows from the number of elements given for initialization; this is also the case in (5), because of the trailing null character that is present in **"ABC"**. Although in (2) only three characters are given for initialization, **'C'** will be followed by **'\0'** because of a general rule for initializing arrays: if we explicitly initialize some array elements, any trailing elements for which we do not give values are set to zero (see the end of Section 3.4).
By contrast, the following definition is not equivalent to those above:

```
char s[] = {'A', 'B', 'C'};          // (6)
```

No trailing null character will be added in this case (6), so here we will have an array of only three elements. The following line (7) is incorrect:

```
char s[4] = "ABC\0";      // Error.    (7)
```

If we write a string literal "..." in our program a trailing null character is automatically added, so the string in memory will take one byte more than the number of characters surrounded by quotes. In (7) the four characters **'A'**, **'B'**, **'C'** and **'\0'** are within quotes, so **"ABC\0"** will occupy five bytes. It is not allowed to specify more elements for initialization than the number of array elements.

5.5 String Operations

It would be very unfortunate if assigning a string such as **"ABC"** to a character array **s** always had to be done by means of a sequence of assignment statements, as we did at the end of the last section. The practical way of doing this and many other string operations is by calling standard functions declared in *string.h*. We therefore write

```
#include <string.h>
```

after which the task mentioned is performed by the statement

```
strcpy(s, "ABC");
```

Those who are not familiar with C++ or C may be inclined to write

```
s = "ABC"; // Error
```

to achieve this, but this is wrong for two reasons. First, the right-hand side would yield an address, so if the statement were valid then an address would be copied (as was done in program POINTER) instead of the characters themselves. Second, the name of an array, such as **s**, is not a *(modifiable) lvalue* and can therefore not be used as the left-hand side of an assignment. Recall that we have discussed lvalues in Section 3.8.

(Incidentally, we will see in Chapter 6 that in C++ constructions such as this assignment statement can be made legal by overloading the assignment operator.) Now that we are familiar with pointer types, we should know a little more about lvalues. Based on the definitions

```
char ch, *p, s[100];
int i, j;
```

the examples of the following table may be helpful to tell lvalues from other expressions:

Lvalue	No lvalue
ch	&ch
p	s
*p	ch + 1
*(s + 99)	s + 99
s[99]	5
*"ABC"	"ABC"
i	-i
*&i	&*p
(i<j ? i : j)	(i<j ? i : ch)
*p++	p++

As we have seen in Section 3.8, the following statement assigns zero to the smaller of the two variables i and j, while the other left unchanged:

```
i < j ? i : j = 0;
```

This statement is valid only in C++. In C, conditional expressions cannot be lvalues, so the line just shown is not a valid statement in C. We can nevertheless realize the same effect in C by writing

```
*(i < j ? &i : &j) = 0;
```

which, incidentally, is also valid in C++. Here the left-hand side is not a conditional expression (although such an expression is part of it).

As our last example illustrates, any expression that begins with the indirection operator * is an lvalue; any expression that begins with the 'address of' operator & is not. On the other hand, the latter operator can only be applied to lvalues. Thus, in the following form the *operand* that follows & must be an lvalue, but the whole expression is not:

```
& operand
```

Let us now revert to the function **strcpy**. We call it with two arguments, which can be any expressions of type pointer-to-**char**. In other words, the expressions that we write as *destination* and *source* in the call

> **strcpy**(*destination*, *source*)

must yield addresses. Bytes are copied from the source area to the destination area until the null character has been copied. It is our responsibility to take care that the destination area is large enough for all characters to be copied, the null character included. As we have seen at the beginning of Section 5.4 and elsewhere, there are several kinds of expressions whose values are addresses, which implies that the destination need not be the beginning of an array, as the following program shows:

```
#include <iostream.h>
#include <string.h>

int main()
{  char s[100]="Program something.", t[100];
   strcpy(t, s);
   strcpy(t + 8, "in C++.");
   cout << s << endl << t << endl;
   return 0;
}
```

Its output is

```
Program something.
Program in C++.
```

The expression **t + 8** yields the address of the **s** in **Program something.** This is the start position of the destination, to which the characters of **"in C++."** of the source are copied. After copying these seven characters, the null character (actually present in the source) is copied as well, which causes the copying process to terminate. It is essential that this null character is included in the copying process, because its presence in array **t** is the only means to prevent the subsequent output statement from printing any undefined characters that may follow the null character in this array.

As we have seen, we cannot use an assignment statement to place a string into a character array. The *initialization* of array **s** in the above program seems to contradict this. However, initialization is a language concept entirely different from assignment, even though they look similar because of the equal sign being used in both cases. Recall that we have discussed array initialization at the end of Section 4.5.

This is perhaps a good opportunity to mention another subtle point in connection with this subject. In the following two lines, **s** is an array with four elements; it is just large enough for the string **"ABC"**, the null character included:

```
char s[4] = "ABC";
char *p = "DEF";
```

During initialization, the four characters of this string are copied to **s**; we can, of course, place other characters into this array later, but its (physical) length will always remain 4. Things are essentially different with the pointer variable **p**. Here the address of **"DEF"**, not the character sequence itself, is copied to **p** (not to ***p**). We can split up the last line into a declaration and an assignment:

```
char *p; p="DEF";
```

We cannot do this with the declaration of **s** (unless we use **strcpy**). Another point in which **p** is different from **s** is that **p** is by no means restricted to an array of only four characters, as is the case with **s**. In **p** only an address is stored, and we can write, for example,

```
p = "ABCDEFG";
```

later, to use **p** for the address of a larger string. Now that we have focused on their differences, we must also remember that **s** and **p** are similar in many respects; for example, the following four expressions are all valid:

```
s[i]        *(s + i)
p[i]        *(p + i)
```

Substrings

Although **strcpy** is quite a useful function, copying everything from the given source until the null character is encountered may not be what we want. We often want to replace only some portion (sometimes called a *substring*) in the middle of a given string. This can be done by means of the function **strncpy**. This has not only the letter **n** in the middle of its name but also a third parameter, which says how many characters are to be copied at most. The call

```
strncpy(destination, source, n)
```

copies *n* characters from *source* to *destination*, unless in *source* a null character is encountered before *n* characters have been copied. In that case, the null character is copied and the copying process terminates. For example, after

```
char s[100];
strcpy(s, "These are discrete structures.");
```

we can use the statement

```
strncpy(s + 10, "con", 3);
```

to give array **s** the following new contents:

```
These are concrete structures.
```

After copying the letters, **c**, **o**, and **n**, the given maximum number of characters to be copied has been reached, so copying stops; this implies that the null character is not copied. If the final argument had been greater than 3, precisely four characters (**c**, **o**, **n**, and '\0') would have been copied. The characters in **"crete structures."** would then no longer have been considered to belong logically to the string stored in **s**.

The results of **strcpy** and **strncpy** are undefined if the destination and the source overlap. For example, if we want to insert the string **"The "** at the beginning of the string stored in **s** after

```
char s[100] = "programming language C++",
     temp[100];
```

we should use the temporary variable **temp**, writing, for example,

```
strcpy(temp, s);
strcpy(s, "The ");
strcpy(s + 4, temp);
```

Return values

The functions **strcpy** and **strncpy** return the start address of the destination. We often ignore these returned values, but we can use them if we like, as is done in

```
cout << strcpy(s, "William Shakespeare");
```

which can be used instead of

```
strcpy(s, "William Shakespeare"); cout << s;
```

String length and concatenation

The standard function **strlen** (declared in *string.h*) returns the length of a string, so we can write, for example:

```
#include <string.h>
...
int length;
char s[100]="ABC";
length = strlen(s);
```

That length is 3 in this example: it says how many characters precede the null character. We can also say that it indicates the position of the null character: in our example, the null character can be found in **s[3]**. Because of this null character the number of characters logically used in **s** is equal to **strlen(s) + 1**.

If we want to append a string **t** with string **s**, we could do this as follows:

```
strcpy(t + strlen(t), s);
```

However, there is a special function, **strcat**, for this *concatenation* operation, which in this case we would use as follows:

```
strcat(t, s);
```

Again, it is possible to limit the number of characters to be copied, by using a related function, **strncat**. If we write

```
strncat(t, s, n);
```

then the first **n** characters of **s** are copied, unless a null character is encountered (and copied). In the latter case, the copying process terminates immediately.

It is the programmer's responsibility that there is enough memory available in the 'target' **t** to contain the concatenation result, consisting of both its old value and the characters copied from the 'source' **s**.

String comparison

If we want to compare two strings, we normally should not use the relational operators ==, !=, <, <=, >, >=, because, if we do, *start addresses* are compared, not the characters stored there. For example, the test in the second line of

```
strcpy(s, "ABC");
if (s == "ABC") ...
```

will fail: although **s** contains the string **"ABC"**, the address of **s** is different from the address of the constant **"ABC"** that in the program follows the equality operator ==. Instead of the operator ==, we should use the function **strcmp** (declared in *string.h*). The last program line should be replaced with

```
if (strcmp(s, "ABC") == 0) ...
```

It may seem curious for **strcmp** to return 0 in case of equality, but the reason for this is that this function can also be used for the other relational operations, which here refer to the alphabetical order of words as these appear, for example, in a telephone directory. For example, we have

```
strcmp("Walker", "Wood")          < 0
strcmp("Morrison", "Morris")      > 0
strcmp("Johnson", "Johnson")      = 0
```

When we use the call **strcmp(s, t)**, first the characters **s[0]** and **t[0]** are compared. If these are equal, **s[1]** and **t[1]** are compared, and so forth. This process can terminate in two ways. Either

-   two unequal characters **s[i]** and **t[i]** are encountered, or
-   the null character is encountered in both **s[i]** and **t[i]**.

In either case, the value returned by **strcmp** is **s[i] − t[i]**. Note that this also gives the correct result if **s[i]** or **t[i]** is the null character (which is equivalent to integer 0).

Again, there is a special version, **strncmp**, to limit the number of characters to be compared. For example, if two character arrays **s** and **t** are given and we want to know if the characters stored in **s[7]**, **s[8]**, and **s[9]** are equal to those in **t[0]**, **t[1]**, and **t[2]**, we can write

```
if (strncmp(s + 7, t, 3) == 0) ...
```

The keyword const

The string functions we have been discussing are declared in *string.h* as follows:

```
int strlen(const char *s);
int strcmp(const char *s1, const char *s2);
int strncmp(const char *s1, const char *s2, int maxlen);
char *strcpy(char *dest, const char *src);
char *strncpy(char *dest, const char *src, int maxlen);
char *strcat(char *dest, const char *src);
char *strncat(char *dest, const char *src, int maxlen);
```

Notice the use of the keyword **const**, also discussed in Sections 2.2 and 3.4. The advantage of this keyword is that we can immediately see the distinction between what we may call 'input' and 'output' parameters. For example, the second parameter, **src**, of **strcpy** denotes the source area; it is used only to copy characters from, so this area will not be modified. The keyword **const** can therefore be used for it. We may call it an 'input parameter' because the function 'receives' data through it. In contrast to this, the first parameter, **dest**, of **strcpy** is the destination area, which will be overwritten. We must not use **const** for it. We may call it an 'output parameter' because data is written to the destination area, to be used later by the caller of **strcpy**. Note that the keyword **const**, as it is used here, does not apply to the arguments themselves but only to the memory areas they denote.

We can also use the keyword **const** for normal pointer variables; if it occurs at the beginning, as with the above parameters, it again indicates that the memory areas they point to will not change. Instead, we can write **const** between **char*** and the variable to indicate that the pointer itself will not change. The following example illustrate both usages:

```
char s[10] = "Pim";

const char *p = s;          // We can change p, not *p
p++;                        // O.K.
*p = 'T';                   // Error
*(p + 1) = 'o';             // Error
p[2] = 'n';                 // Error

char* const q = s;          // We can change *q, not q
*q = 'T';                   // O.K.
*(q+1) = 'o';               // O.K.
q[2] = 'n';                 // O.K.
q++;                        // Error
```

Finally, we can use **const** for both purposes at the same time:

```
const char* const r = s;   // We can change neither r nor *r
```

This form is to be recommended if we intend to use a long string at many places in our program. For example, by writing

```
const char* const publisher =
"John Wiley & Sons\n"
"Baffins Lane\n"
"Chichester\n"
"West Sussex PO19 1UD\n"
"England";
```

we can use **publisher** instead of this long string. The first occurrence of **const** indicates that we will not change any characters of this string, the second that we will not assign another string to **publisher**.

It should also be pointed out that using a pointer here is more economical than using an array. Consider replacing the first of the above six lines with

```
char publisher[] =
```

In this case, the long string **"John Wiley..."** would occur twice in memory: first, it is there simply because the string occurs in the program, and, second, a copy of it is stored in array **publisher**. In our original definition, the variable **publisher** is not an array but a pointer, which uses much less memory space, and the actual characters of the string occur only once in memory.

5.6 Dynamic Memory Allocation

When declaring an array, we have to specify its length as a constant expression, as is done with length 100 in

```
char s[100];
```

Sometimes we would rather use a variable, or some expression containing variables, for this purpose, if that were possible, so that we would have, for example,

```
int n;
...
cin >> n;
char s[n];              // Error
```

There is an error in this program fragment: we cannot use variables, such as **n**, in array declarations. Still, what is aimed at here can be accomplished, and in C++ this can even be done in two ways. Let us first discuss the new method, which can be used only in C++, not in C. It works as follows:

```
int n;
char *s;
...
cin >> n;
s = new char[n];
```

The **new** operator is immediately available in C++, so we need not use any header file for it, as would be the case for standard functions. This operator yields a pointer. In the above example, this is a pointer to a character; the value assigned to **s** is the start address of a block of **n** bytes. As we can write **s[i]** instead of ***(s+i)**, we can say that the array elements

```
s[0], s[1], ..., s[n-1]
```

(each of type **char**) are now available.
   Another example is

```
int *p;
p = new int;
```

In this case, memory space for only one integer is allocated, and its address is assigned to **p**. If we want to allocate memory space for a block of **m** integers, we can write

```
p = new int[m];
```

In all this, we have assumed the requested block of memory space to be available. If this block is very large or if we have already requested much memory previously, there may not be enough free memory available. In that case, the **new** operator traditionally yields the value 0 (also written as **NULL**). Unfortunately, due to proposals by the C++ standard committee, this is no longer automatically the case with all C++ compilers. If memory allocation by means of the **new** operator fails, then, according to the new proposed C++ standard, a so-called *new-handler*, will be called. We will discuss this in more detail in Section 12.3. If we prefer the traditional behavior, with **new** returning 0, it has been proposed that we should write

```
set_new_handler(0);
```

before the first use of **new**. This proposal has been adopted by Borland, so this call to **set_new_handler** is really required with their popular C++ compiler if we want the value 0 to be returned in the case of memory-allocation failure. Program TESTMEM illustrates this. It tests approximately how much memory can be allocated in this way:

```
// TESTMEM: This program tests how much memory is available.
#include <iostream.h>
#include <new.h> // Required for set_new_handler (see below)

int main()
{   char *p;
    set_new_handler(0);      // Required with Borland C++
    for (int i=1; ; i++)
    {   p = new char[10000];
        if (p == 0) break;
        cout << "Allocated: " << 10 * i << "KB\n";
    }
    return 0;
}
```

Repeatedly a block of 10KB is allocated. As long as this is possible, the amount of memory allocated so far is printed. As soon as the attempt to allocate memory fails, the loop terminates.

It goes without saying that the allocated memory will be 'given back' to the computer system when the program terminates. However, we sometimes want this memory to be released sooner because we want it to be available for other purposes, such as other uses of **new**. Memory space allocated by **new** can be released by means of the **delete** operator. The way this should be done depends on how memory was allocated. We write

```
delete p;        if p = new int;    was used for allocation, but
delete[] p;      if p = new int[m]; was used for allocation.
```

Like **new**, the **delete** operator is only available in C++, not in C.

Pointers as truth values

As we know, a logical expression such as **a < b** has type **int** and its value is 1 or 0, denoting *true* or *false*, respectively. Any arithmetic expression is permitted in a context that requires a truth value, and any nonzero value can be used as *true*. Although pointers do not have arithmetic types, they can assume the value 0, as a code for 'invalid address'. Like arithmetic expressions, pointers are permitted as truth values. A zero pointer value denotes *false*; any nonzero pointer *true*. For example, if **p** is a pointer, we can use the constructions below on he left, and they are equivalent to those on the right:

```
if (!p) ...               if (p == NULL) ...
if (p && ...) ...         if (p != NULL && ...) ...
```

Note that the value 0 is the only arithmetic value that can be assigned to a pointer **p** without using a cast: **p = 0;** is a correct assignment statement, but **p = 1;** is not.

The functions malloc, calloc, free, and realloc

Instead of using the C++ operator **new**, we can allocate memory by means of the standard function **malloc**, which is very often used in C programs, and declared in the header file *stdlib.h*. For example, we can dynamically allocate an 'array' **s** of **n** characters as follows:

```
#include <stdlib.h>
int n;
char *s;
...
cin >> n;
s = (char *) malloc(n);
```

The function **malloc** is declared in *stdlib.h* as follows:

```
void *malloc(unsigned nbytes);
```

The argument of **malloc** is the number of (contiguous) bytes to be allocated. Its return value is the start address of this block of memory. Its type is pointer-to-**void**, so that the address can be assigned to any pointer, provided that we use a cast, as discussed in Section 5.3. For example, we can use **malloc** to allocate memory for a **float** array with 1000 elements as follows:

```
#include <stdlib.h>

int main()
{  float* a = (float *)malloc(1000 * sizeof(float));
   ...
```

Note that **malloc** requires the size of the memory block to be expressed in bytes, regardless of what these bytes will be used for. As one **float** object takes **sizeof(float)** bytes, the argument of **malloc** in this example will be clear. If this call to **malloc** succeeds, the 'array elements'

```
a[0], a[1], ..., a[999]
```

are available as if we had written

```
float a[1000];
```

Success and failure of malloc

If enough memory is available, **malloc** works as we have discussed in the above examples. If not, it returns the value 0. This is possible because of a special language rule, not yet discussed, which says that, unlike other numeric values, the special integer value 0 may be assigned to pointers and may also be compared with them. Furthermore, any real address in C++ is guaranteed to be nonzero. Instead of 0, it is customary to use the symbolic constant **NULL**, defined as 0 in the header file *stdlib.h* (and in *stdio.h*). The fact that **malloc** returns the special value **NULL** if the call to this function fails due to lack of memory enables us to take whatever action we like. The simplest way to cope with this problem is to test if **NULL** is returned, and, if so, to print an error message and terminate program execution:

```
s = (char *)malloc(n);
if (s == NULL)
{  cout << "Not enough memory.\n";
   exit(1);
}
```

The function **exit**, used here, is also declared in *stdlib.h*. It terminates program execution and returns its argument to the operating system. It is customary to use argument 0 for 'normal' and 1 for 'abnormal' program termination. This argument value is returned to the calling process, which normally is the operating system. It would be very unwise not to test the value returned by **malloc**. If this value happens to be **NULL**, the effect of ignoring this using **NULL** as a real address may be very unpleasant and similar to using undefined pointers or to storing data outside array boundaries.

Some functions related to malloc

There are some other useful functions for memory allocation; like **malloc**, they are declared in *stdlib.h*. If we want the allocated memory to be initialized with zero values, we can use **calloc** instead of **malloc**. Another new point of **calloc** is that is takes two arguments, the number of data elements and the number of bytes required for each data element. Clearly the product of these two arguments is the number of bytes that **malloc** would require as an argument. For example, if we want to allocate memory for an 'array' of **n** integers, with 0 as their initial values, we can write

```
#include <stdlib.h>
...
int *p;
...
p = (int *)calloc(n, sizeof(int));
if (p == NULL) ...
```

Memory allocated by **malloc, calloc,** or **realloc** (to be discussed shortly) can be released by calling the function **free**. The argument of this function must be an address previously obtained by a call to **malloc, calloc,** or **realloc**. We often use something of the following form:

```
s = (char *)malloc(...);
xxx
free(s);
```

The memory locations **s[0], s[1], ...** can be used only in program fragment *xxx*. There is no point in calling **free** if, after this call, program execution terminates immediately or very soon, since in that case memory will be released anyway. On the other hand, calling **free** is very important at the end of a function that is called a great many times. If we call **malloc** in such a function and omit calling **free**, the amount of memory in use will cumulate unnecessarily. This is a rather tricky point, since with a normally defined array we are used to the fact that its memory space is automatically released on return from the function. For memory allocated with **malloc** (or **calloc** or **realloc**) we should not forget to do this ourselves.

We sometimes want to alter the size of the block of memory previously allocated by **malloc** or **calloc**; for example, it may turn out that more memory is needed than we had anticipated. The function to use for this purpose is **realloc**. It takes two arguments: an address, previously obtained by **malloc, calloc,** or **realloc**, and the new length of the block of memory, expressed in bytes. It can be used as follows:

```
#include <iostream.h>
#include <stdlib.h>
...
char *s;
...
s = (char *)malloc(1000); // Anticipated length: 1000 bytes
if (s == NULL)
{   cout << "malloc fails with n = 1000";
    exit(1);
}
```

```
...
// Here s[0], ..., s[999] can be used.

cin >> n;
     // New length n, possibly greater than 1000
s = (char *)realloc(s, n);
if (s == NULL)
{   cout << "realloc fails with n = " << n;
    exit(1);
}
...
// Here s[0], ..., s[n-1] can be used.
```

If, in the above call to **realloc**, the argument **n** is greater than 1000, then after this call s[0], ..., s[999] have the same contents as before, which means that we have added the elements s[1000], ..., s[n–1] at the end. All **n** bytes are again contiguous, that is, they form one block. To achieve this, it may be necessary for **realloc** to move the previously allocated block, which means that frequent use of this function may be very time consuming. If **n** is less than 1000, the 'array size' is decreased. In this case, only the elements s[0], ..., s[n–1] are available after the call to **realloc**, and we must no longer use s[n], ..., s[999]. The most drastic way of reducing previously allocated memory is by writing **realloc(s, 0)**, which we can use instead of **free(s)**.

C++ vs. C memory-allocation methods

When comparing the new, typical C++ operators **new** and **delete** on the one hand with **malloc** and related C functions on the other, we find that in most cases the new facilities are easier to use than the older ones, especially if, for example, a sequence of integers is to be allocated. In Section 6.7 we will see that we sometimes prefer **new** to **malloc** for reasons other than notational convenience. There is a situation in which using **new** and **delete** is rather inconvenient: altering the size of previously allocated memory is done much easier with **realloc**. An attractive aspect of **malloc**, **free** and so on is that these functions are well standardized, which is not (yet) the case with **new** and **delete**. If memory allocation fails, **malloc** and **realloc** simply return zero, while, as we have seen, this point is more complicated with the **new** operator. In the case of memory-allocation failure the C++ **new** operator may or may not return zero, depending on the compiler we are using. There is no such problem with **malloc**, **calloc** and **realloc**, so these functions are more portable.

It is wise to use either the new or the old facilities consistently, so **new** and **malloc** had better not be used in the same program. The operator **new** may be based on low-level memory-allocation routines that are different from those used by **malloc**, and mixing these facilities may cause serious problems.

5.7 Input and Output of Strings

Input

After declaring

```
char s[40];
```

the following ways of reading a string from the keyboard into array **s** are very simple but, as we will see in a moment, they are not completely safe:

```
scanf("%s", s);    // ???
cin >> s;          // ???
gets(s);           // ???
```

Note that we need the header file *stdio.h* for the **scanf** and **gets** functions and *iostream.h* for the >> operator. In one respect, both the **scanf** function and the >> operator read a string in a way that is similar to the way they read a number: any leading white-space characters are skipped, and the reading process ends at the first white-space character that follows the string. That white-space character is then regarded as not yet read: it is still present to be read by the next read operation. By contrast, the **gets** function reads an entire line, which may include blank spaces; although the newline character is read in, it is not placed in **s**. For example, suppose this text is entered, in which *b* denotes a blank space and ¶ a newline character:

```
bbCharlesbDickens¶
```

If we are using **scanf** or the >> operator as shown above, only the name **Charles** (followed by a null character) will be placed in array **s**. On the other hand, the entire line of text, including the blanks but excluding the newline character, will appear in **s** if we are using the above call to **gets**.

The above three ways of performing input are unsafe because array **s** will overflow if, for example, the following character sequence is entered on the keyboard:

```
ABCDEFGHIJKLMNOPQRSTUVWXYZabcdefghijklmnopqrstuvwxyz
```

Since this line consists of 52 letters and because a null character will be added at the end, the length of array **s** should be at least 53 instead of 40.

Since we normally want to prevent array overflow by all means, the above three program lines are suspicious, to say the least. Fortunately, we can do better, as the following four program lines illustrate:

```
scanf("%39s", s);        // Reads a word of at most 39 chars.
cin >> setw(40) >> s;    // The same with stream I/O.
fgets(s, 40, stdin);     // Reads a line of at most 39 chars.
cin.getline(s, 40);      // Slightly different, see below.
```

By specifying "%39s" in the above call to **scanf**, at most 39 characters will be read so there is still room in array **s** for the null character at the end. Again, any leading white-space characters are skipped. The process of reading characters (other than white-space) ends either by encountering a white-space character or by having read 39 characters, whichever happens first.

The **setw** manipulator, as used above, also prevents array overflow. By using the limit **40** here, a word of at most 39 characters will be read. Here, too, any leading white-space characters are skipped and any white-space character will signal the end of the input.

The standard C input function **fgets** (declared in *stdio.h*) is primarily intended for the input of an entire line of text from a file, as we will see in Chapter 8. By using the identifier **stdin** as its third argument, we can also use it for the 'standard input device', which is normally the keyboard. The second argument, **40**, indicates how many positions are available in the memory area given by the first argument, **s**. Besides offering a provision to prevent array overflow, this function is also different from **gets** in that it normally places a newline character ('\n'), if it finds one, in the array. For example, if we enter the three characters **ABC** and then press the Enter key, the above call to **fgets** will place the following five characters in array **s**:

```
ABC\n\0
```

Of course, we can easily overwrite '\n' by '\0' as follows:

```
s[strlen(s) - 1] = '\0';
```

It goes without saying that, in our example, **fgets** will not place a newline character in **s** if the input process ends because 39 normal characters (possibly including blanks) have been read. In that case these characters, followed by '\0' are placed in **s**. Both **gets** and **fgets** normally return a pointer to a character, equal to the address (**s** in our example) of the memory location where the first character is placed. In case of 'end-of file' (see Section 8.4) they return zero.

Using stream I/O, we can read an entire line of text by means of the curious above function call to **cin.getline**. Its effect is similar to that of **fgets** but for the newline character at the end: in our example with **ABC** as input line, **cin.gets(s, 40)** places only these four characters in **s** (although the newline character is read in):

```
ABC\0
```

In Chapter 9 we will see how constructs such as **cin.getline** fit nicely into the C++ language. In the meantime you can already use this call if you prefer using stream I/O to standard I/O.

Output

If we want to display the string stored in the usual way (that is, with a terminating null character) in array **s**, there are several ways of doing this. To begin with, we can use each of the following, rather simple operations:

```
printf(s);              // Display just the contents of s.
printf("%s", s);        // The same result as previous line.
cout << s;              // The same result as previous line.
printf("%s\n", s);      // Display s followed by newline.
puts(s);                // The same result as previous line.
```

Note that **puts**, unlike its counterpart **gets**, is perfectly safe and quite useful. It provides a newline character at the end. For example, instead of **printf("Ready.\n");**, we can write

```
puts("Ready.");
```

with exactly the same result.

If we want to produce a table with a column of strings followed by another column, we must obviously supply a field width for that first column. Then we are faced with the problem that, without precautions, both **printf** and **cout << setw(...) ...** would cause a field width the column to be right adjusted, producing, for example, the following table, which is clearly not what we want:

```
Charles 21
    Tim  5
  Peter 12
```

The following program, based on standard I/O shows how to realize left alignment for the first column:

```
// ALIGN1: Strings in a table, based on standard I/O.
#include <stdio.h>

int main()
{   char *p[3] = {"Charles", "Tim", "Peter"};
    int age[3] = {21, 5, 12}, i;
    for (i=0; i<3; i++)
        printf("%-12s%3d\n", p[i], age[i]);
    return 0;
}
```

(In this program, **p** is an array of pointers, a subject that we will discuss in detail in Section 5.9.) If we had written **%12s** instead of **%-12s** in the above call to **printf**, the strings of the first column would have been right aligned, so that the output would have been as shown above. The minus sign in **%−12s** causes left alignment to take place, so program ALIGN1 produces output in the following, desired form:

```
Charles      21
Tim           5
Peter        12
```

Program ALIGN2, based on stream I/O, produces the same output as ALIGN1. A discussion of the curious way left alignment is achieved here can be found in Section 9.2:

```
// ALIGN2: Strings in a table, based on stream I/O.
#include <iostream.h>
#include <iomanip.h>

int main()
{  char *p[3] = {"Charles", "Tim", "Peter"};
   int age[3] = {21, 5, 12}, i;
   for (i=0; i<3; i++)
      cout << setw(12) << setiosflags(ios::left) << p[i]
            << setw(3) << resetiosflags(ios::left) << age[i]
            << endl;
   return 0;
}
```

5.8 Strings as Arguments and as Return Values

In Section 5.5 we have discussed how to use the important string functions **strlen**, **strcpy**, **strncpy**, **strcmp**, **strncmp**, **strcat**, and **strncat**. If we like, we can write such functions ourselves. Although we need not do this for these seven functions, writing them down is a very good exercise. There are several solutions. For example, consider the following versions of **strlen**:

```
// Version 1
int strlen(const char *s)
{  int n=0;
   while (s[n] != '\0') n++;
   return n;
}

// Version 2
int strlen(const char *s)
{  int n=0;
   while (*s++ != '\0') n++;
   return n;
}
```

```
// Version 3
int strlen(const char *s)
{   char *p=s;
    while (*p != '\0') p++;
    return p - s;
}
```

In all three versions

```
const char *s
```

indicates that an address is expected as an argument, and that the contents of the memory area given by this address will not be altered. (Recall our discussion of **const** at the end of Section 5.5.) In version 1 the array notation **s[n]** is used, which, incidentally, may be replaced with ***(s+n)**. Version 2 shows that we can use **s** as a real variable: the pointer **s** is altered, which does not affect the corresponding argument. Version 3 shows the initialization of a pointer. Here the initial value of **p** is **s**. After execution of the while-statement, **p** points to the null character and **s** to the given start point, which means that the desired string length is equal to the difference **p – s**.

Note that we can write all three versions slightly shorter and more efficiently by simply omitting

```
!= '\0'
```

This will be clear if we replace **'\0'** with the equivalent notation **0** and recall Example 6 at the end of Section 2.4.

We will now compare two versions of **strcpy**. The first is no doubt the more readable one, but the second is shorter and possibly faster:

```
/* This function copies from source 'src'
       to destination 'dest'.
    (Well-readable version)
*/
char *strcpy(char *dest, const char *src)
{   int i=0;
    while (dest[i] = src[i], dest[i] != '\0') i++;
    return dest;
}
```

```
/* This function copies from source 'src'
       to destination 'dest'.
    (Fast version)
*/
char *strcpy(char *dest, const char *src)
{   char *start=dest;
    while (*dest++ = *src++)  ;
    return start;
}
```

In the last version the unary operators * and ++ are used. According to Section 3.5, these associate from right to left, which means that the assignment

```
*dest++ = *src++
```

is to be read as

```
*(dest++) = *(src++)
```

Since we have written src++, not ++src, the indirection operator * is to be applied to src before this variable is incremented. This yields a character that is placed into the location whose address is given by dest before that variable is incremented. The while-loop terminates when the null character has been copied, since then the value of the whole assignment is zero.

Like strlen and strcpy, the other functions mentioned can be written in a very compact form. Here is a version for each of the functions strcmp and strcat.
You are strongly recommended to write strncpy, strncmp and strncat yourself as an exercise.

```
int strcmp(const char *s, const char *t)
{   int i=0;
    while (s[i] == t[i])
        if (s[i++] == '\0') return 0;
    return s[i] - t[i];
}

char *strcat(char *dest, const char *src)
{   strcpy(dest+strlen(dest), src);
    return dest;
}
```

Each of the functions strcpy and strcat alters the area that starts at the address given through its first parameter, so we must not use const for this parameter. That address is also used as the return value of these functions. When we do the same in functions of our own, a warning may not be superfluous. We must always remember that the memory area used by local variables is released when the function is left. The following function will therefore lead to problems:

```
char *incorrect(void)
{   char str[100] = "ABC";
    return str;
}
```

Suppose we use this function as follows:

```
char *p;
...
p = incorrect();
```

Although **p** is assigned the address of a memory area, it would not be wise to use it, because the contents of that area, that is, the character sequence **ABC\0**, may already have been destroyed or will at any rate be used for other purposes. Still, we can allocate a memory area, place some data in it, and return its start address, as the following corrected version shows:

```
char *correct()
{  char *str;
   str = new char[100]; // or: str = (char *)malloc(100);
   strcpy(str, "ABC");
   return str;
}
```

5.9 Multi-dimensional Arrays

We can regard a *table* or *matrix* as an array whose elements are again arrays. The notation for such a table element is in accordance with this; we can write

```
table[i][j]
```

to denote the element in the *i*th row and the *j*th column of the two-dimensional array **table** (where, as usual, we count from 0). If we want **table** to have 20 rows and 5 columns, and elements of type **float**, for example, we declare

```
float table[20][5];
```

If you are familiar with Pascal, you must be on your guard not to make the mistake of writing **table[i, j]** instead of **table[i][j]**. Since

```
i, j
```

is a comma expression whose value is the same as that of **j**, the expression **table[i, j]** would be equivalent to **table[j]**.

Initialization

In Section 4.5 we saw how to initialize a one-dimensional array. We can easily extend this to two-dimensional ones. Suppose that we want the **int** array **a** to have two rows and three columns with the following initial values:

```
60  30  50
20  80  40
```

We can write either of the following two lines to achieve this:

```
int a[2][3] = {{60, 30, 50}, {20, 80, 40}};
int a[2][3] = {60, 30, 50, 20, 80, 40};
```

The first of these two lines clearly shows that there are two rows and three columns. This is not the case with the second, which is also allowed.

Arrays of strings can be initialized very conveniently. The following example shows both an initialization of an array of strings and the way these strings can be used:

```
char namelist[3][30] = {"Johnson", "Peterson", "Jacobson"};
for (i=0; i<3; i++) cout << namelist[i] << endl;
```

A pointer to an array

As we have seen in Section 5.1, the expressions a[i] and *(a + i) are equivalent. The former is more natural if a is an array, the latter if a is a pointer, but in either case we can replace one with the other if we like. The same principle applies to the following program, where we have a table (or *matrix*) consisting of two rows, each row being a one-dimensional array of three **int** elements:

```
// PARRAY: A pointer to an array.
#include <iostream.h>

int main()
{  int i, j, a[2][3] = {{8, 3, 6}, {5, 7, 0}}, (*p)[3];
   p = a;
   for (i=0; i<2; i++)
   {  for (j=0; j<3; j++) cout << p[i][j] << " ";
      cout << endl;
   }
   cout << sizeof(a)/sizeof(int)
        << " elements in array a.\n";
   cout << sizeof(*p)/sizeof(int)
        << " elements in each row.\n";
   return 0;
}
```

The most interesting variable in this program is **p**. It is a pointer to a one-dimensional array of three **int** elements. The way **p** is defined helps us to verify this. It suggests that (*p)[i] is of type **int**. This implies that *p (without [i]) is an array of **int** elements, so that **p** must be a pointer to such an array. In other words, while **a** is an array of two rows, **p** is a pointer to a row. The statement

```
p = a;
```

which, as usual, could also be written as

```
p = &a[0]
```

assigns the address of the first row to **p**. The following four expressions are then equivalent:

```
a[i][j]
(*(a + i))[j]
p[i][j]
(*(p + i))[j]
```

Rather arbitrarily, the third of these was used in program PARRAY. Note that **p + 1** is the address of the second row (**p** being equal to the address of the first row).

Since **p** is a pointer to a row, the expression ***p** (also known as **p[0]**) denotes a complete row. Because a row consists of elements of type **int**, the number of elements in each row is equal to

```
sizeof(*p)/sizeof(int)
```

This is confirmed by the fourth of the following output lines, produced by program PARRAY:

```
8  3  6
5  7  0
6 elements in array a.
3 elements in each row.
```

Note that in expressions such as **(*(p + i))[j]** the outer parentheses **( )** are necessary because, according to Section 3.6, **[ ]** has higher priority than the unary operator *****. In other words, if we wrote ***(p + i)[j]** this would mean ***((p + i)[j])**, which is not what we want here.

In the above program and discussion we have retained array notation, using **[j]**, in all expressions denoting individual elements of array **a**. If we wanted, we could also have used pointer notation instead of array brackets here: ***((*(p + i)) + j)** would be a very inconvenient but valid form for **(*(p + i))[j]**, which in turn is an inconvenient form for **p[i][j]**. This equivalence also holds if we replace **p** with **a** in these three expressions.

Function parameters

Let us return to the example of the beginning of this section, a table of three rows and five columns, defined as

```
float table[20][5];
```

If we want to use **table** as an argument of a function, writing **f(table),** for example, we can write the first line of that function as follows:

```
int f(float t[][5])
```

The first dimension (20) of parameter **t** may be omitted; the second (5) (and any further dimensions) must be present. Remember that inside function **f** it must be possible to compute the address of each element **table[i][j]**. Since the elements of a two-dimensional array are stored row by row, element **table[i][j]** is stored at position $5i + j$ (with **table[0][0]** being stored at position 0). For example, element **table[2][3]**, that is, the element in row 2 and column 3, lies at position $5 \times 2 + 3 = 13$, as you can see below:

	Col. 0	*Col. 1*	*Col. 2*	*Col. 3*	*Col. 4*
Row 0	0	1	2	3	4
Row 1	5	6	7	8	9
Row 2	10	11	12	13	14
...	...	...	...	...	...
Row 19	95	96	97	98	99

It will now be clear that the value 5 must be available to the compiler when it is compiling function **f**.

Instead of the above line, we can write

```
int f(float (*t)[5])
```

This is similar to what we discussed at the end of Section 5.2, where we could use either of the following lines as the beginning of function **minimum:**

```
int minimum(int a[], int n)
int minimum(int *a, int n)
```

With this **minimum** function, **a** points to the first element of an array of **int** values, and **a[0]** (equivalent to ***a**) is of type **int**. Analogously, **t** points to the first element of an array of rows, each row consisting of five **float** values, and **t[0]** (or ***t**) is the first row. The first element of this first row is **t[0][0]**, for which we can also write **(*t)[0].**

Arrays of pointers

In the example we have been discussing, **table[0]**, ..., **table[19]** are 20 one-dimensional arrays of five elements each. It is, of course, possible to store the start addresses of such one-dimensional arrays in an array of twenty pointers. This leads to a more dynamic data structure, because the sequences pointed to no longer need to have the same length. Because of this dynamic aspect, we will use the name **dtable** to distinguish it from **table**. We begin by replacing

```
float table[20][5];
```

with

```
float *dtabel[20];
```

It is very important to realize that with this new version the memory space for the actual floating-point numbers still has to be allocated. For example, if we want a table of five columns again, we can write

```
set_new_handler(0); // See Section 5.6
...
for (i=0; i<20; i++)
{  dtable[i] = new float[5];
   if (dtable[i] == NULL)
   {  cout << "Not enough memory"; exit(1);
   }
}
```

After this, we can use the elements **dtable[i][j]** in exactly the same way as we could use the elements **table[i][j]** before. The situation is illustrated by Figure 5.2.

However, it is by no means necessary for all 'rows' **dtable[i]** to have the same length. Instead of the constant 5 in the above loop, we can use any expression, the value of which may different for different values of **i**.

Although arrays of pointers are normally used in combination with the **new** operator (or the **malloc** standard function), this is not absolutely necessary. For example, suppose that we want to use the **float** 'array elements' **a[i][j]**, with **i** = 0, 1, 2, and with

length 20 for row **a[0]**,
length 1000 for row **a[1]**, and
length 100 for row **a[2]**.

Instead of using **new** or **malloc**, we can also achieve this as follows:

```
float *a[3], a0[20], a1[1000], a2[100];
a[0] = a0;
a[1] = a1;
a[2] = a2;
```

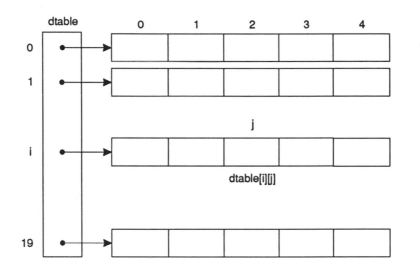

Figure 5.2. Array of pointers, used as a two-dimensional array

5.10 Program Parameters

The **main** function of a program can have parameters, which we call *program parameters*. The idea is that the user, when starting the program, can supply arguments, in the form of character strings. The program can detect how many arguments are supplied and then use them. The way of parameter passing is essentially different from what we are used to. Program PROGPARM will make this clear:

```
// PROGPARM: Demonstration of using program parameters.
#include <iostream.h>

int main(int argc, char *argv[])
{   cout << "argc    = " << argc << endl;
    for (int i=1; i<argc; i++)
       cout << "argv[" << i << "] = " << argv[i] << endl;
    return 0;
}
```

To run this program, we enter a command line consisting of the program name followed by number of *program arguments*, written as character sequences and separated by blanks, as, for example, in

```
PROGPARM ABC DEFG HIJKL
```

With this command line, the output of the program is

```
argc     = 4
argv[1]  = ABC
argv[2]  = DEFG
argv[3]  = HIJKL
```

The parameter **argc** is equal to the number of program arguments if we regard the program name also as a program argument. This name, in the form of the complete path name of the executable program, such as C:\PR\PROGPARM.EXE, will be available through **argv[0]**. The array elements **argv[1]**, ..., **argv[argc–1]** are pointers to the program arguments proper, as Figure 5.3 illustrates.

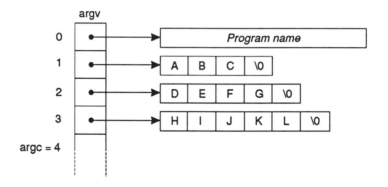

Figure 5.3. Program parameters

Each of the pointers **argv[i]** (i = 1, 2, ..., **argc – 1**) points to a character sequence, that is, to the first character of that sequence. As usual, these character sequences are terminated by null characters. Here we have, for example,

```
argv[1][0] = 'A'
argv[1][1] = 'B'
argv[1][2] = 'C'
argv[1][3] = '\0'
```

As this example illustrates, the number of *arguments* is arbitrary, but we gain access to them by means of two program *parameters*, traditionally named **argc** and **argv**, denoting *argument count* and *argument vector*. Their types must be as they are here.

The concept of program parameters enables us to write programs that are similar to conventional operating-system commands. For example, using a copy command, written as

```
copy a:aaa.txt b:bbb.txt
```

can now be regarded as executing a program named **copy** with **a:aaa.txt** and **b:bbb.txt** as program arguments.

5.11 The Functions sscanf and sprintf

If a character string is stored in an array, we can 'read' data from that array in a way similar to reading data from the keyboard, by using the function **sscanf** instead of **scanf**. The first argument of **sscanf** is the name of the array, or, in general, an expression whose value is an address. This new function is useful when numbers are given in their usual external format, that is, as character sequences, and we want them to be converted into their internal, binary format. We therefore say that we use **sscanf** (and **sprintf**, discussed below) for *in-memory format conversion*. For example, the call to **sscanf** in

```
#include <stdio.h>
...
char s[50]="123    456\n98.765";
int i, j;
double x;
sscanf(s, "%d %d %lf", &i, &j, &x);
```

causes the variables i, j and x to assume the values 123, 456, and 98.765, respectively. Like **scanf**, the function **sscanf** returns the number of values that have been successfully read and assigned to variables, so in this example that return value is 3.

It should be noted that, unlike **scanf**, the function **sscanf** has no side effect, that is, it does not keep track of what has been read already. Therefore we cannot replace the above call to **sscanf** with the three calls

```
sscanf(s, "%d", &i);
sscanf(s, "%d", &j);
sscanf(s, "%lf", &x);
```

for if we did, not only the first but also the second and the third statement would start reading at the beginning of s, so that j and x would also be given the value 123.

We use **sprintf** for conversion in the opposite direction, that is, from the internal, binary to the external, character-string format. This means that **sprintf** fills an array with the character sequence that a similar call to **printf** would 'print'. As usual with string functions, **sprintf** stores a null character at the end. For example, with **s** declared as above, the statement

```
sprintf(s,
"Sum: %6.3f  Difference: %6.3f\n, 45 + 2.89, 45 - 2.89);
```

writes the following character sequence, followed by '\0', into **s**:

```
Sum: 47.890  Difference: 42.110
```

Unlike **printf**, we must not split this **sprintf** call into two separate calls for the sum and the difference, for then the difference would again be written at the beginning of **s**, overwriting the sum just placed there. Like **scanf** and **printf**, the new functions **sscanf** and **sprintf** are declared in *stdio.h*.

Stream facilities for in-memory format conversion

If you prefer the typical C++ stream I/O to standard I/O, you can find information about stream facilities (based on the **>>** and **<<** operators) equivalent to **sscanf** and **sprintf** in Section 9.6.

5.12 Pointers to Functions

Like data, functions are stored in memory and have start addresses. In most languages we perform operations on data only, not on functions, but in C++ (and in C) we can assign the start addresses of functions to pointers. Later, such a function can be called in an indirect way, namely by means a pointer whose value is equal to the start address of the function in question. For example, if we declare

```
float (*p)(int i, int j);
```

then we can assign the start address of the function

```
float example(int i, int j)
{  return 3.14159 * i + j;
}
```

to the pointer **p** by writing

```
p = example;
```

After this assignment, we can write the following function call:

```
(*p)(12, 34)
```

Its effect is the same as that of

```
example(12, 34)
```

Incidentally, we are also allowed to omit the asterisk (as well as the parentheses) in the call **(*p)(12, 34)**, which gives

```
p(12, 34)
```

On the one hand, this is an advantage because of its simplicity, but, on the other, we can no longer tell from this call alone whether **p** is a function or a pointer.

The usefulness of pointers to functions becomes clear if we imagine a large program in the beginning of which we want to choose one out of several functions; the chosen function is then to be called a great many times. By using a pointer, the choice has to be made only once: after assigning (the address of) the selected function to a pointer, we can later call it through that pointer.

Pointers to functions also enable us to pass a function as an argument to another function. We will use a very simple example: once you understand the principle, you will be able to write more interesting applications of it yourself. Suppose that we want to write a general function to compute the sum of some values, say,

$$f(1) + f(2) + ... + f(n) \tag{5.1}$$

for *any* function f with return type **double** and with one **int** argument. Our general summation function, say, **funsum**, takes two arguments: n, the number of terms in the sum (5.1), and f, the function to be used. To show that **funsum** is really a general function, we will call it twice, and compute the sum of

$$reciprocal(k) = 1.0/k \qquad (k = 1, 2, 3, 4, 5)$$
$$square(k) = k^2 \qquad (k = 1, 2, 3)$$

The following program shows how this can be done:

```
// PFUN: A function with a function as its argument.
#include <iostream.h>

int main()
{   double reciprocal(int k), square(int k),
            funsum(int n, double (*f)(int k));
    cout << "Sum of five reciprocals: "
         << funsum(5, reciprocal) << endl;
    cout << "Sum of three squares: "
         << funsum(3, square) << endl;
    return 0;
}
```

```
double funsum(int n, double (*f)(int k))
{   double s=0;
    int i;
    for (i=1; i<=n; i++) s += f(i);          // or: (*f)(i)
    return s;
}

double reciprocal(int k)
{   return 1.0/k;
}

double square(int k)
{   return (double)k * k;
}
```

This program computes the two sums $1 + 1.0/2 + 1.0/3 + 1.0/4 + 1.0/5$ and $1.0 + 4.0 + 9.0$, so its output is

```
Sum of five reciprocals: 2.28333
Sum of three squares: 14
```

Exercises

5.1   Write a program which reads a line of text and prints this line in the reverse order. Write a version that uses an array and no pointer notation, and compare it with another version that uses pointers and no array notation.

5.2   Write the function **reverse(s, t)** which examines the strings s and t to see if either of these is the reverse of the other. The value to be returned is 1 if this is the case and 0 if it is not.

5.3   Write a program which reads a sequence of integers, followed by a nonnumeric character, and, for each of the integers 0, ..., 99, counts how often that integer occurs in the sequence. You need not, and, for reasons of efficiency, must not, use nested loops. The output is a table with two columns: the first column lists the integers 0, ..., 99, as far as they have occurred at least once in the input data; the second column shows how often these integers have occurred.

5.4   Write a program that reads a sequence of 20 integers and, for each element of this sequence, counts how many smaller elements follow in the sequence.

5.5   Write a program that merges two sequences of integers. First, a_1, ..., a_{10} are read. This sequence is monotonic nondecreasing, which means that $i < j$ implies $a_i \leq a_j$.

Then the sequence $b_1, ..., b_{10}$ is read, which is also monotonic nondecreasing. Finally, the 20 integers read are printed as one monotonic nondecreasing sequence.

5.6 Write the program PARSORT, which takes three program arguments and prints them in alphabetic order. For example, the command line

```
PARSORT John Albert Jack
```

leads to the following output:

```
Albert
Jack
John
```

5.7 Write a program that reads lines of text from the keyboard and prints only the longest of these lines.

5.8 Write a program to solve the *Josephus* problem. The program reads two positive integers, n and k. Suppose that n persons form a circle. In clockwise order, we assign the numbers 1, 2, ..., n to them. Starting at person 1 and counting clockwise, we remove the kth person from the circle. In the reduced circle, we continue with the person following the one just removed and, resuming counting from 1 to k, again eliminate the kth person. This process is repeated until only one person remains: we want to know the number of this person.

5.9 Read a positive integer n from the keyboard and print the first $n + 1$ lines of *Pascal's triangle*. This triangle consists of lines of integers. Starting at the top, these lines are numbered 0, 1, ..., n, and there are $i + 1$ integers on line i. Each line starts and ends with integer 1. Except for all these integers 1, each integer in the triangle is computed as the sum of the two nearest integers on the line immediately above it. For example, with $n = 8$, Pascal's triangle is as shown below:

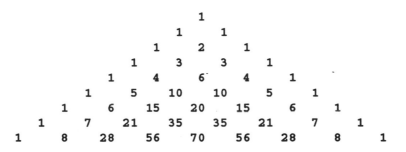

As you may know, the integers on line n, in the given order, are the coefficients $a_n, a_{n-1}, ..., a_1, a_0$ that occur in the right-hand side of

$$(x + 1)^n = a_n x^n + a_{n-1} x^{n-1} + ... + a_1 x + a_0$$

5.10 Predict the output produced by the following statements. Use your computer to see if your predictions are correct.

    a.   `cout << "ABCDEFG\n" + 3 << endl;`

    b.   `cout << "\nABCDEFG\n" + 3 << endl;`

    c.   `cout << "ABCDEFG"[3] << endl;`

    d.   `cout << ("GFEDCBA" + 1)[3] << endl;`

    e.   `cout << char("GFEDCBA"[1] + 3) << endl;`

    f.   `cout << &("ABCDEFG\n"[2]) << endl;`

    g.   `cout << *"ABCDEFG" << endl;`

6

Classes and Objects

6.1 Classes and Structures

Instead of using only individual variables of the types discussed so far, we can group some variables together. The new types built in this way are called *classes*. In some other languages, objects of such types are called *records*. A class is a generalization of what is a *structure* in C. Compared with C structures, classes have two important extensions:

1. Classes (including C++ structures) can have functions as their members. These functions operate on the data members; this combination of functions and data in classes is called *encapsulation*.

2. Unlike structures in C, classes provide for member-access control: we can protect data and functions in classes from unauthorized use, which is similar to declaring local variables in functions or (global) static variables in program modules. This concept is referred to as *data hiding*. For each component in a class or structure, we can indicate whether or not data hiding is to apply. If we omit such explicit indications, data hiding applies to the components of a class by default, while those of a structure are by default publicly accessible.

In the C language, the keyword **struct** is available, the keyword **class** is not. In C++ these keywords are both available, and, apart from default access rights, they are used in the same way and have the same meaning. We will therefore use the term *class* in our discussions even when the keyword **struct** actually occurs in the program text. Remember, a class is a *type*; if we define a variable of such a type, this variable is an *object*, or, more specifically, a *class object*, but not a class.

Classes can be regarded as a means of *extending* the language we are using: they enable us to define our own types, along with operators that can be applied to objects of these types.

As far as data is concerned, classes are somewhat similar to arrays, but their elements, normally called *members*, are not identified by subscripts but by *member names*. Suppose we have objects for each of which we want to store its code number, its name, its weight, and its length. We can define a class for these objects as follows:

```
struct article {
    int code;
    char name[20];
    float weight, length;
};
```

This *structure* is a *class* with only public members. We will discuss private members in Section 6.6. The above fragment is equivalent to

```
class article {
public:
    int code;
    char name[20];
    float weight, length;
};
```

As long as our classes are as simple as this example, with all members public, we will frequently use the keyword **struct**, rather than **class**, in our programs, so we can omit **public:**. If you do not like the apparent inconsistency of talking about *classes* and writing **struct**, you can simply replace **struct** with **class** in any program, provided you insert **public:** immediately after {, as the above example shows.

The position of the open brace, {, in the above examples may look strange. However, this way of defining a class is very usual, and it is more compact, that is, it saves one line of text in the latter example, which would otherwise look like this:

```
class article
{
public:
    ...
}
```

In the above two fragments, only **struct**, **class** and **public** are keywords; the other names, **article, code, name, weight,** and **length** are chosen by ourselves. This *class declaration* does not declare any variables. Yet it is useful, because it enables us to use the type **article**, in the same way as standard types, such as **int, float**, and so on. For example, we can now declare (and, at the same time, 'define') the two class variables **s** and **t**:

```
article s, t;
```

In C++ the keyword **struct** need not be not used in this line, while in C we would have to write

```
struct article s, t;
```

The short form in C++, without **struct**, is very similar to the declarations that we already know, such as

```
float x, y;
```

We could have combined the declaration of type **article** and that of the variables **s** and **t** by writing

```
struct article {
   int code;
   char name[20];
   float weight, length;
}  s, t;
```

In this case we should regard the whole part of the form

```
struct article { ... }
```

as the type, comparable with the keyword **float**, for example. If we use this combined declaration, we can omit the name **article**, although that would deprive us of a short-hand notation for this new type. Remember that in large programs we often need to use the same class several times; in particular, the type name **article** may occur in several functions, while the variables **s** and **t** are local to one of these functions. It is then very convenient to separate the (global) declaration of this class from the (local) variable declarations. If the program consists of several modules and some class type is to be used in more than one, it is highly recommended to define that type in a header file and to use a **#include** line for this file in all modules in which that type is used. After declaring the class variables **s** and **t** in one of the above ways, we can use them as follows:

```
s.code = 123;
strcpy(s.name, "Pencil");
s.weight = 12.3;
s.length = 150.7;
t = s;
```

This program fragment assigns values to all members of **s**; then these are all copied to **t**. The latter is remarkable: recall that we cannot use a single assignment to copy an entire array. We can copy a class object, even if this has an array among its members, as is the case here. The situation is now as shown in Figure 6.1.

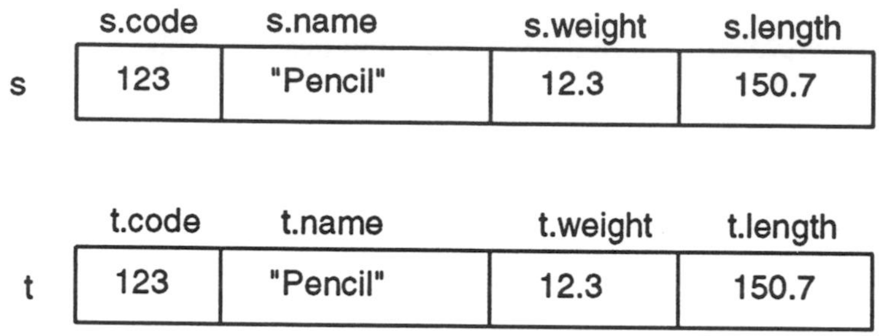

	s.code	s.name	s.weight	s.length
s	123	"Pencil"	12.3	150.7

	t.code	t.name	t.weight	t.length
t	123	"Pencil"	12.3	150.7

Figure 6.1. Situation after the execution of **t** = **s**;

The above fragment shows that class members are written with a dot between the class-variable name and the member name. These members are in fact normal variables. We can use them in the same way as other variables. For example, reading the **code** and **name** members can be done by writing

```
cin << s.code << s.name;
```

or, in the way this is done in C:

```
scanf("%d %s", &s.code, s.name);
```

Since **s.name** is an array, it is not preceded by **&**. Class objects (such as **s** and **t**) and arrays are sometimes called *aggregates*. Classes can also have other classes as their members. If an aggregate is part of another aggregate, as is the case with **s.name**, we call it a *subaggregate*.

In many applications we use pointers to class objects. For example, if **p** points to an **article** object, we can write **(*p).code**, which is similar to **s.code**, used above. The parentheses are really required here because the dot (.) has higher precedence than the asterisk (*), as you can see in Section 3.6. Since such rather awkward expressions would occur very often, a special, more convenient notation is available. Instead of

```
(*p).code
```

we can write

```
p->code
```

with exactly the same meaning. We will be using the latter notation frequently in this book.

Like arrays, class objects can be *initialized* by means of constant expressions separated by commas and enclosed in braces. Also, they are implicitly initialized with zeros if they have permanent memory space. In our example, we can write

```
struct article {
   int code;
   char name[20];
   float weight, length;
};

int main()
{  static article s = {246, "Pen", 20.6, 147.0}, t;
   ...
}
```

Since **t** is static, it is implicitly initialized with zeros (with 20 null characters in array name). If we had omitted **static** in this example, the members of **t** would have had undefined initial values. The initialization of **s**, however, would in that case be valid as well. The list of constant expressions between braces must not contain more elements than there are members in the class. If it contains fewer, the remaining members of the class object are initialized with zeros (even for 'automatic' variables).

There is another way of initializing class objects. Instead of writing a list of expressions enclosed by braces, we may use any expression without braces, provided it has exactly the right type. For example, in function **f**, we can initialize **t** using the global variable **s**; in the following example, **t** is in turn used to initialize **u**:

```
...
article s = {246, "Pen", 20.6, 147.0};
...

void f(void)
{  article t=s, u=t;
   ...
}
```

Another aspect that class objects have in common with arrays is that we cannot use them as a whole in comparisons, as is attempted in

```
if (s == t) ...    // Error
```

However, C++ offers facilities for 'overloading' operators; this enables us to extend the meaning of == (and other operators), after which this comparison is valid. We will discuss this in more detail in Section 6.8.

The size of class objects

A class object may be larger than the sum of its members, so there may be gaps between these members. For example, we have

sizeof(s) ≥ sizeof(s.code) + sizeof(s.name) + sizeof(s.weight) + sizeof(s.length)

In this example, it is to be expected that the equal sign will apply because the name member takes 20 bytes, which is a round number. However, if the length of array **name** had been 21, there would probably have been a gap of either one or three bytes to round up this odd length of 21 to 22 or 24.

Subaggregates

Class members can have any type, so they can again be classes. We have already seen that class members can be arrays. In our example, the characters of the member **name** are also available as individual array elements. For example, we can write

```
s.name[3]
```

Both the dot and the brackets have the highest precedence, but since they associate from left to right the above means the same as

```
(s.name)[3]
```

It is also possible to use arrays of class objects. On the basis of our example, we can declare

```
article table[2];
```

after which we can write, for example,

```
table[i].length
```

and even

```
table[i].name[j]
```

If we want to initialize array **table**, we can do this, for example, as follows:

```
article table[2] = {{123, "Pencil", 12.3, 150.7},
                     {246, "Pen", 20.6, 147.0}};
```

As with arrays, we can omit the innermost braces and write

```
article table[2] = {123, "Pencil", 12.3, 150.7,
                     246, "Pen", 20.6, 147.0};
```

The former way of initializing is more logical and should therefore be preferred to the latter. It also enables us to omit trailing values for some array elements; for example, the **weight** and the **length** members of both **table[0]** and **table[1]** are given the initial value 0 if we write

```
article table[2] = {{123, "Pencil"},
                     {246, "Pen"}};
```

6.2 Classes as Arguments and as Return Values

If we have to pass class objects as function arguments, we can do this in three ways, and the same applies to the way return values are passed back. We will demonstrate this using type **article**, declared in the following header file:

```
// ARTICLE.H: Header file for three demonstration programs.
struct article {
    int code;
    char name[20];
    float weight, length;
};
```

Although we could pass arguments in one way and return values in another, we will not do this in the following examples.

a. Entire class objects as arguments and return values

It is possible to use class objects as arguments and return values. Remember, this involves copying these objects, which may take more time than copying only their addresses (to be discussed in b. and c.). Yet this method may sometimes be useful and reasonably efficient. Let us discuss it by using a very simple example: in a complete program, we will define the function **largeobj**, which takes an object of our class **article** as its argument and returns a similar object, which has a **code** member equal to the old one plus 1, the same **name** member as the old one, and of which the **weight** and **length** members are twice as large as the corresponding old members:

```
// ENTOBJ: Passing an entire class object.
#include <iostream.h>
#include "article.h"

article largeobj(article x)
{   x.code++;
    x.weight *= 2;
    x.length *= 2;
    return x;
}

int main()
{   article s = {246, "Pen", 20.6, 147.0}, t;
    t = largeobj(s);
    cout << t.code << endl;
    return 0;
}
```

In function **largeobj**, parameter **x** is a copy of argument **s**. In the return statement, **x** is again copied. Parameter **x** is used as a local variable; the return statement would also be correct if **x** were a local variable, declared in function **largeobj** in the normal way.

b. Addresses as arguments and as return values

The following program demonstrates how to pass addresses both as arguments and as return values, using pointers:

```
// PTROBJ : Pointer parameter and pointer return value.

#include <iostream.h>
#include <string.h>
#include "article.h"

article *plargeobj(article *px)
{   article *p = new article;
    p->code = px->code + 1;
    strcpy(p->name, px->name);
    p->weight = 2 * px->weight;
    p->length = 2 * px->length;
    return p;
}

int main()
{   article s = {246, "Pen", 20.6, 147.0}, *pt;
    pt = plargeobj(&s);
    cout << pt->code << endl;
    return 0;
}
```

Although this program is even less realistic than the previous one, it shows clearly how an address of a class object can be passed not only as an argument but also as a return value. But for the latter aspect, we could have used a more realistic example by using a **void** function, as shown in this fragment:

```
void plargeobj(article *p)
{   p->code++;
    p->weight *= 2;
    p->length *= 2;
}
...
plargeobj(&s);
```

This example shows that we can change an object if we pass its address, as we have also seen in Section 4.3.

We now revert to program PTROBJ, since it offers a good opportunity to discuss a serious programming error, which occurs in the following, incorrect version of function **plargeobj**:

```
article *plargeobj(article *px)   // Error
{  article obj;
   obj.code = px->code + 1;
   obj.weight = 2 * px->weight;
   obj.length = 2 * px->length
   return &obj;
}
```

As we know, an automatic variable exists only as long as the function in which it is defined is being executed. In this example, memory for **obj** is automatically allocated when **plargeobj** is entered and released when it is left. This means that in the function in which **plargeobj** is called, after that call, the memory occupied by **obj** a short while ago may already be in use for other purposes, although its start address is still available! (This is similar to entering a house the key of which was given to us some time ago by the previous owner who no longer lives there.)

c. References as arguments and return values

In the following program, a reference to a class object is passed both as an argument and as the return value of function **rlargeobject**:

```
// REFOBJ: Reference parameter and reference return value.
#include <iostream.h>
#include <string.h>
#include "article.h"

article &rlargeobj(article &x)
{  article *p = new article;
   p->code = x.code + 1;
   strcpy(p->name, x.name);
   p->weight = 2 * x.weight;
   p->length = 2 * x.length;
   return *p;
}

int main()
{  article s = {246, "Pen", 20.6, 147.0}, *pt;
   pt = &rlargeobj(s);
   cout << pt->code << endl;
   return 0;
}
```

The above function **rlargeobj** returns a reference to a new object; in other words, it returns an lvalue, so we can assign its address to pointer **pt** in the **main** function. We could use a variable t of type **article** instead of a pointer **pt**, with the following two lines replacing similar ones in the above **main** function:

```
{ article s = {246, "Pen", 20.6, 147.0}, t;
  t = rlargeobj(s);
```

However, that would be bad programming practice. The object generated by **new** in function **largeobj**, after being copied into variable t, would still be present in memory while it is unreachable. This is like copying, say, a sheet of paper to use this copy later and at the same time making it impossible to use the original version ever again. By contrast, the object generated in program REFOBJ is not copied, but its address is placed in variable **pt** so the very object generated by **new** is used later.

Again, we will more often use reference parameters in a **void** function, is done in the following fragment:

```
void plargeobj(article &x)
{ x.code++;
  x.weight *= 2;
  x.length *= 2;
}
...
plargeobj(s);
```

Another example

Functions returning a reference can be called in unusual contexts, as the following example demonstrates:

```
article &heavier(article &x, article &y)
{ return x.weight > y.weight ? x : y;
}
```

With three given **article** variables s, t, and u we can write, for example,

```
u = heavier(s, t);
heavier(s, t).weight = 0;
```

After the selected object has been saved by copying it into **u**, its **weight** member is set to zero. In other words, the last line assigns zero to either **s.weight** or **t.weight**.

Dynamic data structures

Since class members can have any type, there can be a pointer member **p** pointing to another object that is of the same type as the one of which **p** is a member:

```
struct element {int num; element *p;};
```

Such types, combined with dynamic memory allocation, offer very interesting new possibilities. They enable us to create objects dynamically, each containing one or more pointers to similar objects, also created dynamically, and so on. The new aspect of such *dynamic data structures* is that the objects in question are variables that have no names by which we can have access to them. Instead, they are accessed by following chains of pointers. Examples of dynamic data structures are *linked lists* and *binary trees*. We will use linked lists in Sections 7.7 and 7.8. A very instructive problem about binary trees, along with its solution, can be found in Appendix A, Exercise 42.

6.3 Unions

With the class objects we have seen so far, all data members are in memory at the same time. In other words, the amount of memory used by a normal class object is at least the sum of the amounts of memory used by its data members. In contrast to this, there is another special case of the class concept, called *union*. The notation of unions is similar to that of other classes. However, union members overlay each other. The amount of memory a union object takes is only as large as that of its largest member, which implies that there is only one member actually present at a time. For example, after writing

```
union intflo {int i; float x;} u;
```

we can use **u.i** and **u.x**, in the same way as if the above keyword **union** were replaced with **struct**. However, the members i and x share memory space, so by executing

```
u.i = 123;
u.x = 98.7;
```

the second statement destroys the value just assigned to **u.i**. The above declaration declares not only the variable **u** but also the type **intflo**. For example, we can now declare

```
intflo v;
```

Unions can be useful if we want to store only one of their members. In that case, they are more economical with memory space, especially if we use arrays of union objects. However, it is the programmer's responsibility to remember which of the members have been used. One way of realizing this is to use a class with two members: a 'flag' and a union, the flag being a code for the current member choice in the union. For example, we can write

```
enum choice{intflag, floatflag};
struct {choice flag; union {int i; float x;} num;} a[1000];
...
if ( ... ) {a[k].flag = intflag; a[k].num.i = 123;}
     else {a[k].flag = floatflag; a[k].num.x = 98.7;}
...
if (a[k].flag == intflag)
  cout << "Integer value: " << a[k].num.i; else
if (a[k].flag == floatflag)
  cout << "Float value: " << a[k].num.x; else
  cout << "Unknown flag";
```

6.4 Bit Fields

Normally, the smallest unit of memory used for variables is one byte. However, it is possible for classes to have members that are smaller than one byte. As their sizes are expressed in bits, they are called *bit fields*. In the following example we have a class object **s**, with bit fields **b4**, **b1**, **b2**, consisting of 4, 1, and 2 bits, respectively. Besides, there is a **char** member **ch**:

```
struct example {
    unsigned b4:4, b1:1, b2:2;
    char ch;
} s;
```

Bit fields are similar to other class members, with one exception: since several of them may be located in the same byte, we cannot uniquely identify them by their addresses, and we must therefore not apply the 'address of' operator **&** to them. We can write

```
s.b4 = 7;
```

which implies that **s.b4** is an *lvalue* (discussed in Section 5.5), but, unlike other lvalues, it must not be preceded by the unary operator **&**.

6.5 Member Functions and Encapsulation

This section is about an important C++ language aspect that is not available in C. Although we will again write **struct** in some examples, this new aspect applies to classes in general.

When declaring classes, we usually also define functions that manipulate variables of these types. In complex programs, we often work with many classes and with several functions for each of these. As this might easily lead to confusion, there is a need for a language facility to group things together in an orderly way. The C++ language offers this facility. In order to make clear that certain functions belong to some class, we make those functions members of that class. Since member functions are declared (or even defined) inside classes, the technical term for this idea is *encapsulation*. For example, in program VEC1 the functions **setvec** and **printvec** are defined inside the class **vector**:

```
// VEC1: A class in which two functions are defined.
#include <iostream.h>

struct vector {
   float x, y;
   void setvec(float xx, float yy) {x = xx; y = yy;}
   void printvec()const {cout << x << ' ' << y << endl;}
};

int main()
{  vector u, v;
   u.setvec(1.0, 2.0); u.printvec();
   v.setvec(3.0, 4.0); v.printvec();
   return 0;
}
```

Notice the four function calls in this program. In

```
u.setvec(1.0, 2.0);
```

the variable name **u** and the dot at the beginning indicate that function **setvec** is to be applied to the variable **u**. The notations **u.setvec** (for the function member **setvec**) has the same form as **u.x** (for the data member x).

As a result of the calls **u.printvec( )** and **v.printvec( )**, program VEC1 produces the following output:

```
1 2
3 4
```

Using **const** in

```
void printvec()const { ... }
```

is not absolutely necessary, but it is recommended for functions that do not change the value of data members. In this example, we can use **const** for **printvec** because this function does not alter x or y, but we must not use it for **setvec** because this function changes these data members.

In program VEC1, the functions **setvec** and **printvec** have been *defined* inside the class. Their definitions are therefore dealt with as if we had used the **inline** keyword, discussed in Section 4.10. Instead, we could only have *declared* them there and defined them outside the class, as program VEC2 shows:

```
// VEC2: A class in which two functions are declared.
//          These functions are defined outside the class.

#include <iostream.h>

struct vector {
    float x, y;
    void setvec(float xx, float yy);
    void printvec()const;
};

int main()
{   vector u, v;
    u.setvec(1.0, 2.0); u.printvec();
    v.setvec(3.0, 4.0); v.printvec();
    return 0;
}

void vector::setvec(float xx, float yy)
{   x = xx; y = yy;
}

void vector::printvec()const
{   cout << x << ' ' << y << endl;
}
```

The functions **setvec** and **printvec** in program VEC2 are not inline functions. We see that in the function definitions the part

```
vector::
```

has been inserted. This is necessary indicate that the functions are members of class **vector**. A consequence of this is that we can use the names x and y in these functions, without specifying explicitly that these are **vector** members. Incidentally, in the functions **setvec** and **printvec**, we could replace x and y with

```
this->x
this->y
```

respectively, to express more clearly that x and y members of class objects. The name **this** is a C++ keyword. In a member function, it is always available as a pointer to the object specified in the call to that function. This object is said to be *the object for which the function is called*. For example, **printvec** is called for **u** in

```
u.printvec
```

During the execution of this function, **this** is a pointer to **u**, so we can write **this–>x** to denote the member **u.x**. Although such use of **this** would be superfluous in program VEC2, this keyword is useful in other cases, as we will see in Section 6.8.

Although notations such as

```
u.x
u.printvec()
```

look very similar, there is an important distinction in the implementation of data members and functions: each of the objects **u** and **v** has its own data member **x**, but there is only one function **printvec**, shared by these two objects. The value of **sizeof(vector)** will therefore be equal to **sizeof(point)**, where type point is defined as

```
struct point{float x, y;};
```

6.6 Member Access Control

In programs VEC1 and VEC2, we could have used the class members **x** and **y** in the **main** functions, if we had wanted to do so. We did not, because access to these members was delegated to the member functions **setvec** and **printvec**. This is a situation which frequently occurs. Especially in more complicated applications of classes, we feel a need to make a distinction in the access control of members (applying to both data and functions):

1. Some members, such as the functions **setvec** and **printvec** in Section 6.5, should be *public*. They belong to the *interface*; the 'user' needs only to know what can be done with them.

2. Other members, such as **x** and **y** should be *private*. They belong to the *implementation*, that is, users need not know their details, unless they want to know how operations on the data type in question are implemented.

When we are using the keyword **struct**, all members are public by default. If we use the keyword **class** they are by default private. In both cases we can explicitly indicate what we want by using the keywords **public** and **private**. (If we omit these last two keywords when using the keyword **class**, we have no access to any class member at all, which does not make sense.) Apart from this distinction in **access control**, **struct** and **class** have the same meaning. In a class declaration, we can insert **public:** and **private:**, including the colons, as demonstrated by program VEC3, which has been derived from program VEC2 in Section 6.5.

```
// VEC3: A class with private members x and y.
#include <iostream.h>

class vector {
public:
   void setvec(float xx, float yy);
   void printvec()const;
private:
   float x, y;
};

int main()
{  vector u, v;
   u.setvec(1.0, 2.0); u.printvec();
   v.setvec(3.0, 4.0); v.printvec();
   return 0;
}

void vector::setvec(float xx, float yy)
{  x = xx; y = yy;
}

void vector::printvec()const
{  cout << x << ' ' << y << endl;
}
```

Since class members are by default private, we could have omitted the keyword **private** in VEC3 if the order of the class members had been different, as in

```
class vector {
   float x, y;
public:
   void setvec(float xx, float yy);
   void printvec()const;
};
```

However, placing private class members at the end is recommended. If there are a great many members, it is a good idea to begin by listing the public members because those are the ones that we have access to from outside the class.

   The only essential difference between the programs VEC2 and VEC3 is that the members x and y are public in VEC2 while they are private in VEC3. For example, using **u.x** in the **main** function is possible in VEC2, not in VEC3. Recall that the form

```
struct name { ... }
```

is equivalent to

```
class name { public: ... }
```

If we use the words **private** or **public** for each member, **struct** is equivalent to **class**, but **class** is more often used. In C, we have structures (no classes) but these cannot contain function members as they can in C++, nor are the keywords **private** and **public** available in C.

Using :: for functions that return pointers

In the definition of a member function outside its class, the scope-resolution operator :: is immediately followed by the function name. For a function that returns a pointer, this implies that the asterisk is to be written in front of the class name preceding this operator, as in

```
char *classname::myalloc()
{   ...
}
```

This member function **myalloc** of class **classname** returns a pointer to a character. Obviously, the blank in the first line of this function is not significant, so each of the following lines are equivalent to that line:

```
char* classname::myalloc()
char * classname::myalloc()
char*classname::myalloc()
```

It would not be correct if the asterisk were written between :: and **myalloc**.

6.7 Constructors and Destructors

In many applications, we want certain actions to be performed when a class object is created. In C++ this can be done very elegantly by means of a *constructor*, which is a member function that has the same name as the class in question. For example, let us consider a class with two data fields:

1. A pointer **ptr**, pointing to a sequence of integers.
2. An integer **len**, which is the length of that sequence.

Figure 6.2 shows two objects, **r** and **s**, of such a class type, along with two sequences of three and five integers, respectively.

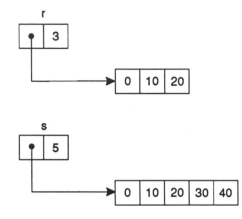

Figure 6.2. Variable-length sequences

Now suppose we have declared class type **row** with only the two members **ptr** and **len**, mentioned above. Then the declaration on the second line of the function

```
void tworows()
{   row r, s;
    ...
}
```

will create the two objects **r** and **s**, excluding the integer sequences. In order to allocate memory space for these sequences, we could insert

```
r.ptr = new int[3]; r.len = 3;
s.ptr = new int[5]; s.len = 5;
```

in this function. When the function is left, the memory space is automatically released for **r** and **s**, but not for the two integer sequences pointed to. It would therefore be necessary to insert

```
delete r.ptr;
delete s.ptr;
```

at the end of function **tworows**. All this is not particularly convenient, and it is a potential source of programming errors. It would be much better if we could arrange for all required memory space to be automatically allocated and released. We can do this by including both a *constructor* and a *destructor* in the class **row**, as is done in program CONSTR:

```
// CONSTR: Demonstration of a constructor and a destructor.
#include <iostream.h>

class row {
public:
    row(int n=3)
    {  len = n; ptr = new int[n];
        for (int i=0; i<n; i++) ptr[i] = 10 * i;
    }
    ~row() {delete ptr;}
    void printrow(char *str)const;
private:
    int *ptr, len;
};

void row::printrow(char *str)const
{  cout << str;
    for (int i=0; i<len; i++) cout << ptr[i] << ' ';
    cout << endl;
}

void tworows()
{  row r, s(5);
    r.printrow("r: ");
    s.printrow("s: ");
}

int main()
{  tworows();
    return 0;
}
```

Class **row** has not only the two data members **ptr** and **len** but also the function
members **row( )**, **~row( )**, and **printrow( )**. Since the first of these is named after the
class **row**, it is the constructor of this class. Analogously, the name of the destructor is
formed by writing the tilde-symbol ~, followed by the class name. When defining
constructors and destructors, we do not write **void, int**, or any other type at its beginning. Constructors and destructors must not contain return-statements. For the objects
r and **s** of the class **row**, the constructor **row( )** is implicitly called when they are
created, the destructor **~row( )** when they cease to exist. In function **tworows( )**, both
the constructor **row( )** and the destructor **~row( )** are implicitly called twice: the
constructor is called when **r** and **s** are created in their declarations, and the destructor
on return from **tworows** to **main**. Thanks to these implicit calls, memory for the integer
sequences is automatically allocated and released in the same way as it is for the
(smaller) objects **r** and **s**.

In this example, the constructor **row** has a default argument 3, which applies to **r**,
since no argument is given for it in the declaration

```
row r, s(5);
```

For **s**, however, the argument 5 is given. As a result of this declaration, the constructor **row( )** is executed twice, first with the default argument 3 and then with argument 5. In the above declaration, it is not allowed to replace **r** with **r( )**.

Instead of providing the **row** constructor with a default argument, we could have used two distinct constructors, one with a parameter and one without. In other words, we could have written the two constructors

```
row(int n)
{  len = n; ptr = new int[n];
    for (int i=0; i<n; i++) ptr[i] = 10 * i;
}
row()
{  len = 3; ptr = new int[3];
    for (int i=0; i<3; i++) ptr[i] = 10 * i;
}
```

instead of the single **row** constructor of program CONSTR. Then the above definitions of **r** (without an argument) and **s** (with argument 5) would have had the same effect as they have in program CONSTR. A constructor without parameters is called a *default constructor*; the one shown above would be used in program CONSTR for the definition of **r**. If we had not used the default argument (= **3**) in program CONSTR and we had not supplied a default constructor either, the definition

```
row r;
```

would not have been correct.

The constructor **row** in program CONSTR initializes the data members **len** and **ptr**. We can do this in a different way. Instead of using the assignment-statement **len = n;**, we could write **:len(n)** just before the open brace:

```
row(int n=3): len(n)
{  ptr = new int[n];
    for (int i=0; i<n; i++) ptr[i] = 10 * i;
}
```

If we also want to initialize **ptr** in this way, we can even write

```
row(int n=3):len(n), ptr(new int[n])
{  for (int i=0; i<n; i++) ptr[i] = 10 * i;
}
```

These two versions are equivalent to the original **row** constructor. The text of the form

```
: ...
```

written between) and {, is called a *constructor initializer*. We will return to this subject in a moment.

You may wonder what would happen if we omitted the destructor ~**row( )** in program CONSTR. Apparently, the program would run correctly. However, if function **tworows** were called a great many times, we might run out of memory, since without the destructor the memory for the integer sequences, allocated by the constructor, would not be released until program termination.

In our above discussion, we have considered **r** and **s** to be limited to the two data members **ptr** and **len** of class **row**. Now that the integer sequences pointed to (as illustrated in Figure 6.2) are automatically created and destroyed, we would rather consider these to be part of **r** and **s**. This point of view makes it easier to think in terms of *abstract data types*: we simply regard objects of type **row** as rows of integers, without bothering about implementation details.

Constructor initialization vs. assignment

In many cases it makes no difference whether constructor initialization or assignment is used. Suppose, in the following fragment, we want to replace *xxx* with a constructor that makes class member **i** equal to its argument:

```
class test {
public:
   xxx   // Constructor
   int i;
};
```

The following lines are equivalent solutions to this problem:

```
test(int ii): i(ii){} // Initialization
test(int ii){i = ii;} // Assignment
```

However, we cannot always freely choose between initialization and assignment. This is demonstrated by the following program:

```
// INIT_ASS: Constructor initialization vs. assignment
#include <iostream.h>
int g;

class test {
public:
   test(const int cii, int &rii)
      : ci(cii), ri(rii) // Initialization required.
   {  g = ri;            // Assignment required.
      ri++;
   }
   void pr(){cout << ci << "   " << ri << endl;}
```

```
private:
   const int ci;
   int &ri;
};

int main()
{  int i=123;
   test t(5, i);
   cout << "t.pr(): "; t.pr();
   cout << "i = " << i << endl;
   cout << "g = " << g << endl;
   return 0;
}
```

A constructor initializer can initialize only class members. We can therefore not replace the assignment g = ri in the **test** constructor with an initializion **g(ri)** similar to **ci(cii)**. On the other hand, we cannot use assignments instead of the initialization :ci(cii), ri(rii). Recall that for normal definitions, outside a class, the two lines

```
const int ci;
int &ri;
```

would not be correct: both constants and reference variables must be initialized, as we have seen in Sections 2.2 and 4.3, respectively. These two lines, occurring in the above **test** class, are correct only because **ci** and **ri** are initialized here by a constructor initializer. Besides, the lines

```
ci = cii;
ri = rii;
```

would be impossible because neither a constant (**ci**) nor a reference variable (**ri**) can be given an initial value by means of an assignment.

   If you have difficulty in understanding program INIT_ASS, you may find it helpful to see its output:

```
t.pr(): 5   124
i = 124
g = 123
```

Constructors and dynamically created objects

In program CONSTR, the constructor **row( )** was invoked when the objects **r** and **s** were created by the declaration

```
row r, s(5);
```

Objects can also be created by dynamic memory allocation. In our example, we could write

```
row *p;
```

which would not immediately lead to a call to the constructor **row( )**. After all, this declaration causes memory to be allocated only for the pointer **p**, not for any objects that **p** may point to later. As we have seen in Section 5.6, we can dynamically allocate memory in two ways, either by using the C++ operator **new** or by calling the (older) function **malloc**. There is, however, an important distinction between these two methods. If we write

```
p = new row;
```

the constructor **row( )** is called; this is not the case if we call **malloc** instead, writing

```
p = (row *)malloc(sizeof(row));
```

Analogously, the destructor **~row( )** is called by **delete p**, not by **free(p)**. (Recall that **delete** is the counterpart of **new**, and **free( )** that of **malloc( )**.)

In the above statement **p = new row;** we did not specify an argument, so this statement generates a **row** object with the default length of 3. We can also write, for example,

```
p = new row(5);
```

to generate a row of length 5.

Constructors and arrays of class objects

As we have seen, the definition

```
row r, s(5);
```

generates a row **r** of length 3 and a row **s** of length 5. If we define arrays of **row** objects, the constructor is called for every array element. Arguments for the constructor can be specified by initializing the array in the normal way. Consider, for example, the definition of the arrays **a** and **b** in the following **main** function:

```
int main()
{   row a[2], b[6] = {5, 1, 2};
    cout << "Array a (two elements)\n";
    for (int i=0; i<2; i++){cout << i; a[i].printrow(": ");}
    cout << "\nArray b (six elements)\n";
    for (int j=0; j<6; j++){cout << j; b[j].printrow(": ");}
    return 0;
}
```

If this **main** function replaces that of program CONSTR, the modified program will have the following output:

```
Array a (two elements)
0:  0 10 20
1:  0 10 20

Array b (six elements)
0:  0 10 20 30 40
1:  0
2:  0 10
3:  0 10 20
4:  0 10 20
5:  0 10 20
```

This output shows that for the class objects **b[0]**, **b[1]** and **b[2]** the row lengths are 5, 1 and 2, respectively, as specified in the above initialization of array **b**. No initial values were given for **a[0]**, **a[1]**, **b[3]**, **b[4]** and **b[5]**, so the default row length of 3 applies to these **row** objects.

6.8 Operator Overloading and Friend Functions

In Section 4.8 we discussed function overloading; we saw that, to identify a function, not only its name but also the types and number of its arguments are required. The situation is similar with operators. For example, the division operator / performs integer arithmetic if its two operands have integer type, and floating-point arithmetic if at least one of its operands has floating-point type. This example shows that operator overloading is not an entirely new idea: it is used for / even in the C language. In contrast to C, C++ also enables us to overload operators ourselves. (Incidentally, this was already possible in Algol 68, back in 1968, so it is not a unique concept of C++.) We saw in Section 4.8 that we can use the name of a standard function, such as **sqrt**, for a function of our own. *Operator overloading* always works this way. Although we can define operators of our own, we can only do this with the following characters (or character sequences), which are already in use as operators:

```
new   delete
+     -     *     /     %     ^     &     |     ~
!     =     <     >     +=    -=    *=    /=    %=
^=    &=    |=    <<    >>    >>=   <<=   ==    !=
<=    >=    &&    ||    ++    --    ,     ->*   ->
()    []
```

The precedence of these operators cannot be changed. For example, if we define our own operators + and *, the precedence of * will be higher than that of +.

To discuss operator overloading, we will again use type **vector**. With two given vectors

$$\mathbf{u} = (x_u, y_u)$$
$$\mathbf{v} = (x_v, y_v)$$

we can compute their sum

$$\mathbf{s} = (x_s, y_s)$$

as follows:

$$x_s = x_u + x_v$$
$$y_s = y_u + y_v$$

Figure 6.3 illustrates this for the vectors $\mathbf{u} = (3, 1)$, $\mathbf{v} = (1, 2)$, which have $\mathbf{s} = (4, 3)$ as their sum vector.

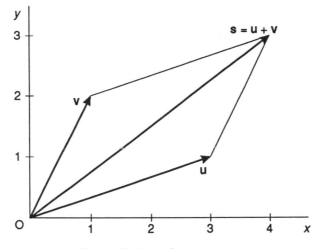

Figure 6.3. Sum of two vectors

We will now *overload* the addition operator + for vectors, so that in our program we can write

```
s = u + v;
```

in which **s**, **u**, and **v** are vectors. Program OPERATOR shows how this can be done:

```
// OPERATOR: An operator function for vector addition.
#include <iostream.h>

class vector {
public:
   vector(float xx=0, float yy=0): x(xx), y(yy) {}
   void printvec()const;
   void getvec(float &xx, float &yy)const{xx = x; yy = y;}
private:
   float x, y;
};

void vector::printvec()const
{  cout << x << ' ' << y << endl;
}

vector operator+(vector &a, vector &b)
{  float xa, ya, xb, yb;
   a.getvec(xa, ya); b.getvec(xb, yb);
   return vector(xa + xb, ya + yb);
}

int main()
{  vector u(3, 1), v(1, 2), s;
   s = u + v;      // Computes the sum of two vectors!
   s.printvec(); // Output: 4 3
   return 0;
}
```

As this program shows, we can define a plus operator of our own by means of a function whose name consists of the keyword **operator** followed by +. Other operators can be defined analogously. Note that the first line

```
vector operator+(vector &a, vector &b)
```

of our operator definition has almost the same form as

```
vector sum(vector &a, vector &b)
```

of a function **sum**, which we could have defined instead. In that case we would have written

```
s = sum(u, v);
```

instead of the more convenient notation

```
s = u + v;
```

In spite of this notation with two operands and an operator, **operator+** is a real function. This is best illustrated by comparing the above statement with the following one, which we can really write in our program instead of the above assignment statement:

```
s = operator+(u, v);
```

Unlike ordinary functions, operator functions can have only one or two parameters; at least one of these must be a class. Here we have used reference parameters (by writing **vector &a** instead of **vector a**) for the sake of efficiency: in this way, no new copies of the arguments **u** and **v** are made.

The **vector** constructor in this program shows a constructor initializer, discussed in the previous section. Instead, we could have done without it, using this constructor version, equivalent to the one in program OPERATOR:

```
vector(float xx=0, float yy=0){x = xx; y = yy;}
```

The program also defines and uses the function **getvec**, which did not occur in Section 6.5. We use this in the **operator+** function to fetch the individual components **x** and **y** of its parameters **a** and **b**. After all, we could not have written **a.x** and **a.y** in this operator function because, in class **vector**, the members **x** and **y** are private. You may argue that it would be preferable if, in some way or other, the function **operator+** would have direct access to these members (without these being made public). There are two ways to achieve this, and we will discuss these successively.

Note also the expression

```
vector(xa + xb, ya + yb)
```

in the return-statement of the **operator+** function. This is an explicit call to the constructor of class **vector**, and it works as a cast. We will discuss this aspect in more detail in Section 6.9.

Friend functions

For a given class, we can define *friend functions*, which have access to the private members of the class. It is necessary for friend functions to be declared inside the class. At the beginning of such declarations, we use the keyword **friend**. Although friend functions are declared in a class, they are not member functions. In program FRIEND, the **operator+** function is a friend function of class **vector**:

```
// FRIEND: The 'friend' keyword applied to an
//         operator function.

#include <iostream.h>

class vector {
public:
   vector(float xx=0, float yy=0): x(xx), y(yy){}
   void printvec()const;
   friend vector operator+(vector &a, vector &b);
private:
   float x, y;
};

void vector::printvec()const
{  cout << x << ' ' << y << endl;
}

vector operator+(vector &a, vector &b)
{  return vector(a.x + b.x, a.y + b.y);
}

int main()
{  vector u(3, 1), v(1, 2), s;
   s = u + v;       // The sum of two vectors is computed here!
   s.printvec();  // Output: 4 3
   return 0;
}
```

Thanks to the **friend** prefix in the declaration of the **operator+** function, the private members x and y are now directly accessible in this function, as the above modified version of this function illustrates.

Curiously enough, although a friend function is not a class member, we may *define* it inside a class, if we like. For example, in program FRIEND we can define class **vector** as follows:

```
class vector {
public:
   vector(float xx=0, float yy=0): x(xx), y(yy){}
   void printvec()const;
   friend vector operator+(vector &a, vector &b)
   {  float xa, ya, xb, yb;
      return vector(a.x + b.x, a.y + b.y);
   }
private:
   float x, y;
};
```

If we do, we will obviously not define the **operator+** function *after* class **vector**, as we did in program FRIEND.

In a class A, we can specify that all member functions of a class B are to be friend functions by declaring *class* B as a friend of A. We then write

```
friend class B;
```

Operators as member functions

Our goal, having direct access to private members of class **vector**, can also be obtained by including the **operator+** function as a member of this class. However, this method requires a notation that at first sight looks odd: although we are defining a *binary* operator, the operator function must have only one parameter, namely one that corresponds to the second operand. The following program shows how we can use a member function for our vector addition:

```
// OPMEMBER: An operator function as a class member.
#include <iostream.h>

class vector {
public:
   vector(float xx=0, float yy=0): x(xx), y(yy){}
   void printvec()const;
   vector operator+(vector &b);
private:
   float x, y;
};

void vector::printvec()const
{  cout << x << ' ' << y << endl;
}

vector vector::operator+(vector &b)
{  return vector(x + b.x, y + b.y);
}

int main()
{  vector u(3, 1), v(1, 2), s;
   s = u + v;     // Computes the sum of two vectors!
   s.printvec(); // Output: 4 3
   return 0;
}
```

Note the following statement in the **operator+** function:

```
return vector(x + b.x, y + b.y);
```

The unqualified **x** and **y** refer to the first operand, that is, to the vector variable **u**. The operator definition shows only the parameter **b**, which corresponds to the second operand, **b**. The first operand is *implicit* because the statement

```
s = u + v;
```

is to be regarded as an abbreviated form of

```
s = u.operator+(v);
```

This is in accordance with normal member functions (not necessarily operators). Since **u** is written here before the dot to indicate that the function **operator+** is to be called for **u**, it would not make sense if **u** were also given as an argument. This explains why a member function that defines a binary operator has only one parameter.

Another possibly confusing point in this program is the double occurrence of the word **vector** in the first line

```
vector vector::operator+(vector &b)
```

of the operator function. The first word **vector** on this line is the type to be returned by this function. Then **vector::** follows to indicate that the function is a member of class **vector**. We would have omitted this second occurrence of **vector** and this double colon if we had defined the function inside the class declaration.

Besides aesthetic advantages of defining **operator+** as a friend function, there is a more practical argument in favor of friend functions, which is related to type conversions of the first operand, as we will see almost at the end of Section 6.10.

The above discussion might suggest that, when overloading any operator, we can freely choose between member and friend functions. This is not the case. The four operators =, [ ], ( ) and –> are required by the language to be defined as class member functions, so we cannot use friend functions for them.

Overloading applied to unary operators

So far, we have discussed how to define operators that have two operands. We can also apply the principle of operator overloading to *unary* operators. For example, let us define the minus sign as the unary operator for vectors, so that we will be able to write

```
vector u, v;
...
v = -u;
```

Once we have defined both a unary minus and a binary plus operator, we can use these to define a binary minus operator, since we have

```
a - b = a + (-b)
```

As we define a binary operator by means of an operator member function with only one parameter, it is only logical for a unary operator function to have no parameters at all: in both cases the number of parameters is one less than the number of operands. Program UNARY puts all this into practice:

```
// UNARY: An unary operator, along with two binary ones.
#include <iostream.h>

class vector {
public:
   vector(float xx=0, float yy=0): x(xx), y(yy){}
   void printvec()const;
   vector operator+(vector &b); // Binary plus
   vector operator-();          // Unary minus
   vector operator-(vector &b); // Binary minus
private:
   float x, y;
};

void vector::printvec()const
{  cout << x << ' ' << y << endl;
}

vector vector::operator+(vector &b)  // Binary plus
{  return vector(x + b.x, y + b.y);
}

vector vector::operator-()           // Unary minus
{  return vector(-x, -y);
}

vector vector::operator-(vector &b)  // Binary minus
{  return *this + -b;
}

int main()
{  vector u(3, 1), v(1, 2), sum, neg, diff;
   sum = u + v;
   sum.printvec();    // Output:  4  3
   neg = -sum;
   neg.printvec();    // Output: -4 -3
   diff = u - v;
   diff.printvec();   // Output:  2 -1
   return 0;
}
```

This program also shows how the C++ keyword **this** can be used. Recall that **this** is a pointer to the current object, as discussed in Section 6.5. We use it here in the function that defines the binary minus operator. Since ***this** is the object pointed to by **this**, it denotes the object **u**, used in the call

```
u.operator-(v)
```

In the **main** function, this call actually occurs in the more convenient form

```
u - v
```

6.9 Type Conversion for Classes

As we know, constructors are functions, so if **vector** is a constructor (for the class with the same name) and if this function allows calls with only one argument, we can regard

```
vector(5)
```

as a function call. On the other hand, it is also the typical C++ notation for a *cast*, comparable, with, for example,

```
float(5)
```

After all, **vector**, like **float**, is a type. As its notation suggests, **vector(5)** (with class **vector** defined as in Section 6.8) indeed means both a cast and a function call. Since the **vector** constructor is defined as in

```
class vector {
public:
    vector(float xx=0, float yy=0): x(xx), y(yy){}
    ...
private:
    float x, y;
}
```

this function can be called with zero, one, or two arguments. By writing **vector(5)**, a vector object with x = 5 and y = 0 is created, and this object is the result of the cast. In general, we can define type conversions (written as casts) for class types simply by defining appropriate constructors. The beauty of this is that we can define type conversions for classes any way we like, and that their use can be as simple as those for standard types. For example, compare these two lines:

```
float x; x = float(5);
vector v; v = vector(5);
```

This program fragment can be simplified by initializing the variables **x** and **v** in their declarations. Doing this in a straightforward way, we obtain

```
float x = float(5);
vector v = vector(5);
```

Again, note the similarity between these two lines. Although correct, they are not in their most convenient forms. We may replace them with the following two lines:

```
float x = 5;
vector v = 5;
```

There is even a third way to obtain the same effect, as far as the initialization of **v** is concerned:

```
vector v(5);
```

Except for the number of arguments, this form is similar to

```
vector v(1, 2);
```

which we have already used in several demonstration programs. Remember that our constructor for type **vector** has two parameters (for which arguments may or may not be supplied). There is no such constructor for type **float**, so that

```
float x(5);    // Error
```

is not possible. Here is another rather strange, but instructive program fragment:

```
x = 5;
v = 5;
```

The assignment **v** = 5 is regarded as an abbreviated form of **v** = **vector(5)**. We now see that constructors are also useful to define *implicit* type conversions (in which no cast is used). Such conversions also occur in contexts other than assignments. Some examples of implicit conversion are

1. The expression **v + 1**, which is shorthand for **v + vector(1)**.
2. The call **f(1)**, where **f** is a function that takes a vector as its argument.
3. The statement **return 1;**, occurring in a function that returns a vector.

So much for invoking the constructor **vector** with one argument. Since not only its second but also its first parameter is given the default value 0, it follows that the declaration

```
vector v;
```

creates a vector with both private members x and y initialized to 0. As for the remaining case, in which we use two arguments, recall that we have already seen examples such as

```
vector u(3, 1), v(1, 2);
```

and

```
return vector(-x, -y);
```

If we want to add the constant vector (7, 3) to a given vector **v**, we must write

```
v + vector(7, 3)
```

It would be incorrect if we tried to achieve the same effect by writing

```
v + (7, 3)
```

because here the comma would act as the comma-operator (discussed in Section 3.2). Consequently, that line would be interpreted as

```
v + 3
```

which is valid and in turn equivalent to

```
v + vector(3, 0)
```

Beware of a similar pitfall in declarations with initializations:

`vector v=5;`	is equivalent to	`vector v(5);`
`vector v=vector(7,3);`	is equivalent to	`vector v(7,3);`
`vector v=(7, 3);`	is *not* equivalent to	`vector v(7, 3);`

Other new aspects of constructors with several arguments

In Section 6.7 we have initialized an array of **row** objects, using a constructor with one argument. By contrast, the **vector** constructor has two arguments. The following example shows how to use this constructor to initialize an array of **vector** objects:

```
vector M[5] = {vector(3, 2), vector(4, 5), vector(2, 7)};
```

Although array **M** has five elements, only three initial values are specified. Because of the default arguments 0 of the **vector** constructor, the elements **M[3]** and **M[4]** obtain the initial value (0, 0).

It is also possible to initialize a **vector** object that is created by the **new** operator, as shown by the second of these three lines:

```
vector *p, *q;
p = new vector(4, 2);
q = new vector;
```

After this, the values of ***p** and ***q** are (4, 2) and (0, 0), respectively.

6.10 Copying a Class Object

A class object that contains a pointer to dynamically allocated memory can be copied in two ways. If, as often is the case, a class contains only member functions and 'simple' data members (which are not classes themselves), copying is by default done 'bitwise': all members, including pointers, are copied literally. We call the result a *shallow* copy; the contents of the memory area pointed to are not copied, and the copied pointer is identical with the original one. This way of copying is illustrated in Figure 6.4(a). Second, we can copy that memory area as well, using newly allocated memory for it. As Figure 6.4(b) shows, the pointer of the *deep* copy differs from the original one.

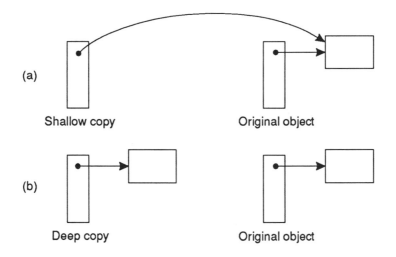

Figure 6.4. Two kinds of copies: (a) shallow copy; (b) deep copy

A shallow copy and its original object share the area pointed to, while a deep copy has such an area of its own. The distinction between these two copying methods is particularly important if the memory area in question is allocated by a constructor and deleted by a destructor. What we need is deep copies. If shallow copies were made, applying the destructor to both the original object and the copy would result in deleting the shared area twice, which is an illegal and a dangerous thing to do.

Copy constructors

Copying an object occurs more frequently than you may expect. For example, in

```
mytype x(123), y=x;
```

the object x is copied into object y. Also, in a call to the following function f, the argument is copied into the parameter w:

```
mytype f(mytype w)
{  mytype z;
   ...
   return z;
}
```

(If we use 'call by reference' instead, writing **mytype f(mytype &w)**, the argument would not be copied.) In this example, copying occurs once again in the return-statement.

For all copying operations other than by assignment, we need a special constructor, known as a *copy constructor*, which for this example is declared as

```
mytype(const mytype &v);
```

This constructor has the task to specify how copying is to be done. Note that the class name **mytype** is used here both as a function name and as a parameter name. Remember also that a copy constructor always has a reference parameter, as the ampersand indicates. The keyword **const** indicates that the copy constructor will not change the value of the argument. How copy constructors can be defined will be demonstrated shortly in a complete program.

Copying by assignment operators

It goes without saying that copying also takes place in assignments, such as in the second line of

```
mytype x(123), y;
y = x;
```

However, this example is essentially different from the one in our discussion of copy constructors: there the equal sign was used in a declaration while it occurs here in an assignment. Although initialization and assignment look very much the same, they are distinct language constructs. A special measure, other than a copy constructor, is required to prevent shallow copying taking place in assignments. We must define a special assignment operator, as declared in

```
mytype operator=(mytype v);
```

to specify how a deep copy is to be made in assignments. As mentioned in Section 6.8, the assignment operator must be a member function; it cannot be a friend function.

Copying demonstrated by an example

Let us clarify these two important aspects (copy constructor and assignment) by means of the following example. We want to define and use a special string type, which we will call class **cstring**. (The name **string** might be confusing because of the standard header file **string.h**, hence our name **cstring**, which stands for 'character string'.) Objects of this type can contain strings of any length, and the + operator can be used to concatenate such strings. For example, our **cstring** class enables us to write

```
cstring s="ABC", t="DEF", u;
u = s + t + "GH";                    // u = "ABCDEFGH"
```

Furthermore, we want to be able to declare **cstring** objects of a given length, initialized with blanks. If we write

```
cstring x(20);
```

then x will be a string of 20 blanks, followed by a null character.

So far, we have paid much attention to conversions from standard types to class types. It is sometimes also desirable to enable the opposite conversions, that is, from class types to more elementary types. For example, our **cstring** objects are very much like normal strings but since **cstring** objects are not pointers to characters, some special measure is required to use them as such, as, with the above declaration of **x**, is done in

```
cout << x;
```

or

```
char a[80];
strcpy(a, x);
```

We will discuss the method to convert class types to other types in more detail shortly. Let us first have a look at a complete program in which all this is realized:

```
// CSTRING: This program demonstrates how to make deep copies.

#include <iostream.h>
#include <string.h>

class cstring {
public:
   cstring(int n=0);              // First constructor.
   cstring(const char *str);      // Second constructor.
   cstring(const cstring &x);     // Third constructor
                                  // ('copy constructor')
                                  // to make deep copies.
   ~cstring(){delete p;}          // Destructor.
   cstring operator=(cstring x);  // Assignment operator.
   friend cstring operator+(cstring x, cstring y);
                                  // Concatenation.
   operator const char*() {return p;}
                // Conversion from cstring to const char*,
                // to be discussed shortly.
private:
   char *p;
};

cstring::cstring(int n):p(new char[n+1]) // First constructor.
{  for (int i=0; i<n; i++) p[i] = ' ';
   p[n] = '\0';
}

cstring::cstring(const char *str)
   :p(new char[strlen(str)+1])        // Second constructor.
{  strcpy(p, str);
}

cstring::cstring(const cstring &x)
   : p(new char[strlen(x.p)+1])
                   // Third constructor (= copy constructor
{  strcpy(p, x.p);  // to make a deep copy).
}

cstring cstring::operator=(cstring x)
{  if (p != x.p)
   {  delete p;                        // Assignment operator
      p = new char[strlen(x.p)+1];     // makes a deep copy.
      strcpy(p, x.p);
   }
   return *this;
}
```

```
cstring operator+(cstring x, cstring y)
{ cstring s(strlen(x.p)+strlen(y.p)+1);
  strcpy(s.p, x.p);
  strcat(s.p, y.p);
  return s;
}


int main()
{ cstring b2(2),       // "  "   (Two blanks).
         b3=3,         // "   "  (Three blanks).
         s="Hello,",
         t=s,          // s copied into t  ("Hello,").
         s1=t,         // t copied into s1 ("Hello,").
         x,            // "" (empty string).
         y;            // "" (empty string).
  t = "world";         // New value for t  ("world").
  x = s1 + b2 + t;     // "Hello,  world".
  y = "Message: " + (x = x + "!") + b3 + "How are you?";
  cout << x << endl;   // Here x and y are converted
  cout << y << endl;   // from type cstring to type char*.
  return 0;
}
```

Like default assignment operations (which we cannot use because they make shallow copies), our **cstring** assignments can be used within expressions, as (x = x + "!") on the fourth line from the bottom demonstrates. The output of this program is

```
Hello,  world!
Message: Hello,  world!  How are you?
```

The second constructor, which takes a pointer to a character as its argument, enables us to write strings such as **"How are you?"** in positions that actually require objects of type **cstring**. Recall that we discussed such implicit type conversions by means of constructors in Section 6.9.

We must not omit the two components that make deep copies, namely the copy constructor and the assignment operator function. If we did, the compiler would not detect it, but the program may crash during execution. This is because in that case shallow copies would be made instead of deep ones. As a result, the destructor (present in the header file) would try to release the same memory area more than once. It is instructive to check how often our constructors and destructors are called. If everything is as it should be, the destructor is called exactly as many times as all constructors together are called. We can obtain accurate and detailed information about this by introducing a global count variable for each constructor and a similar variable for the destructor. These variables are initialized to zero and increased by one in each constructor and in the destructor. Note, however, that we also need another program modification to realize this. This is because of destructor calls at the very end of the function in which class variables are declared: if this were the function **main**, we would have to display our count variables before all destructor calls have taken place. We can solve this problem by renaming our function **main** and calling it in a new one, as in

```
// CSTRING1: Modified version to count all calls to
//           the constructors and to the destructor.

int c1, c2, c3, d;
// Count variables for constructors and destructor,
// implicitly initialized to zero and increased by
// one in the constructors and in the destructor.
...
void old_main()  // Original main function
{  ...
}

int main()       // New, very simple main function
{  old_main();
   ... // The values of c1, c2, c3 and d are displayed here.
   return 0;
}
```

Except for very simple programs, it is not easy to predict the frequencies counted in this way. Fortunately, we need not do this. In an experiment with our **cstring** program, the following counting results were found:

Constructor 1:   10
Constructor 2:   5
Constructor 3:   12
Destructor: 27

If we had omitted the third constructor, that is, the copy constructor, not bothering about deep or shallow copies, there would have been only 10 + 5 = 15 constructor calls and as many as 27 destructor calls, which would have been seriously wrong. Constructor 3 is called by the declarations of the variables **t** and **s1** and by the execution of return statements: six for the **operator+** function and four for the **operator=** function. Note that in the **main** function the plus operator occurs six times and the assignment operator four times. This explains that the copy constructor is called 2 + 6 + 4 = 12 times.

Conversion from class types to other types

Another interesting aspect of program CSTRING is the way implicit conversion from **cstring** to **const char*** is defined. All we have to do to realize this is to define the function

```
operator const char*() {return p;}
```

as a member of class **cstring**. In general, we can define a conversion from class type **X** to type **T** by writing a function of the form

```
operator T() { ... return xxx;}
```

as a member of class **X**. In this function, *xxx* is an expression that can implicitly be converted to type **T**.

Member functions vs. friend functions

Our + operator for string concatenation is a friend function. You may wonder why not use a member function instead. The answer is that our choice enables us to use this operator with a normal string (instead of a **cstring** object) as its first operand, as in

```
y = "Message: " + ...
```

Implicit type conversion, made possible by our second constructor, is applied here because the + operator function has two parameters. If it had been a member function, it would have had only one parameter, corresponding to the second operand, so defining the + operator as a member function would have deprived us of the implicit conversion that is applied here.

As for the assignment operator, the C++ language requires **operator=** functions to be member functions; they cannot be defined as friend functions.

Memberwise copying

At the beginning of this section, we restricted our discussion to classes that have no other classes as their members. If classes do have other classes as their members, the default copying method is not exactly 'bitwise', but what is called *memberwise*. Suppose that class **C** has a member class **M** and that an object of class **C** is to be copied. Obviously, copying this object implies copying its **M** member. If **C** has no user-defined copy constructor, but its member **M** has, this copy constructor is called in the process of copying the **M** member. All members of **C** that are not classes are copied bitwise.

Exercises

6.1 Write a program that reads the names and the ages of ten people, and stores these data in structures that are elements of an array. Print the average age of these people. Also, print a table of ten lines, with on each line the given data of a person, along with the (positive or negative) deviation of his or her age from the average age. Store only the first 30 characters (followed by the null character) of names that are longer than 30 characters.

6.2 The same as Exercise 6.1, but full names are to be stored. Each structure must not include a name itself but a pointer. This points to an area of memory which is allocated by means of **new** and in which that name is stored. You may, however, assume each name to be no longer than 100 characters, so that you can initially read it into a buffer of a fixed size.

6.3 Define a class **verylongint**, with a pointer as one of its members. This pointer points to a memory area in which very long integers are stored digit by digit. Besides functions such as constructors and a destructor, which are not directly called by the 'user', there must be the operators +, *, and =, as well as a function **print** to display such long integers, in such a way that we can use this class, for example, as follows:

```
verylongint x = 30000, y = 20000, y1 = y,
            z = "123456789012345", result;
result = x * x * x * x + y * y * y * y1 + z;
result.print();
```

As this example illustrates, string quotes are required for integers that do not fit into type **long int**. For integers below this limit, string quotes may be written or omitted, as the user likes. The output to be produced by this program fragment is

970 123 456 789 012 345

7

Object-oriented Programming

Although the term *object-oriented programming*, or *OOP*, for short, is very popular these days, it is interpreted differently by different people. It seems not unreasonable to use it, as is frequently done, as soon as our attention is focused on class objects, with private data members and associated access functions. However, in *The Annotated C++ Reference Manual*, Ellis and Stroustrup give a more limited meaning to this term:

> "The use of derived classes and virtual functions is often called *object-oriented programming*."

According to this definition, which has the advantage of being very compact and precise, we cannot discuss OOP until Section 7.4. In the meantime, if not already dealing with OOP, we are at least preparing for it: there is very little that can be skipped in this and the previous chapters.

7.1 Interface, Implementation, and Application Files

So far, we have used only one program file for the definition, the implementation, and the application of a class. This was very reasonable for our rather small programs, intended only to demonstrate some basic facts about classes. However, in practice it is usually to be preferred that programs dealing with classes should consist of at least three files:

1. A header file that declares the class type. Except for inline member functions (defined inside the class), functions are only declared, not defined, in this file. This file is the *interface* between the implementation and the application (see 2 and 3).

2. A file that contains both an include line for the interface and the definitions of the functions just mentioned. This file is called the *implementation* of the class in question.

3. A file that also contains an include line for the interface, followed by other functions, including the **main** function. This file is called an *application* of the class.

When writing an application, we regard ourselves as 'class users' and we do not want to bother about implementation details. The interface must supply us with all information we need so that we can *use* the implementation. A class implementation can be quite general. For example, if we write implementation and interface files for vector operations, it must be possible to use these for all kinds of applications. This aspect of *reusability* is an important factor in efficient software construction. The class concept encourages us to write *reusable code* in the form of implementation and interface files.

Splitting up programs into modules is called *modular programming*. In Section 4.6 we saw how to do this for a simple program, in which we did not use the class concept. In large programs, with hundreds of functions and several class types, the application will normally consist of several files, and there will normally be both an implementation and an interface file for each class or for each set of related classes. Instead of presenting a large software project in this book, we prefer dealing with rather small programs, but we will now split these up in the same way as we would do for large ones. Although this approach may not really be advantageous for these rather small and simple programs, you can easily imagine its usefulness in practical program development.

7.2 A Class for Sets

We will now demonstrate the idea discussed in the previous section by means of an example. Suppose that in some application program we want to deal with (finite) sets of integers. With traditional programming, we would begin by thinking about how to represent such a set internally, that is, by designing its implementation. However, it may be more convenient and more logical to specify the *operations* to be applied to our sets first. These operations are:

1. Introducing new sets by simply declaring them to be of the type **iset**, as in

```
iset S, T=1000, U=T, V(1000);
```

Immediately after defining the set **S**, in this way, it should be empty. The sets **T**, **U**, and **V** should initially contain exactly one element, 1000.

2. Adding another integer element x to S by writing

    ```
    S += x
    ```

    If set S already contains this integer, it is not to be altered, because a set cannot contain several copies of the same element. The above expression should be an lvalue and its value should be S. (As usual, appending a semicolon turns this expression into a statement.)

3. Removing an integer x from set S by writing

    ```
    S -= x
    ```

    We want this expression to be valid also if x is not an element of S; in that case S is to be left unchanged. The expression should be an lvalue and its value should be S.

4. Looking to see if integer x belongs to the set S. For example, we want to write

    ```
    if (S(x)) ...    // x in set S.
    ```

5. Displaying all elements of set S, in increasing order and separated by a blank, by writing

    ```
    S.print();
    ```

6. Assigning a set S to another set variable T by means of the following expression, which should be an lvalue and have T as its value:

    ```
    T = S
    ```

7. Inquiring how many elements there are in set S by converting S to type **int**. This also provides a means to test of the set is empty by writing either S == 0 or !S:

    ```
    cout << "There are " << int(S) << " elements in S.\n";
    if (!S) cout << "Set S is empty.\n";
    ```

The points 2, 3, and 4 can be realized by overloading the operators +=, -=, and, curiously enough, the operator formed by a pair of parentheses ( ).

Although the above seven points do not specify how the set is to be represented, there are some elements in them that makes it attractive to store the integers in increasing order. This does not only apply to point 5, which mentions this increasing order explicitly, but also to the points 2, 3, and 4. After all, it is clear that the set S is to be searched for x, and searching large amounts of data is done most efficiently if these data are in a systematic order. As for the definition of U in point 1 and the assignment in point 6, we will supply both a copy constructor and an assignment operator.

As suggested in point 7, it is possible to apply the ! operator to a set without defining such an operator for type **iset**. All we need is an **operator int( )** function to convert type **iset** to type **int**, where the resulting **int** value is equal to the number of elements in the set. The expression !S is then equivalent to !int(S).

We will use a very simple application program, SETAPPL, which nevertheless demonstrates the use of the above seven operations:

```
// SETAPPL: Demonstration program for set operations
//          (application; file name: setappl.cpp)
#include "iset.h"

int main()
{  iset S=1000, T, U=S;
   if (!T) cout << "T is empty.\n";
   if (U) cout << "U is not empty.\n";
   S += 100; S +=10000;
   (((S += 10) += 1) += 20) += 200;
   cout << "There are " << int(S) << " elements in S.\n";
   T += 50; T += 50;
   cout << "S: "; S.print();
   S -= 1000; cout << "1000 removed from S.\n";
   if (S(1000)) cout << "1000 belongs to S (error).\n";
           else cout << "1000 is no longer in S.\n";
   if (S(100)) cout << "100 still belongs to S.\n";
   cout << "S: "; S.print();
   cout << "T: "; T.print();
   cout << "U: "; U.print();
   T = S;
   cout << "After assigning S to T, we have T: "; T.print();
   return 0;
}
```

With the interface and the implementation to be discussed shortly, the output of this program is as follows:

```
T is empty.
U is not empty.
There are 7 elements in S.
S: 1 10 20 100 200 1000 10000
1000 removed from S.
1000 is no longer in S.
100 still belongs to S.
S: 1 10 20 100 200 10000
T: 50
U: 1000
After assigning S to T, we have T: 1 10 20 100 200 10000
```

In this application program, we see that the interface *iset.h* is included. This file does not show all implementation details but it reveals about as much of the implementation as the 'user', that is, the writer of application programs, needs:

```
// ISET.H: Header file for set operations (interface).
#include <iostream.h>

class iset {
public:
    iset(){a = 0; n = 0;}          // Constructor to begin with
                                   // an empty set.
    iset(int x)                    // Constructor to begin with
    {   a = 0; n = 0;              // one element x.
        *this += x;
    }
    ~iset(){delete[] a;}           // Destructor.
    iset &operator+=(int x);       // Adds x to the set.
    iset &operator-=(int x);       // Removes x from the set.
    int operator()(int x) const;   // Is x in the set?
    void print() const;            // Prints all elements of
                                   // the set on one line,
                                   // separated by a blank.
    iset &operator=(iset S);       // Assignment operator.
    iset(const iset &S);           // Copy constructor.
    operator int(){return n;}      // Convert iset to int.
private:
    int n, *a;
};
```

As you can see, there are a few aspects of this interface that are not explicitly required in the seven points specified by the 'user': the private variables **n** (indicating how many elements the set contains), a pointer **a** (to be used as an array), and the destructor ~**iset**. The latter is important in the implementation in order to release all memory required by the set as soon as we no longer need it. All other members of the class **iset** are used in application programs.

Let us now turn to the most technical part, the implementation. Although more advanced dynamic data structures could be used, such as linear lists and binary trees, our set will be represented by a consecutive area of memory, to be used as an array, in which the integers contained in the set are stored in increasing order. We will use the C++ operator **new** for memory allocation, rather than the C function **malloc**. This means that we cannot use **realloc** to extend the memory area in question. Instead, we will allocate **new** once again, copy the integers from the old area to the new one, and release the old area, using **delete**. Since this means that extending an area takes some time (as would be the case with **realloc**), it would not be efficient to do all this work each time an element is to be added to a set. We will therefore extend the area with a block of, say, five integers rather than only one integer, each time an extension is required. The rather small block size, 5, was chosen to make area extension work in the case of our simple demonstration program; for practical applications, some larger value may be taken. With this method, at most **blocksize** – 1 locations are allocated without being used, which makes it more economical with memory space than linear lists or binary trees, since these would require additional memory space, used as pointers. Increasing **blocksize** causes more possible waste of memory but makes this method faster.

Since the integers are stored in increasing order, searching can be done very fast by means of binary search. If the integer searched for is not found, our function **binsearch**, used for this purpose, returns information about the position where it belongs in the sequence. This is useful in case of the operator +=, which inserts the integer in the sequence. Because of all the shifting work, insertion is not an efficient operation with this method, and neither is deletion (by means of the operator –=).

```
// ISET: Implementation file for set operations;
//       file name: iset.cpp.

#include "iset.h"

const int blocksize=5;
    // May be replaced with a larger value.

static int *memoryspace(int *p0, int n0, int n1)
/* If p0 == 0, allocate an area for n1 integers.
   If p0 != 0, increase or decrease the old sequence
   p0[0], ..., p0[n0-1].
   In either case, the resulting new sequence is
   p1[0], ..., p1[n1-1], and p1 is returned.
*/
{   int *p1 = new int[n1];
    if (p0) // Copy from p0 to p1:
    {   for (int i=(n0<n1?n0:n1)-1; i>=0; i--)
            p1[i] = p0[i];
        delete p0;
    }
    return p1;
}


int binsearch(int x, int *a, int n)
/* The array a[0], ..., a[n-1] is searched for x.
   Return value:
       0 if n == 0 or x <= a[0]
       n if x > a[n-1]
       i if a[i-1] < x <= a[i]
*/
{   int m, l, r;
    if (n == 0 || x <= a[0]) return 0;
    if (x > a[n-1]) return n;
    l = 0; r = n-1;
```

```
    while (r - 1 > 1)
    {   m = (l + r)/2;
        (x <= a[m] ? r : l) = m;
    }
    return r;
}

iset &iset::operator+=(int x)
{   int i=binsearch(x, a, n), j;
    if (i >= n || x != a[i]) // x is not yet in the set?
    {   if (n % blocksize == 0)
        a = memoryspace(a, n, n + blocksize);
        for (j=n; j>i; j--) a[j] = a[j-1];
        n++;
        a[i] = x;
    }
    return *this;
}

iset &iset::operator-=(int x)
{   int i=binsearch(x, a, n), j;
    if (i < n && x == a[i])
    {   n--;
        for (j=i; j<n; j++) a[j] = a[j+1];
        if (n % blocksize == 0)
        a = memoryspace(a, n+1, n);  // Release one block.
    }
    return *this;
}

void iset::print() const
{   int i;
    for (i=0; i<n; i++) cout << a[i] << " ";
    cout << endl;
}

int iset::operator()(int x) const
{   int i=binsearch(x, a, n);
    return i < n && x == a[i];
}

static int *newcopy(int n, int *a)
// Copy a[0], ..., a[n-1] to a newly
// allocated area, and return the
// new start address.
{   int *p = new int[n];
    for (int i=0; i<n; i++) p[i] = a[i];
    return p;
}
```

```
iset &iset::operator=(iset S)  // Assignment operator.
{  delete a;
   n = S.n;
   a = newcopy(n, S.a);
   return *this;
}

iset::iset(const iset &S)        // Copy constructor.
{  n = S.n;
   a = newcopy(n, S.a);
}
```

7.3 Derived Classes and Inheritance

Suppose we have declared a certain class type **B**, and we want a new one, **D**, consisting of all members of class **B** and some additional members besides. Instead of copying the members of **B**, we can then simply refer to **B** in the declaration of **D**. The new class **D** is said to be *derived* from the original class **B**, which is called the *base* class of **D**. We say that a derived class *inherits* the members of its *base* class.

For example, let us consider the class **geom_obj** for geometrical objects, declared as follows:

```
#include <iostream.h>

class geom_obj {
public:
   geom_obj(float x=0, float y=0): xC(x), yC(y){}
   void printcenter() const
   {  cout << xC << " " << yC << endl;
   }
protected:
   float xC, yC;
};
```

As for the new keyword **protected**, we will discuss this shortly. We can do only very little with this class type, nor does it give much information about what kind of objects are to be stored in it. We now want to use two types of very specific geometrical objects, namely circles and squares. As usual, a circle is characterized by its center and its radius. As for a square, let us represent it by its center and one of its four vertices. We can now benefit from the class type **geom_obj**, which we have already declared, by declaring the *derived classes* **circle** and **square** as follows:

```
const float PI=3.14159265;

class circle: public geom_obj {
public:
   circle(float x_C, float y_C, float r)
      : geom_obj(x_C, y_C)
   { radius = r;
   }
   float area() const {return PI * radius * radius;}
private:
   float radius;
};

class square: public geom_obj {
public:
   square(float x_C, float y_C, float x, float y)
      :geom_obj(x_C, y_C)
   {   x1 = x; y1 = y;
   }
   float area() const
   {   float a, b;
      a = x1 - xC; b = y1 - yC;
      return 2 * (a * a + b * b); // See Figure 7.1
   }
private:
   float x1, y1;
};
```

In each of these two class declarations, the first line shows the name of the base class
geom_obj. The two derived classes **circle** and **square** are to be regarded as extensions
of their base class **geom_obj**. The keyword **public** as used in, for example,

```
class square: public geom_obj
```

specifies that all public members of the base class **geom_obj** are also regarded as public
members of the derived class **square**. Class **square** is said to be *publicly derived* from
class **geom_obj**. For example, we can write

```
square S(3, 3.5, 4.37, 3.85);
S.printcenter();
```

Although **printcenter** does not occur directly in the declaration of class **square**, it is
nevertheless one of its public member functions because it is a public member of class
geom_obj from which class **square** has been publicly derived. Another point to be
noted is the use of xC and yC in the **area** member function of class **square**. These are
protected members of the base class **geom_obj**, as the keyword **protected** indicates.

'Protected' members are similar to 'private' ones. Their only difference is that a derived class has access to the protected members, not to the private members, of its base class.

User-defined assignment operators

If an assignment operator is defined as a member function of a base class, it is not inherited by any derived class.

Constructors and destructors of derived and base classes

The derived classes **circle** and **square** can be regarded as extensions of their base class **geom_obj**. When an object of, for example, type **square** is created, as is done by the above declaration of the variable S, the constructor of the base class **geom_obj** is called first; then that of **square** is called. Conversely, when an object of a derived class is destroyed, destructors, if any, are called in the reverse order: first that of the derived class and then that of the base class.

We can pass arguments from the constructor in a derived class to the constructor of its base class. As we normally do this to initialize data members of the base class, the way we write this down is in the form of a *constructor initializer*, also discussed in Section 6.7. In the constructors of both **circle** and **square**, this initializer is

```
:geom_obj(x_C, y_C)
```

Since the **geom_obj** constructor has default arguments, this initializer is not obligatory here. If we omit it, the constructor of **geom_obj** is called with its default argument values 0. The initializer would really have been required if there had been no default arguments, that is, if in the constructor

```
geom_obj(float x=0, float y=0): xC(x), yC(y){}
```

(see the beginning of this section) we had omitted the two occurrences of =0. In our example the values of x_C and y_C, as supplied to the derived class, are passed to the constructor of the base class **geom_obj**, and stored as the members xC and yC of this class.

Let us now combine the preceding class declarations of this section with this **main** function:

```
int main()
{  circle C(2, 2.5, 2);
   square S(3, 3.5, 4.37, 3.85);
   cout << "Center of circle: "; C.printcenter();
   cout << "Center of square: "; S.printcenter();
   cout << "Area of circle:   " << C.area() << endl;
   cout << "Area of square:   " << S.area() << endl;
   return 0;
}
```

The resulting program (compiled as one source file) gives the following output:

```
Center of circle: 2 2.5
Center of square: 3 3.5
Area of circle:   12.5664
Area of square:   3.9988
```

Figure 7.1 shows the circle and the square in question. It also shows the meaning of the variables **a** and **b** in the **area** member function of class **square**.

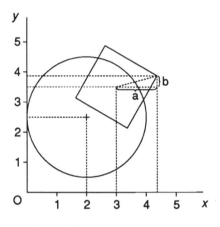

Figure 7.1. Circle and square

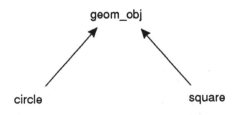

Figure 7.2. Base class and two derived classes

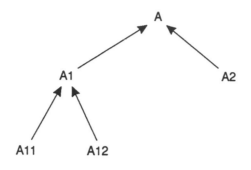

Figure 7.3. A tree of classes

In the example we have been discussing, the relationship between the base class and its derived classes is illustrated by Figure 7.2.

The situation can be more complicated. First, derived classes can act as base classes for other (derived) classes, so that we can build trees of classes, as shown in Figure 7.3. Here class **A1**, although derived from class **A**, is the base class of **A11** and **A12**. Second, base and derived classes need not form a tree, as we will see now.

Conversion from derived to base class

Perhaps contrary to what you would expect, conversion from a derived class to its base class is possible, while the reverse is not. The same applies to the corresponding pointer types, except when casts are used: the compiler allows any pointer conversion by means of a cast. The following fragment illustrates all this:

```
class B { ... };          // Base class B
class D: public B { ... } // Derived class D

...

B b, *pb;
D d, *pd;

...

b = d;        // From derived to base: OK
pb = pd;      // Corresponding pointer types: OK
d = b;        // From base to derive: error
d = (D)b;     // Even with cast: error
pd = pb;      // Corresponding pointer types: error
pd = (D*)b;   // With cast: technically OK, but suspicious
```

Class **D** may contain members that do not belong to class **B**. The assignment **b = d** will omit such members of **d**, since there is no room for them in **b**. Yet this is a safe operation in that it will not cause any members of **b** to be undefined. The reverse assignment, **d** = **b** is not allowed. If it were, those members that are specific for class **D** would have undefined values in **d**. Since this would be undesirable, this assignment is not allowed. Even the cast in **d** = (D)**b** would not make this assignment a valid one.

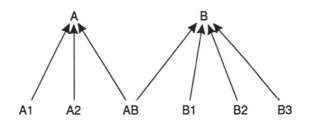

Figure 7.4. Multiple inheritance

Multiple inheritance

So far, it was taken for granted that each derived class should have only one base class. In the first version of C++, this was indeed the case. However, in C++ Release 2 the concept of *multiple inheritance* was introduced. This means that it is possible for a class to be derived from more than one base class. For example, the situation can be as shown in Figure 7.4, where the derived class **AB** has both class **A** and class **B** as its base classes. If we want the public members of **A** and **B** to be public members of **AB**, the class declaration of **AB** is written as follows:

```
class AB: public A, public B {
   ...
}
```

If **AB** has a constructor with parameters, we can pass these to each base class as, for example, in:

```
AB(int n=0, float x=0, char ch='A')
   :A(n, ch), B(n, x)
{  ...
}
```

The creation of an object of class **AB** causes the three constructors for **A**, **B**, and **AB**, in that order, to be called.

7.4 Virtual Functions and Late Binding

Suppose we have declared class **ctype** as follows:

```
class ctype {
public:
   virtual void f() { ... }
   ...
};
```

The new keyword **virtual** is relevant if **ctype** has derived classes, say, **ctype1** and **ctype2**, and if we are using pointers to class objects. When using class **ctype** to define a variable of this type, as in

```
ctype v;
```

we immediately create a class object. Instead, we can only define a pointer **p** and create a class object later, as is done in

```
ctype *p;
...
p = new ctype;
```

The **ctype** object ***p** created in this way is only loosely related to **p**, since **p** can also point to other **ctype** objects. Suppose that we declare the derived classes **ctype1** and **ctype2** as follows:

```
class ctype1: public ctype {
public:
   void f() { ... }
   ...
};

class ctype2: public ctype {
public:
   void f() { ... }
   ...
};

ctype *p;
```

We have seen in the previous section (using the assignment **pb = pd**) that implicit conversion from 'pointer to derived class' to 'pointer to base class' is possible. It follows that in the above example we can write **p = new ctype1** and **p = new ctype2**.

The three class types **ctype**, **ctype1**, and **ctype2** have member functions with the same name (**f**). Because of the keyword **virtual** in the base class **ctype**, function **f** is what we call a *virtual function*. This means that during the execution of the call

```
p -> f()
```

the decision is made which of the three functions (**ctype::f**, **ctype1::f**, or **ctype2::f**) is to be called. This decision is based on the type of the object pointed to by **p**. Since the correct function is not chosen at compile time but rather at execution time, the term *late* (or *dynamic*) *binding* is used for the relationship between the pointer **p** and the function in question. If we had omitted the keyword **virtual** in the declaration of **ctype**, only the *type* of **p** would have been used to decide which function to use. In other words, the function **ctype::f** would have been taken, even if **p** pointed to a **ctype1** or **ctype2** object. This is not unreasonable, since, as we know, a derived type is an extension of its base type(s), so all members of a base class also belong to its derived classes. Without the keyword **virtual**, the decision which function is to be taken is already made at compile time, so in that case we speak of *early* (or *static*) binding.

As for the implementation, there will be an extra (anonymous) member in the class in case of late binding (that is, if there is a keyword **virtual**), so that it can be determined at run time which of the member functions is to be taken. This is shown by program LATE, in which the classes **early** and **late** are identical but for the keyword **virtual**:

```
/* LATE: This program shows that with late binding there
   is an anonymous class member to tell at run time which
   class actually applies.
*/

#include <iostream.h>

struct early {int i; void f(){i=1;}};          // Base
struct late {int i; virtual void f(){i=2;}};   // Base

struct early1: early {void f(){i=11;}};        // Derived
struct late1: late {void f(){i=21;}};          // Derived

int main()
{  cout << "Class sizes in bytes, found by sizeof:\n";
   cout << "early:  " << sizeof(early) << endl;
   cout << "late:   " << sizeof(late) << endl;
   cout << "early1: " << sizeof(early1) << endl;
   cout << "late1:  " << sizeof(late1) << endl;
   return 0;
}
```

(The keyword **struct** is used here only to make the program text as simple as possible: if we used **class** instead, it would be necessary to write **public:** or **protected:** in front of **int i;**.) The program does not do any practical work but is illustrates the point we are discussing. Its output reveals that late binding requires an anonymous member, which in our example (and using Borland C++), takes 4 − 2 = 2 bytes:

```
Class sizes in bytes, found by sizeof:
early:  2
late:   4
early1: 2
late1:  4
```

This output also shows that member functions are not really stored in the class objects themselves: since the **int** member i of class **early** already takes two bytes, which is the size of that whole class, it follows that function **f**, although a member of the class, is not really stored in objects of this class. (If it were, much memory space would be wasted in programs with a great number of objects of the same class type.) You can also see from this output that an object of a derived class type accommodates the data members of its base class type(s). For example, the two bytes of an **early1** object are needed to store the integer i of its base class **early**. In other words, our derived classes **early1** and **late1** take as much room as their base classes **early** and **late**, respectively, because they have no data members other than those inherited from their base classes.

We now turn to a simple but complete program with pointers to base and derived classes, to see a virtual function (named **print**) in action:

```
// VIRTUAL: A virtual function in action.

#include <iostream.h>

class animal {
public:
   virtual void print() const
   {  cout << "Unknown animal type.\n";
   }
protected:
   int nlegs;
};

class fish: public animal {
public:
   fish(int n){nlegs = n;}
   void print() const
   {  cout << "A fish has " << nlegs << " legs.\n";
   }
};

class bird: public animal {
public:
   bird(int n){nlegs = n;}
   void print() const
   {  cout << "A bird has " << nlegs << " legs.\n";
   }
};
```

```
class mammal: public animal {
public:
   mammal(int n){nlegs = n;}
   void print() const
   {  cout << "A mammal has " << nlegs << " legs.\n";
   }
};

int main()
{  animal *p[4];
   p[0] = new fish(0);
   p[1] = new bird(2);
   p[2] = new mammal(4);
   p[3] = new animal;
   for (int i=0; i<4; i++) p[i]->print();
   return 0;
}
```

The most interesting part of this program is the for-statement at the end. The four elements of the pointer array **p** point to objects of four different class types, for each of which there is a **print** function. It is clearly impossible for the compiler to determine from the statement

```
p[i]->print();
```

which of the four functions **fish::print, bird::print, mammal::print**, and **animal ::print** applies. Thanks to the keyword **virtual** in the base class **animal**, this choice is made at run time. Before the for-statement is executed, the **new** operator is called four times to create the objects in question. They accommodate an anonymous member for the actual class type, to enable late binding. The output of program VIRTUAL is:

```
A fish has 0 legs.
A bird has 2 legs.
A mammal has 4 legs.
Unknown animal type.
```

Instead of these four lines, the text of the fourth line would have been printed four times if we had used early binding, that is, if we had omitted the keyword **virtual**.

As mentioned at the beginning of this chapter, the use of derived classes and virtual functions is often called *object-oriented programming*. Another popular term in connection with programs such as VIRTUAL is *polymorphism*. It refers to the fact that objects of different (derived) types, such as **fish, bird**, and **mammal**, are accessed in the same way, as is done in the above call p[i]–>print().

As for terminology, it might be mentioned that member functions are sometimes called *methods* and that calling an object's member function is referred to as *sending a message to the object*. This terminology is particularly popular with users of OOP languages other than C++.

Reusability: programming by difference

An interesting point about derived classes is that they are not specified in their base classes, nor do base classes 'know' how many derived classes there are. Consequently, we can add derived classes later, without modifying either the base class or already existing derived classes. Recall that in realistic C++ software projects, there are interface, implementation, and application files. Now suppose we want to program a new application of some class and we find interface and implementation files which cover almost all we want, but in which some facilities are lacking or different from what we need. With a well-designed class hierarchy of base and derived classes, it will then be possible to write another implementation file for a new derived class, tailored to our application, and to use this file in addition to the already existing interface and implementation files, *without modifying or recompiling these*. This idea can make software more *reusable* than it was with older programming methods. Since programming in this way is limited to what is new, the terms *programming by difference* and *incremental programming* are sometimes used for it. This principle will be illustrated by an example in Section 7.7.

Suppressing the virtual mechanism

In program VIRTUAL, we have seen that

```
p[i]->print();
```

with, for example, $i = 1$, calls the **print** function of the derived class **bird**, not that of the base class **animal**. However, we can use the scope-resolution-operator **::** to suppress this mechanism enabled by the keyword **virtual**. For example, the call

```
p[1]->animal::print();
```

would cause the print function of the base class **animal** to be called, which would produce another output line

```
Unknown animal type.
```

Pure virtual functions and abstract classes

In program VIRTUAL, the function **print** is defined not only in the derived classes **fish**, **bird**, and **mammal**, but also in the base class **animal**. If we had not felt a need for this (and we had been interested only in the first three of the four output lines), it would still have been necessary to write this function (with the keyword **virtual**) in the base class, but then we could have written

```
virtual void print() const {}
```

Instead, we can declare **print** as a *pure* virtual function by writing

```
virtual void print() const = 0;
```

However, doing this has far-reaching consequences. Let us assume that we really write this in the base class **animal** of program VIRTUAL. Then this base class is said to be an *abstract* class. An abstract class type cannot be used to create objects of this type. It can only be used for the declaration of derived classes. Such a program modification would therefore make this line invalid:

```
p[3] = new animal;
```

(If we delete this line, we should also replace 4 with 3 in the for-statement that follows it and in the declaration of pointer array **p**.) With these program modifications, it would also be incorrect to write

```
animal A;
```

which would be correct in the original version of program VIRTUAL. Note the difference between this incorrect declaration of **A** and

```
animal *p[4];
```

Using the abstract class type **animal**, we cannot declare the variable **A** since that would create an object of type **animal**. However, we can declare the pointer array **p**, provided that we use its elements only as pointers to objects of the derived types **fish**, **bird**, and **mammal**. Pointers to objects that have the abstract class type **animal** are out of the question simply because there are no such objects.

Making class **animal** abstract also makes it impossible to omit any of the **print** functions in the derived classes **fish**, **bird** and **mammal**, that is, if we still create objects of these derived class types. In general, if we derive class **D** from the abstract class **B** and we do not provide definitions in **D** for all pure virtual functions of **B**, then this derived class **D** is in turn an abstract class; in that case we can use class **D** only to derive other classes from it, not to define objects.

We have seen that making a class abstract makes its use more restricted. At first this may seem to be a disadvantage. Yet, if a class is to be used only as a base class for other classes, not to create objects of it, it is highly recommended to make it an abstract class. The compiler will then detect any accidental attempts to use the base class for creating objects, and it will also detect any missing member functions for derived classes. You may compare this with using local rather than global variables: although the use of local variables is restricted to the functions in which they are defined, we normally prefer them to global variables because they prevent us from making nasty errors. Remember also that loop constructs such as the while-statement are generally preferred to the goto statement, even though they are more restricted. We will use an abstract class in a more interesting program in Section 7.7.

Virtual base classes

Suppose we have a base class **A**, with two derived classes **A1** and **A2**. As we know, **A1** and **A2** objects are in fact extensions of **A** objects, in other words, each has an **A** sub-object. If we now use multiple inheritance to define another derived class, **A12**, with **A1** and **A2** as its base classes, the situation is as follows:

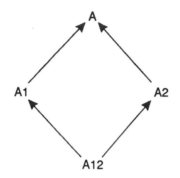

The curious point about this is that each object of class **A12** will have two sub-objects of class **A**. If **A** has a data member **a**, then an **A12** object x would have two data members **a**, one derived through **A1** and the other through **A2**. The following two lines show how we can tell them apart and demonstrate that there are two of them:

```
x.A1::a = 1; x.A2::a = 2;
cout << x.A1::a << " " << x.A2::a;
```

These lines have **1 2** as output. However, this may not be what we want. We can suppress this duplication of indirectly inherited members by using the keyword **virtual** in the declarations of **A1** and **A2** as follows:

```
class A { ... };
class A1: virtual public A { ... };
class A2: virtual public A { ... };
class A12: public A1, public A2 { ... };
```

Thanks to the keyword **virtual** on the second and third of these lines, **A** is a *virtual base class*, and class **A12** has only one sub-object of class **A**. With an **int** member **a** in class **A** and a variable x of type **A12**, as in the above example, the above two lines would still be valid, but their output would be **2 2**. Since **A** is now a virtual base class, there is now only one member **a** in object x.

For the sake of completeness, it must be mentioned that a derived class cannot *directly* inherit the members of a base class more than once:

```
class A12: public A, public A { ... }; // Error
```

7.5 Static Class Members

Normally, a data member of a class type is stored in every object of that type. However, if we use the keyword **static** for a class data member, there will be only one such member for the class, regardless of how many objects there are. In other words, a static class member belongs to its class type rather than to the individual objects of that type. Besides static data members, we can also use static member functions, which differ from other member functions in that they cannot use any data members that are specific for objects; the **this** pointer is not available in static member functions.

Program STATMEM shows how static members can be used. The constructor of **person** increases the static class member **count** by 1 each time it is called. In this way, we count how many objects of type **person** there are.

```
/* STATMEM: Using a static class member to
            count how many times the constructor
            person() is called.
*/
#include <iostream.h>
#include <string.h>

class person {
public:
   person(char *str)
   {  strcpy(name, str);
      count++;
   }
   void print() const
   {  cout << name << endl;
   }
   static void printcount()
   {  cout << "There are " << count
              << " persons." << endl;

   }
private:
   char name[20];
   static int count;
};

int person::count=0;

int main()
{  person A("Mary"), B("Peter"), C("Charles"), *p;
   p = new person("Kate");
   A.print(); B.print(); C.print(); p->print();
   person::printcount();
   return 0;
}
```

The output of this program is as follows:

```
Mary
Peter
Charles
Kate
There are 4 persons.
```

We have to define a static class member outside the class definition, as is done here in the program line

```
int person::count=0;
```

Since the static class member count is associated with the class type **person**, not with objects of that type, we write **person::count**, whereas we would have written, for example, **A.count** if **count** had been a nonstatic member and if we had been interested in the copy of it for object **A**. The same applies to the static member function called in the **main** function as **person::printcount( )**. The notion of static member functions enables us to access the private static **count** member. In contrast to the **print** member function, **printcount** cannot be applied to a particular object, hence the difference in prefix in the calls **A.print( )** and **person::printcount( )**. If we had not been able to use a static member function, it would have been necessary to make the **count** data member public and to write

```
cout << "There are " << person::count
     << " persons." << endl;
```

instead of **person::printcount( )** in the **main** function. The output would then have been the same as it is now.

Note the analogy between static data members and static local variables in functions. In both cases, there is only one copy of them. As for a nonstatic local variable in a function, there is a new copy of it each time the function is called, so in case of recursion there will be several copies. If a local variable is static there is only one copy, even in case of recursion. Things are similar with a static data member of a class: there is only one copy of that member, no matter how many objects of that class there are.

7.6 Pointers to Members

In Section 5.12 we discussed pointers to functions. Unfortunately, we cannot use such pointers for functions that are class members. For example, consider the following program fragment, which defines function **f**, class **example**, pointer **p** and the variables **u, v** and **w**:

```
int f(){return 123;}

class example {
public:
    example(int ii, int jj):i(ii), j(jj){}
    int ivalue(){return i;}
    int jvalue(){return j;}
private:
    int i, j;
};

int (*p)();
example u(1, 2), v(3, 4), w(5, 6);
```

After writing

```
p = f;
```

we can call function **f** by writing **(*p)( )** or even **p( )**, as we have seen in Section 5.12. Although the member function **ivalue** is very similar to function **f**, we cannot assign it to pointer **p**. Each of the following attempts would fail:

```
p = ivalue;          // (1) error
p = example::ivalue; // (2) error
p = u.ivalue;        // (3) error
```

Attempt (1) fails because we should specify to which class **ivalue** belongs. Although (2) looks better, it is not clear at all how to use **p**. If we continued by writing **p( )** (as an indirect call to **ivalue**), it would not be clear whether **u.i**, **v.i** or **w.i** should be the resulting value. Nor could **u.p( )** be correct, since **p** is not a class member. This explains that the C++ language does not allow (2). Finally, (3) is not considered correct because it is at least misleading. Since only one function **ivalue** is physically present in memory and the value of **p** can only be an address, no information about **u** is stored in **p** so we cannot expect the effect of (3) to be any different if we replace **u** with **v** or **w**.

To enable us to use pointers to class member functions, a new operator has been introduced. Instead of

```
int (*p)();
```

we should write

```
int (example::*p)();
```

to express that **p** is intended as a pointer to a member function (without parameters and returning **int**) of class **example**. We can then write

```
p = example::ivalue;    // or: p = &example::ivalue
```

As indicated by comment, we may write or omit the 'address of' operator (&) here as we like. After this assignment, we can use **p** as the second operand of a special operator, .*, as the following examples show:

```
(u.*p)()    // = u.ivalue() = u.i = 1
(v.*p)()    // = v.ivalue() = v.i = 3
(w.*p)()    // = w.ivalue() = w.i = 5
```

Instead of **ivalue**, we could use **jvalue** here, since this member function has the same type as **ivalue**. The values of those expressions would then be 2, 4 and 6.

In the above examples, the operator .* follows the class objects **u**, **v** and **w**. because these variables are class objects. In many applications we deal with class objects via pointers to those objects. Such pointers can be followed by another new operator, –>* (instead of .*). For example, if we replace

```
example u(1, 2), v(3, 4), w(5, 6);
```

with

```
example *p12 = new example(1, 2),
        *p34 = new example(3, 4),
        *p56 = new example(5, 6);
```

we should at the same time replace

```
(u.*p)()    // = u.ivalue() = u.i = 1
(v.*p)()    // = v.ivalue() = v.i = 3
(w.*p)()    // = w.ivalue() = w.i = 5
```

with

```
(p12->*p)()    // = p12->ivalue() = p12->i = 1
(p34->*p)()    // = p34->ivalue() = p34->i = 3
(p56->*p)()    // = p56->ivalue() = p56->i = 5
```

It would be inconsistent if the new operators .* and –>* were available only for function members. They are therefore also made applicable to pointers to data members, even though normal pointers, such as **pf** in the following example, can also be used for data members:

```
class num {public: float x;} u;
float *pf;
pf = &u.x;         // pf is a normal pointer to float.
*pf = 1.23;        // Effect: u.x = 1.23
```

If we want to use a pointer to a member instead, we can write

```
class num {public: float x;} u;
float num::*pm;
pm = &num::x;        // pm is a pointer to a data member.
u.*pm = 1.23;        // Effect: u.x = 1.23
```

Comparing the above two fragments, we see that a pointer to a member enables us to delay specifying the object (**u**) until we actually use the pointer. Apparently, a pointer to a class member is not a real pointer but rather an offset. With a given object **u** and a pointer **pm** to a data member, the expression **u.*pm** indicates where in object **u** the member in question is to be found.

After having seen so many program fragments, it is time to combine all we have been discussing in this section in a complete demonstration program:

```
// PTRMEM: Pointers to class members.
#include <iostream.h>

class example {
public:
   example(int ii, int jj):i(ii), j(jj){}
   int ivalue(){return i;}
   int jvalue(){return j;}
   int i, j;
};

int main()
{  example u(1, 2), v(3, 4), w(5, 6), *pobject = &w;
   cout << "Pointer to function members: ";
   int (example::*pf)();
   pf = example::ivalue;
   cout << (u.*pf)() << "  ";               // 1
   pf = example::jvalue;
   cout << (v.*pf)() << "  ";               // 4
   cout << (pobject->*pf)() << endl;        // 6

   cout << "Pointer to data members:    ";
   int example::*pd;
   pd = &example::i;
   cout << u.*pd << "  ";                    // 1
   pd = &example::j;
   cout << v.*pd << "  ";                    // 4
   cout << pobject->*pd << endl;             // 6
   return 0;
}
```

The output of this program is as follows:

```
Pointer to function members: 1   4   6
Pointer to data members:     1   4   6
```

7.7 Polymorphism and Reusability

As mentioned in Section 7.4, derived classes enable us to reuse code in a very elegant way. We will now demonstrate this by means of a heterogeneous linked list (also called a *linear* list), as shown in Figure 7.5.

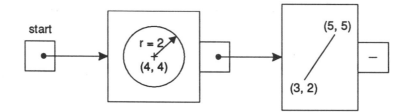

Figure 7.5. A heterogeneous linked list

Suppose that we are given a class in the form of both an interface file *figures.h* and an implementation file *figures.cpp*. These files, listed below, enable us to build a linked list consisting of two types of elements: one type is to store line segments and the other circles. For a line segment we store its two end points A and B, and for a circle its center C and its radius *r*. We are using a pure virtual function (**print**) in the class **element**, which is therefore an abstract class. Consequently, there can be no object of class **element**; this class is used only to derive other classes from, as follows from our discussion in Section 7.4.

```
/* FIGURES.H: Interface file to build linked lists for
              circles and lines.
*/

#include <iostream.h>
#include <stdlib.h>

class point {
public:
    float x, y;
    point(float xx=0, float yy=0): x(xx), y(yy){}
};

class element {                           // Abstract class
public:
    element *next;
    virtual void print() const = 0;  // Pure virtual function
};
```

```
class line: public element {
public:
    line(point &P, point &Q, element *ptr);
    void print() const;
private:
    point A, B;
};

class circle: public element {
public:
    circle(point &center, float radius, element *ptr);
    void print() const;
private:
    point C;
    float r;
};

void pr(const point &P, const char *str=", ");
```

```
// FIGURES: Implementation file (figures.cpp) for
//          linked lists of circles and lines.

#include "figures.h"

line::line(point &P, point &Q, element *ptr)
{  A = P; B = Q; next = ptr;
}

void line::print() const
{  cout << "Line: ";
   pr(A); pr(B, "\n");
}

circle::circle(point &center, float radius, element *ptr)
{  C = center; r = radius; next = ptr;
}

void circle::print() const
{  cout << "Circle: ";
   pr(C);
   cout << r << endl;
}

void pr(const point &P, const char *str)
{  cout << "(" << P.x << ", " << P.y << ")" << str;
}
```

In an application program, we can build a list of, say, a line and a circle, by writing the following three lines:

```
element *start=NULL;
start = new line(point(3, 2), point(5, 5), start);
start = new circle(point(4, 4), 2, start);
```

In the last two lines, the address **start** is placed in the member **next** of the element created by **new**. Lists build in this way are in fact *stacks*: the element last added to the list is the one that is first available to be used, because it is pointed to by **start**. In our example, **start** points to the circle element, and the member **next** of this element points to the line element, as shown in Figure 7.5.

We now want to use the files *figures.h* and *figures.cpp*, but besides lines and circles we also want to deal with triangles. Obviously, a triangle is determined by its three vertices A, B, and C. We can then write the following files of our own as a supplement to those just mentioned:

```
/* TRIANGLE.H: Adding a triangle (interface file).
               Class triangle is derived from class element.
*/

class triangle: public element {
public:
   triangle(point &P1, point &P2, point &P3, element *ptr);
   void print() const;
private:
   point A, B, C;
};
```

```
/* TRIANGLE: Adding a triangle class
             (implementation file triangle.cpp).
*/

#include "figures.h"
#include "triangle.h"

triangle::triangle(point &P1, point &P2, point &P3,
              element *ptr)
{  A = P1; B = P2; C = P3; next = ptr;
}

void triangle::print() const
{  cout << "Triangle: ";
   pr(A); pr(B); pr(C, "\n");
}
```

The new class **triangle** was derived from the abstract base class **element** (designed only to derive other classes from it). It may also happen that some class, originally not intended to be used as a base class, is found useful as such later. Suppose, for example, that after having used our figure classes for some time, we want to introduce line segments that have a certain thickness. Instead of deriving another class from the base class **element**, we can benefit from the existing class **line**. Although this class is a derived class itself, and originally not intended as a base class, we can use it as such and derive another derived class, **fatlines**, from it. We therefore write another extension, again in the form of an interface and an application file:

```
// FATLINE.H: Additional header file for thick lines.

class fatline: public line {
public:
    fatline(point &P, point &Q, float thickness,
            element *ptr);
    void print() const;
private:
    float w;
};
```

```
// FATLINE: Implementation of thick lines (file: fatline.cpp).

#include "figures.h"
#include "fatline.h"

fatline::fatline(point &P, point &Q, float thickness,
                 element *ptr): line(P, Q, ptr)
{  w = thickness;
}

void fatline::print() const
{  this->line::print();
   cout << "    Thickness: " << w << endl;
}
```

Note the constructor initializer :line(P, Q, ptr) in the definition of the constructor **fatline**. As follows from our discussion in Section 7.3, it says that the end points P and Q are to be passed to the constructor **line**.

Program DEMO demonstrates how all these files can be used. To run it, we must first link together the four object files obtained by compiling the files *demo.cpp*, *figures.cpp*, *triangle.cpp*, and *fatline.cpp*. The other files listed, that is, the three header files *figures.h*, *triangle.h*, and *fatline.h*, are as usual included by the preprocessor and therefore not supplied to the linker:

```
// DEMO: This program builds a heterogeneous linked list in
//        which data about a line, a circle, a triangle, and
//        a 'fat' line are stored (file: demo.cpp).
//        To be linked with FIGURES, TRIANGLE and FATLINE.
#include "figures.h"
#include "triangle.h"
#include "fatline.h"

int main()
{   element *start=NULL, *p;
    // Build a heterogeneous linked list:
    start = new line(point(3, 2), point(5, 5), start);
    start = new circle(point(4, 4), 2, start);
    start = new triangle(point(1, 1), point(6, 1),
                            point(3, 6), start);
    start = new fatline(point(2, 2), point(3, 3), 0.2, start);
    for (p=start; p != NULL; p = p->next) p->print();
    return 0;
}
```

When running this program, we obtain the following output:

```
Line: (2, 2), (3, 3)
    Thickness: 0.2
Triangle: (1, 1), (6, 1), (3, 6)
Circle: (4, 4), 2
Line: (3, 2), (5, 5)
```

The for-statement at the end of the **main** function demonstrates *polymorphism*: a heterogeneous linked list is traversed, and, according to the principle of *late binding*, the choice which **print** function is to be used is made at run time.

Although this example is too simple to be realistic, it clearly demonstrates how software components that are to be extended can be reused in an elegant and efficient way. With emphasis on *reusable* code, as in this example, people sometimes use the terms *extensible* and *incremental* programming.

7.8 Iterators

In Section 7.7, the application module DEMO contains an assignment statement of the form

```
start = new ...
```

for each list element to be created. We will now see how we can build and traverse a linked list in a loop in such a way that implementation details (such as the use of the

new operator) are hidden. We will do this by using a set of functions, collectively called *iterator* and to be discussed shortly. This method has the advantage that in principle we can modify the implementation (including the interface) without altering the application file. This time we will use a very simple linked list, with elements of the structure type **element**, which has an integer member **num** and a pointer member **next**. Starting with the pointer variable **start**, a linked list of this type is as shown in Figure 7.6.

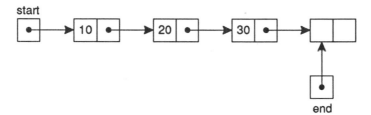

Figure 7.6. A linked list

In this example, the integers 10, 20, and 30 are stored in three elements of the list. The fourth and final element is a so-called *sentinel*, which is frequently used at the end of a linked list because it simplifies list operations and speeds them up. (This is discussed in more detail in *Programs and Data Structures in C*, listed in the Bibliography.)

Instead of using a variable **start** of type pointer-to-**element** in the application module, we will rather use a private member **start** of a class (which we call **list**). Using the typical C++ principle of *encapsulation*, we combine the data and the related functions in this class.

The following application builds a list to store the integers 10, 20, ..., $10n$, in that order, in it and then traverses the list to print these integers in the same order.

```
// LISTDEMO: Application of class 'list'.

#include <iostream.h>
#include "list.h"

int main()
{   int i, n;
    list l;
    cout << "How many integers are to be stored? ";
    cin >> n;
    for (i=1; i<=n; i++) l.append(10 * i);
    cout << "Output:\n";
    l.iteratorSTART();
    while (l.iteratorOK()) cout << l.iterator() << " ";
    cout << endl;
    return 0;
}
```

The function **append** stores its argument at the end of the list. The most interesting aspect of this example is the **iterator** function. We can traverse the linked list l by means of the following three function calls:

l.iteratorSTART( ) To be called only once, to initialize the iteration process.

l.iteratorOK( ) Returns a nonzero value if there is another element in the list and 0 when the process terminates because all elements have been visited.

l.iterator( ) Returns the next **int** value stored in the list.

Viewed from the application module, it is an open question whether class **list** uses a linked list. With the following interface and implementation files it does:

```
// LIST.H: Header file for class 'list'.
struct element {int num; element *next;};

class list {
public:
   list();
   ~list();
   void append(int i);
   void iteratorSTART(){iter_ptr = start;}
   int iteratorOK(){return iter_ptr != end;}
   int iterator();
private:
   element *start, *end, *iter_ptr;
};
```

```
// LIST: Implementation of class 'list'.
#include "list.h"

list::list()
{  start = end = new element; // Sentinel
}

list::~list()
{  element *p;
   while (start != end)
   {  p = start; start = start->next; delete p;
   }
   delete start;
}

void list::append(int i)
{  end->num = i;
   end = end->next = new element;
}
```

```
int list::iterator()
{  int i=iter_ptr->num;
   iter_ptr = iter_ptr->next;
   return i;
}
```

Instead of a linked list, other data structures can be used in such a way that the member functions **iteratorSTART**, **iteratorOK**, and **iterator** are used in exactly the same way. For example, we can use the following very simple interface and implementation files, based on a pointer **a**, used as an array. A drawback of this implementation is its less flexible memory usage: for each object of type **list**, the constructor allocates a memory area of 1000 integers, which must not be exceeded. More general and more economical schemes, such as the method used in Section 7.2, are left as an exercise to the reader.

```
// LIST1.H: Alternative header file for class 'list'.

const int N=1000;

class list {
public:
   list();
   ~list();
   void append(int i);
   void iteratorSTART(){iter = 0;}
   int iteratorOK(){return iter < n;}
   int iterator();
private:
   int *a, n, iter;
};
```

```
// LIST1: Alternative implementation of class 'list'.

#include <iostream.h>
#include <stdlib.h>
#include "list1.h"

list::list()
{  a = new int[N];
   n = 0;
}

list::~list()
{  delete a;
}
```

```
void list::append(int x)
{  if (n == N){cout << "Too many items.\n"; exit(1);}
   a[n++] = x;
}

int list::iterator()
{  return a[iter++];
}
```

If we want to use this alternative implementation, we must not forget to change **#include "list.h"** into **#include "list1.h"** in the application module. Of course, we can instead rename the file *list1.h* into *list.h*. Note, however, that even in this case the application module must be recompiled.

7.9 A Calculator for Rational Arithmetic

We will now declare a class **rational** for *rational numbers*, also called *fractions*. As you probably know, the set of integers is a subset of the set of rational numbers, which can be written in the form i/j, with integers i and j. This set of rational numbers is in turn a subset of the set of real numbers, which also contains irrational numbers, such as $\sqrt{2}$. Normally, real numbers other than integers are approximated by some decimal representation, such as 0.3333333 instead of the exact value 1/3. We will now deal with exact rational numbers, not with their decimal representations. Our class **rational** will enable us, for example, to compute

$$1 + \frac{1}{3} + \frac{5}{12} \times 2 = \frac{13}{6}$$

by means of the following application program:

```
// RATDEMO: A simple example dealing with rational numbers.
#include "rational.h"
int main()
{  rational x(1, 3), y(5, 12), z(2), u;
   u = 1 + x + y * z;
   cout << "u = " << u << endl;
   return 0;
}
```

This application, like many others, clearly illustrates that declaring and implementing a class in files other than that of the main program can be viewed as extending our programming language. After all, in program RATDEMO we use type **rational** and the operators + and * as if these were built-in language facilities.

We will write interface and application files for class **rational** with some more operators than only those used in program RATDEMO, so that they may also be useful for other, more interesting applications. One such an application, a calculator for rational arithmetic will be discussed at the end of this section.

Here is the interface file that provides us with the facilities we need and some more besides:

```
/* RATIONAL.H: Header file for rational numbers
                (interface).
*/

#include <iostream.h>
#include <stdlib.h>

class rational {
public:
    rational(long i=0, long j=1, int ok=0);
    friend rational operator-(rational a);
    friend rational inverse(rational a);
    friend rational operator+(rational a, rational b);
    friend rational operator-(rational a, rational b);
    friend rational operator*(rational a, rational b);
    friend rational operator/(rational a, rational b);
    friend int operator==(rational a, rational b);
    friend int operator!=(rational a, rational b);
    friend int operator<(rational a, rational b);
    friend int operator>(rational a, rational b);
    friend int operator<=(rational a, rational b);
    friend int operator>=(rational a, rational b);
    friend ostream &operator<<(ostream &s, rational a);
    friend long numerator(rational a){return a.num;}
    friend long denominator(rational a){return a.denom;}
    operator double(){return double(num)/double(denom);}
private:
    long num, denom;
};
```

There is one aspect that is entirely new, namely the declaration of the operator << to output rational numbers. We will not discuss this until Section 9.2, but use it already to make class **rational** more useful for real applications. We could have used a member function **print** instead, but the operator << is more convenient to display rational numbers in combination with other data. Note that this operator has been used in program RATDEMO, since it is applied to the variable **u**, which has type **rational**.

As you can see, we store the numerator **num** and the denominator **denom** of the rational number *num/denom* as two **long ints**. They will be 'normalized': the greatest common divisor (GCD) of **num** and **denom** will be 1, and **num** will be negative if and only if the rational number is negative; **denom** will always be positive. The implementation file for this class is listed below:

```
/* RATIONAL: A class for rational numbers
              (implementation).
*/
#include "rational.h"

long gcd(long a, long b) // Greatest Common Divisor
{  a = labs(a); b = labs(b);
   return (b ? gcd(b, a % b) : a);
}

long lcm(long a, long b) // Least Common Multiple
{  return (a % b == 0 ? a :
            b % a == 0 ? b : (a/gcd(a, b)) * b);
}

void simplify(long &i, long &j)
{  long d = gcd(i, j);
   i /= d; j /= d;
}

rational::rational(long i, long j, int ok) // default 0 1 0
{  if (!ok) // ok = 1 if i/j is given in simplified form
   {  if (j == 0)
      {  cout << "Division by zero in class rational\n";
         exit(1);
      }
      if (j < 0){i = -i; j = -j;}
      simplify(i, j);
   }
   num = i; denom = j;
}

rational operator-(rational a)
{  return rational(-a.num, a.denom, 1);
}

rational operator+(rational a, rational b)
{  long comdenom=lcm(a.denom, b.denom),
        sumnum = a.num * (comdenom / a.denom) +
                 b.num * (comdenom / b.denom);
   if (comdenom < a.denom || comdenom < b.denom)
   {  cout << "Long int overflow in addition.\n";
      exit(1);
   }
   return rational(sumnum, comdenom);
}

rational operator-(rational a, rational b)
{  return a+(-b);
}
```

```
rational operator*(rational a, rational b)
{   long anum=a.num, adenom=a.denom,
    bnum=b.num, bdenom=b.denom,
    prodnum, proddenom, apnum;
    simplify(anum, bdenom);
    simplify(bnum, adenom);
    prodnum = anum * bnum; proddenom = adenom * bdenom;
    apnum = labs(prodnum);
    if ((apnum != 0 &&
        (apnum < labs(anum) || apnum < labs(bnum))) ||
         proddenom < adenom || proddenom < bdenom)
    {   cout << "Long int overflow in multiplication.\n";
        exit(1);
    }
    return rational(anum * bnum, adenom * bdenom, 1);
}

rational operator/(rational a, rational b)
{   long i=b.num, j=b.denom;
    if (i < 0){i = -i; j = -j;}
    return a * rational(j, i, 1);
}

int operator==(rational a, rational b)
{   return a.num == b.num && a.denom == b.denom;
}

int operator!=(rational a, rational b)
{   return !(a == b);
}

int operator<(rational a, rational b)
{   return (a - b).num < 0;
}

int operator>(rational a, rational b)
{   return b < a;
}

int operator<=(rational a, rational b)
{   return !(b < a);
}

int operator>=(rational a, rational b)
{   return !(a < b);
}

ostream &operator<<(ostream &s, rational a)
{   return s << a.num << '/' << a.denom;
}
```

As usual in elementary arithmetic, in order to add two rational numbers we find their least common denominator (LCD). Care is taken to avoid **long int** overflow wherever possible. This means that in function **lcd** the LCD is computed by performing the division first in **(a / gcd(a, b)) * b**, while the more natural notation **a * b / gcd(a, b)** would be risky, since **a * b** might be too large. Also, in the definition of **operator***, the function **simplify** is called twice so that all components are as much simplified as possible before the multiplication of the numerators and that of the denominators take place. In spite of these efforts, overflow may take place, as we will see shortly. Some simple checks are therefore included: the absolute product of two nonzero numerators must not be less than the absolute values of these numerators themselves; a similar test applies to the product of the denominators. If such a test fails, the answer is wrong due to **long int** overflow, and the program terminates. The following program can be used to demonstrate this:

```
/* SERIES: Computation of 1/1 + 1/2 + ... + 1/n
           for a given n.
*/
#include <math.h>
#include "rational.h"
#include <iomanip.h>

int main()
{  rational s;
   long i, n;
   double s_quot=0;
   cout << "1/1 + 1/2 + ... + 1/n is computed for your n.\n";
   cout << "Enter n: "; cin >> n;
   for (i=1; i<=n; i++)
   {  s = s + rational(1, i);
      s_quot += 1.0/i;
   }
   cout << "Answer: s = " << s << endl;
   cout << "Converting this to type double gives      "
      << setprecision(15) << double(s) << endl;
   cout << "Computation without class rational gives "
      << s_quot << endl;
   return 0;
}
```

Here is the output of this program for the highest value **n** = 24 for which it can be successfully executed with Borland C++:

```
1/1 + 1/2 + ... + 1/n is computed for your n.
Enter n: 24
Answer: s = 1347822955/356948592
Converting this to type double gives      3.77595817775351
Computation without class rational gives 3.77595817775351
```

A rational calculator

So far, our application files were simpler than their implementation files. This is normally not the case with real programs. Even though implementation details are delegated to the class implementation file, such as *rational.cpp*, application files can be quite complex. An example of an application of rational arithmetic that is more advanced than the programs RATDEMO and SERIES is the calculator program CALCUL, which we can use to evaluate any rational expression, that is, as long as there is no **long int** overflow. You may also call it an *interpreter*, since it works in the same way as certain interpreters for programming languages. The 'programs' interpreted by this interpreter are rational expressions, followed by an equal sign and entered on the keyboard. Its output is the exact rational value of the given expression, represented by its numerator and denominator, in normalized form.

Program CALCUL uses the *recursive descent* method; a similar interpreter is explained in detail in *Programs and Data Structures in C*, listed in the Bibliography. The 'language', that is, set of allowed input strings to be interpreted, can very precisely be defined by means of syntax diagrams. Such a precise definition is very useful because the program is based upon it. Here is another way of defining the set of input strings; it is sufficient for our purposes because our language is very simple compared with a real programming language:

1.   An input string consists of an *expression*, followed by an equal sign.

2.   An *expression* consists of one or more *terms*, separated by + and –.

3.   A *term* consists of one or more *factors*, separated by * and /.

4.   A *factor* consists of:
     -   an unsigned integer (that is, a sequence of decimal digits), or
     -   an *expression* in parentheses ( ), or
     -   a minus sign (–) followed by a *factor*.

Any white-space characters in the input string are skipped.

For each of the terms *expression*, *term*, and *factor*, there is a function which has the task to read a substring and to return its value. For example, the function **factor** can read and evaluate each of the following three substrings, which, according to the above definition, are factors:

```
123
(-5 / 3 + 8 / (9 + 3 / 4) - 30 * 2 / 7)
-53
```

Note that the above definition is *recursive*: an *expression* consists of *terms*, which consist of *factors*, and a *factor* may in turn contain an *expression*. The corresponding functions are therefore also recursive. This is why this program, although rather small, may be more difficult to understand than many others in this book.

```
/* CALCUL:
   A calculator that interprets any rational expression
   read from the standard input stream. You may use integers,
   the four binary operators +, -, *, /, the unary operator
   -, and parentheses, grouped together in the usual way and
   followed by an equal sign. Here is an example of an input
   line:

      (4 - 3)/5 + 3/(15 - (2 * 4 + 13)) =

   In this case, the answer is -3/10.
   The module RATIONAL is to be linked in.
*/

#include <ctype.h>
#include "rational.h"

rational term();
rational factor();

int num_input(long &x)     // Reads an integer, if possible.
{  char ch;
   cin >> ch; cin.putback(ch);
   if (isdigit(ch)){cin >> x; return 1;}
   return 0;
}

int ischar(char chgiven)   // Reads character chgiven,
{  char ch;                // if possible.
   cin >> ch;  // Skips any leading white-space characters.
   if (ch == chgiven) return 1;
   cin.putback(ch); return 0;
}

void error(char *msg)
{  cout << "Error: " << msg << endl; exit(1);
}

rational expression()
{  rational x, y;
   int plus;
   x = term();
   while ((plus = ischar('+')) || ischar('-'))
   {  y = term();
      if (plus) x = x + y; else x = x - y;
   }
   return x;
}
```

```
rational term()
{  rational x, y;
   int times;
   x = factor();
   while ((times = ischar('*')) || ischar('/'))
   {  y = factor();
      if (times) x = x * y; else x = x / y;
   }
   return x;
}

rational factor()
{  long i;
   rational x;                              // Default: 0,
   if (ischar('-')) return (x - factor()); // so x = 0
   if (num_input(i)) return i;
   if (!ischar('('))
      error("Open parenthesis or integer expected.");
   x = expression();
   if (!ischar(')'))
      error("Close parenthesis expected.");
   return x;
}

int main()
{  cout << "Enter an expression consisting of:\n";
   cout << "   integers\n";
   cout << "   the arithmetic operators + - * /\n";
   cout << "   parentheses ( )\n";
   cout << "   blanks, tabs and newline characters\n";
   cout <<
   "The expression is to be followed by an equal sign =\n\n";
   cout << expression() << endl;
   if (!ischar('=')) cout << "No equal sign entered.\n";
   return 0;
}
```

Here is a demonstration of this program:

```
Enter an expression consisting of:
   integers
   the arithmetic operators + - * /
   parentheses ( )
   blanks, tabs and newline characters
The expression is to be followed by an equal sign =
(4 - 3)/5 + 3/(15 - (2 * 4 + 13)) =
-3/10
```

Exercises

Solve the following exercises by using modular programming. Each program is to consist of an interface, an application and an implementation, as discussed in Section 7.1.

7.1 Declare a class **time** with two **int** members **h** and **m**, which represent the time as shown on a digital clock:

  h = 0, 1, ..., 23
  m = 0, 1, ..., 59

Define the operator + for adding a number of minutes to a given time. For example, the following must be possible:

```
time t0(23, 59), t1;
t1 = t0 + 120;
// Now t0 and t1 represent 23.59h and 01.59h,
// respectively.
```

Write a simple application program which reads a given time and a number of minutes to be added to it, and print the resulting time.

7.2 (This exercise requires familiarity with complex numbers.) Declare class **complex** with operators +, −, *, /, ==, !=, and functions **abs, arg, real, imag, csqrt**. Write an application program to demonstrate this class.

7.3 Declare a class for (possibly negative) integers of any length, along with the operators + and * and a **print** function for these very long integers. Write also a demonstration program for this class.

7.4 Declare class **bits** to store bit arrays of arbitrary length. Store eight bits in a byte. Define member functions **ones, zeros**, and **print**, to be used in application programs such as

```
#include "bits.h"

int main()
{  bits a(20);     // Array of 20 bits, initialized to 0.
   a.ones(1, 11); // Set a[1], ..., a[11] to 1.
   a.zeros(2, 5); // Set a[2], ..., a[5] to 0.
   for (int i=0; i<20; i++) cout << a[i];
   cout << endl;  // Output: 01000011111100000000
   a.print();     // The same output!
   return 0;
}
```

The output of this program consists of two identical bit sequences. As follows from the above comments, the function **a.print( )** prints all elements of array **a**, starting at **a[0]**. Define also the function **operator[ ]**, which you can declare in class **bits** as follows:

```
int operator[](int i)const;
```

7.5 Add some more set operations to class **iset**, discussed in Section 7.2. With **iset** variables **A**, **B**, **C**, **D**, **E**, we want to write

```
C = A + B;
D = A * B;
E = A - B;
```

to compute the union, the intersection, and the difference of the sets **A** and **B**, respectively. The union **C** of **A** and **B** contains all elements of **A** and **B**; their intersection **D** contains only those elements which are both in **A** and in **B**. The difference **E** of **A** and **B** consists of those elements of **A** that are not in **B**.

Standard I/O

8.1 Introduction

There are several types of facilities for input and output (or I/O, for short). One category of I/O facilities, inherited from the C language, is the subject of this chapter. It is called *standard I/O* and it requires the following program line:

```
#include <stdio.h>
```

The fact that standard I/O is not a specific C++ facility is no reason to ignore it. It is well-standardized and its use therefore leads to very portable programs. If you are an experienced C programmer and already familiar with standard I/O, you may skip to Chapter 9, where the typical C++ *stream I/O* is discussed.

Although we have already used the two functions **printf** and **scanf** very often, they still present some possibilities worth discussing, so we will look at them in more detail in this chapter. Then we will extend the subject of this chapter in various directions:

- Input from and output to files (on disk)
- Unformatted I/O
- Random access.

The header file *stdio.h*, mentioned above, not only declares functions; it also contains other useful information, such as macro definitions. Before dealing with **scanf** and **printf**, we will first have a look at the two macros **getchar** and **putchar**, defined in *stdio.h*. The macro call

```
putchar(ch);
```

writes the character (stored in the variable) **ch** to the video screen. Analogously, we can read a character from the keyboard by writing

```
ch = getchar();
```

Most operating systems enable us to use **getchar** also for reading a character from a file (on disk) by means of a facility called *redirection*. For example, if our program is called COMPUTE and we want to read something from the file *mydata*1 by means of **getchar** (or **scanf**) when using MS-DOS, we can start it as follows:

```
compute <mydata1
```

Analogous to < for input, we can use the character > for redirection with output. For example, **putchar** in program COMPUTE writes characters to the file *mydata*2 instead of to the video screen if we start this program as follows:

```
compute >mydata2
```

We can also redirect both input and output, which in our example can by done by typing

```
compute <mydata1 >mydata2
```

Because of this possibility of redirection, it is customary to say that **getchar** and **scanf** read data from the *standard input stream*, named **stdin**, rather than 'from the keyboard' as we have said so far. Analogously, **putchar** and **printf** write data to the *standard output stream* **stdout**, rather than 'to the video display'. The names **stdin** and **stdout** do not often occur in our program text. However, in Section 8.4 we will see that we can use these names explicitly.

  We have not yet discussed how, when using **getchar** with redirection, we can detect the end of the input file, nor have we mentioned the type of the variable **ch** in our example. We will now deal with these two points at the same time because they are related to each other. If the type returned by **getchar** were **char**, the only way of signaling 'end of file' by means of a special character would be to reserve one of the 256 possible values of **char** for this purpose. It would then not be possible to read arbitrary files, in which all possible bytes might occur as real data. Therefore a different approach has been taken. The value returned by **getchar** has type **int**, and in case of 'end of file' this return value is equal to a symbolic constant **EOF** (in *stdio.h* normally defined as –1). In all other cases **getchar** returns the value of the byte that has been read. The latter value is nonnegative and less than 256. In most cases, these values are even less than 128, as the ASCII table in Appendix B shows. Do not confuse these character values with integers to be read. For example, the integer 13 is represented externally by the two characters 1 and 3. You should not expect **getchar** to read these in one call and return the value 13. Instead, two calls to **getchar** could be used, the first returning '1' = 49, the second '3' = 51 (see Appendix B). Of course, if we wanted to read some digits such as 1 and 3 and to store the value (13) of the number they represent into the **int** variable **i**, the way to do this would be

```
scanf("%d", &i)
```

It will now be clear that it makes sense to use type **int** rather than **char** for the variable **ch** in the following program fragment:

```
#include <stdio.h>
...
int ch;
...
while ((ch = getchar()) != EOF)
{ ...  // Use ch as if it had been of type 'char'
}
```

Recall that conversion from type **int** to type **char** does not cause any problems. For example, it would be correct to write **str[i] = ch** in the above loop with **ch** of type **int** and **str[i]** of type **char**.

Although **putchar** differs from **getchar** in that we often use it as if it were a **void** function, it actually returns a value of type **int**, which is equal to the argument **ch** or to **EOF** in case of an output error. Thanks to the close relationship between the types **char** and **int**, the argument of **putchar** can be of type **char**, if we like, in which case it is converted to type **int**.

The fact that **getchar** and **putchar** are macros makes their use not much different from that of functions. Note, however, that the possibility of using pointers to functions, as discussed in Section 5.12, does not apply to macros. Another point to be remembered is that any error messages about the way we use macros refer to their expanded forms, which may be confusing.

8.2 The Function **printf**

We use **printf** for formatted output to the stream **stdout**. As we have seen in the last section, **stdout** normally corresponds to the video screen. We often speak about 'printing' rather than 'writing to **stdout**'. A call to **printf** has the form

```
printf(format string, arg1, arg2, ...)
```

in which the *format string* can be followed by any number of arguments. (Variable-length argument lists, as used here, will be discussed in Section 12.9.) Although **printf** is often used as a 'void' function, it returns a value, which is normally equal to the number of characters that are written. In case of an error, the return value is negative.

As discussed in Section 5.4, the format string is passed to **printf** in the form of an address. For example, in

```
printf("Temperature: %4.1f degrees centigrade.", temp);
```

the address of the first character, **T**, is passed to **printf**, and this function itself can determine the length of the string because of the null character, internally stored at its end. The fact that an address is passed as an argument explains that the first argument of **printf** can have other forms that also result in addresses. Examples are the name of an array in which a format string is stored, and a conditional expression, as in:

```
char fstr[80] = "If x = %f and y = %f, then z is ";
float x, y, z;
...
printf(fstr, x, y);
printf(z < 0 ? "negative." : z > 0 ? "positive." : "zero.");
```

The format string can contain two kinds of objects:

- Characters to be printed literally
- Conversion specifications

There must be a conversion specification for each of the arguments *arg1*, *arg2*, and so on. Each conversion specification begins with **%** and ends with a *conversion character*. There may be something, such as a 'precision', between these two characters. Let us start with the conversion characters themselves:

d   The (**int**) argument is converted to decimal representation. (Instead of **d**, we may use **i** with the same meaning.)

o   The (**int**) argument is converted to octal representation, without a leading zero.

x   The (**int**) argument is converted to hexadecimal representation, without a prefix **0x**. In addition to the digits **0**, ..., **9**, the lower case letters **a**, ..., **f** are used. We can also write **X** instead of **x**, with the effect that capital letters **A**, ..., **F** are used instead of lower case letters.

u   The (**int** or **unsigned**) argument is converted to 'unsigned' decimal representation. This implies that the leftmost bit of the argument is used as a value bit, not as a sign bit.

c   The (**char** or **int**) argument is (or is interpreted as) a single character.

s   The argument is a string, or, technically, the address of the first element of a character array. The characters starting at this address are printed until a null character is reached or until as many characters have been printed as indicated by the precision (between **%** and **s**).

f   The (**float** or **double**) argument is converted to decimal representation of the form [–]*mmm.dddddd*, in which the default precision (that is, the number of digits *d* in the form just mentioned) is 6. The result is neatly rounded. If we use **0** as a precision, the decimal point is suppressed.

e   The (**float** or **double**) argument is converted to decimal representation of the form $[-]m.dddddd\mathbf{e}{\pm}xx$, in which the number of digits d is given by the precision (between % and **e**). The default precision is 6. If we write **0** as a precision, the decimal point is suppressed. If we write **E** instead of **e**, then **E** instead of **e** appears in the output.

g   The (**float** or **double**) argument is converted by means of % **f** or % **e** (or % **E** if we write **G** instead of **g**). In most cases, % **f** will be used; % **e** (or % **E**) is used if the exponent is either less than –4 or greater than the given precision. Neither a point at the end nor any trailing zeros are printed.

p   The argument must have a pointer type, that is, it must be an address. This address is printed in a system-dependent way.

n   The argument must be the address of an integer variable. The number of characters printed so far by the current call to **printf** is placed into that variable. (Nothing is printed.)

%   This is not really a conversion character, and there is no corresponding argument. We simply write % % if we want to include the character % in the output.

Between % and the conversion character, we can insert:

1. 'Flags' (in any order):
    –   The converted argument is left aligned in the positions that are available. (Normally, we do not want this for numerical output, but we do for strings.)
    +   The number being printed is preceded by a plus sign if it is positive and by a minus sign it is negative. (Without this flag, a negative number is preceded by a minus sign but a positive one not by a plus sign.)
    blank If a plus or minus sign is omitted, a blank is printed instead. (We use the term *blank* for a *space character*.)
    0   Numbers are padded with zeros (not with blanks) on the left.
    #   An alternative form is used. This form depends on the conversion character as follows. If used in combination with **o**, the first digit is **0**. With **x** or **X**, there is a prefix 0x or 0X if the value is unequal to zero. With **e**, **E**, **f**, **g**, and **G**, a decimal point always appears in the output; with **g** and **G** trailing zeros are printed.

2. A number (written as a sequence of decimal digits), indicating the *field width*. The converted argument is printed in a field of that width or more if more positions are needed. Any room not needed is padded on the left, or, in case of the '– flag', on the right. The padding character is a blank, or, in case of the '0 flag', it is **0**. See also the remark below.

3. A period, which separates the field width (see 2) from the precision (see 4).

4. A number (written as a sequence of decimal digits), indicating the *precision*. In the case of a string, this is the maximum number of characters to be printed. With **f**, **e, E**, it is the number of digits printed after the decimal point; with **g** and **G**, it is the number of significant digits. In case of an integer, it is the minimum number of digits to be printed, with leading zeros, if needed. See also the remark below.

5. A 'length modifier' **h, l** or **L**. We use **h** if the argument is **short** or **unsigned short**, **l** if it is **long** or **unsigned long**, and **L** if it is **long double**.

Remark:
We can write an asterisk (*) for the field width (see 2) and/or for the precision (see 4). If we do, the argument in question must be preceded by one or two special arguments (depending on whether one or two asterisks are being used). These additional arguments must be of type **int**, and their numerical values are taken as the field width and the precision, respectively. In the following program, the value of x is printed with both the field width and the precision given by special arguments, while **k** has only one special argument, used for its width:

```
#include <stdio.h>

int main()
{   int width=5, precision=2, k=1234;
    double x=9.87654321;
    printf("x =%*.*f   k =%*d\n",
           width, precision, x, width, k);
    return 0;
}
```

The output of this program is:

```
x = 9.88   k = 1234
```

8.3 The Function scanf

We use **scanf** for input from **stdin**, which, as discussed in Section 8.1, usually corresponds to the keyboard. A call to this function has the following form:

    scanf (*format string*, *arg1*, *arg2*, ...)

Actually, **scanf** expects an address as its first argument, in the same way as **printf** does. The arguments that follow, *arg1, arg2, ...* are also addresses: they specify where the data items that are read are to be placed.

    The return value of **scanf** is equal to the number of data items that have been read and assigned to variables, or to **EOF** if nothing could be read because we were reading from a file the end of which was encountered. (In Section 8.1 we have seen that **stdin** can be redirected to read data from a file.)

The format string contains conversion specifications, each of which starts with % and ends with a conversion character. The following conversion characters can be used with **scanf**:

d   The input is a decimal integer and the corresponding argument has type **int***. (The latter notation means pointer-to-**int**. Don't forget to use **%ld** for a **long*** and **%hd** for a **short*** argument, as will be discussed shortly.)

i   The input is an integer in decimal, octal, or hexadecimal representation. For example, 19 is decimal, 023 octal, and 0x13 hexadecimal. The argument has type **int***.

o   The input is an octal integer, with or without leading 0. The argument is **int***.

u   The input is an unsigned integer: it cannot be negative, but, on the other hand, its value can be about twice as large as that of type **int**. The argument has type **unsigned int***.

x   The input is a hexadecimal integer, with or without a prefix **0x** or **0X**. The argument has type **int***.

c   The input consists of a character sequence, the length of which is given by the precision (between % and **c**); if no precision is given, only one character is read. In contrast to the other conversion specifications, the character being read can be a white-space character (unless **%c** is preceded by a blank). No null character is added at the end. The argument has type **char***.

s   As with numeric input data, any leading white-space characters are skipped. Then all characters are read, either until as many have been read as indicated by the precision or until a white-space character follows. A null character is added at the end. The argument has type **char*** and must be the start address of an area large enough to store all characters read, including the null character.

f   The input consists of a number, represented as a floating-point or an integer constant, and possibly preceded by a sign. The argument has type **float***. Instead of **f**, we may write **e** or **g**. (Don't forget to write **%lf** in case of a **double*** argument, as discussed below.)

p   The input is an address, as printed by **printf("%p", ...)**. The argument is the address of a pointer (to any type).

n   The number of characters read so far in the current call to **scanf** is stored in the variable the address of which is given by the argument. The argument has type **int***. Nothing is read.

[...]   Characters are read only as far as they occur between these brackets. The first character not belonging to this set terminates reading and is considered not

to be read. A null character is added at the end. The argument has type
char*. (The set of characters between the brackets must not be empty; this
convention makes it possible to recognize the first] in []...] as a character that
belongs to the set.)

[^...]   As [...], except that now characters are read that do *not* occur between the
brackets.

The following example illustrates how **%n** and **%[...]** work. First, all characters different
from the five characters **. , ; ? !** are read and stored in array **str**. Then one more
character is read (which can only be one of the five characters just mentioned) and
stored in the variable **ch**. The total number of characters that are read is stored in the
variable **k**:

```
#include <stdio.h>

int main()
{   int k;
    char str[80], ch;
    scanf("%[^.,;?!]%c%n", str, &ch, &k);
    printf("str=%s  ch=%c  k=%d\n", str, ch, k);
    return 0;
}
```

Executing this program and typing

```
Good morning!
```

as input data gives the following output:

```
str=Good morning  ch=!  k=13
```

Between % and the conversion character there can be

-   An asterisk (*); a data item is skipped in the input stream, that is, it is read but not
    assigned to a variable. There must be no argument corresponding to the conversion
    specification in question.
-   A number (written as a sequence of decimal digits) indicating the maximum field
    width. This is particularly useful when we are reading strings, because it enables
    us to prevent 'array overflow' in case more characters are read than the data area
    in which they are stored permits. For example, in

```
char str[10];
scanf("%9s", str);
```

not more than nine characters will be read; with the null character at the end, at
most ten array elements of **str** will be used, as is permitted.

-   One of the letters l (to be used for the types **double*** and **long***), **L** (for type **long double***), and **h** (for type **short***). For example, the letter l must precede the conversion characters **f**, **e**, and **g**, if the argument has type pointer-to-**double**, as is the case in

```
double xx;
scanf("%lf", &xx);
```

Writing "%f" here would be a very serious error: the compiler would not detect this, but things would go wrong during program execution. With an argument of type **long double***, we would need %Lf. Similarly, the letter l must precede the conversion characters **d**, **i**, **n**, **o**, **u**, and **x**, if the argument is **long***, and the letter **h** must precede them if it is **short***.

With **printf**, it is quite usual to include text other than conversion specifications in format strings. This is done far less often with **scanf**, because such text is not printed but expected in the input! For example, in

```
scanf("%d/%d/%d", &day, &month, &year);
```

the slashes in the format string force the user to separate the numerical values for **day**, **month**, and **year** by slashes, as in

```
31/12/1989
```

Since %**d** permits the data items to be preceded by white-space characters, the input can also have other forms, such as

```
31/      12/
1989
```

However, in the input data, white-space characters must not precede the slashes. If we want them to be permitted, we must write at least one blank immediately before the slashes in the format string. (We may as well write blanks following the slashes to make the format string more readable, although this has no effect.) The following call to **scanf** is therefore more practical:

```
scanf("%d / %d / %d", &day, &month, &year);
```

For example, it accepts the following input:

```
31    /    12/1990
```

Note that the presence of blanks in the format string does not oblige us to enter corresponding blanks in the input, as the final part, **12/1990**, in this example illustrates.

Blanks in the format string are particularly important in combination with **%c**. If the input data

```
123    A
```

is read by

```
scanf("%d %c", &n, &ch);
```

then the character **A** is stored in the variable **ch**. However, if it is read by

```
scanf("%d%c", &n, &ch);
```

(in which there is no blank between **%d** and **%c**), then, after reading 123, the first character that follows is read and stored in **ch**. In our example, this is a blank.

When we are using **scanf** (or **getchar**) to read data from the keyboard, program execution resumes only after we have pressed the Enter key, or, in other words, after we have entered a newline character. Although obviously the computer has 'seen' this newline character, it is considered not to have been read yet. In most cases this will not cause any trouble in any call to **scanf** that follows because the latter will skip over leading white-space characters. However, **%c** skips over white-space characters only if, in the format string, this conversion specification is preceded by a white-space character. Therefore the blank in the format string on the fourth line of the following program fragment is by no means superfluous:

```
printf("Enter an integer: ");
scanf("%d", &n);
printf("Enter a character: ");
scanf(" %c", &ch);
```

Note that you cannot skip over the newline character following the integer by replacing the second of these program lines with

```
scanf("%d\n", &n); // Error
```

If you try this, you will notice that **\n** (or, in general, a white-space character) at the end of the format string has a very undesirable effect. It is interpreted as a command to skip over any white-space characters in the input, until a different character is entered. This means that after entering an integer and pressing the Enter key, the machine will wait until a different character is entered and the Enter key is pressed again. (Recall that the latter is usual: only when the Enter key is pressed is the input, as far as needed by the program, actually processed.) Although all this is already very unpleasant, things may even be worse if there are subsequent calls to **scanf** (or to **getchar**), for then all these additional characters entered are still available in the input stream and will therefore turn up when we do not want or expect them.

8.4 Files

As we have seen in Section 8.1, some operating systems offer the facility of *redirection*, by which we can read from and write to files on disk, using functions (and macros) that are normally associated with the keyboard and the video display. We will now discuss other means for using files, because:

1. We often want to use more than one file for input or output and to use the keyboard or the video display as well.
2. It may be undesirable for the user to start programs in the somewhat complicated way as discussed in Section 8.1.

The header file *stdio.h* contains a program fragment of the following form:

```
typedef struct { ... } FILE;
```

Type **FILE**, defined in this way, is used in *stdio.h* for some function declarations, such as:

```
FILE *fopen(const char *filename, const char *mode);
int fclose(FILE *fp);
```

Although we need not write these declarations ourselves, seeing them makes it easier for us to understand programs that deal with files. We begin with a very simple one. It writes the integers 1, 2, ..., 10, each in two positions and followed by a newline character, to the file *num.txt*. If a file with this name already exists, its old contents are erased; if not, a new file with that name is created:

```
/* OUTNUM: This program writes the integers 1, 2, ..., 10
           in the file num.txt.
*/

#include <stdio.h>

int main()
{  FILE *fp;
   int i;
   fp = fopen("num.txt", "w");
   for (i=1; i<=10; i++) fprintf(fp, "%2d\n", i);
   fclose(fp);
   return 0;
}
```

As mentioned above, the identifier **FILE** is defined in *stdio.h* as the name of a certain structure type. In our program, we declare a pointer to an object of this type by means of

```
FILE *fp;
```

With standard I/O all input and output operations are performed by means of a special kind of pointers, called *file pointers*, or *streams*. The variable **fp** is an example of such a file pointer. Initially, its value is undefined, and we assign a value to it by means of

```
fp = fopen("num.txt", "w");
```

The function **fopen** creates a structure of type **FILE** (in the same way as **malloc** would do this) and stores appropriate initial values in it. It also returns its start address, so that we can assign this to **fp**. We say that the function **fopen** *opens* a file (or a 'stream'). Its first argument, **"num.txt"** is the name of the file on disk. There are several possibilities for its second argument; they are all based on those which, together with their meanings, are given below:

"r"	'Read'	The file must already exist and will be used for input.
"w"	'Write'	If the file already exists, its old contents are erased; if not, the file is created. The file will be used for output.
"a"	'Append'	If the file already exists, new data will be added at its end. Otherwise, **"a"** works like **"w"**.

After calling **fopen** and assigning its return value to **fp** in our example, we use the latter variable as the first argument of **fprintf**. This function is similar to the well-known function **printf**, except for this first argument, which indicates the output stream to be used.

Note that, although we say that we are writing integers, actually *characters* are written. For example, in our first call to **fprintf**, a blank, the character '1', and a newline character are written to the file *num.txt*. We can format data written to this file in the same way as with files written to the video screen, and we therefore speak about *formatted* output and about *text files*.

The function **fclose** does the opposite of **fopen**: the file is *closed*, which means that the structure of type **FILE** is released (in the same way as **free** releases memory), and, in the case of output, the 'buffer is flushed'. To understand what the latter means, we should know that for reasons of efficiency output is normally buffered so that the drive of the disk we are writing to need not be activated each time we perform output operations in our program. We often omit calls to **fclose**, since files are automatically closed when a program terminates in the normal way. For the sake of completeness, it should be mentioned that **fclose** returns a value of type **int**, namely 0 if it succeeds and **EOF** (see Section 8.1) if it fails.

We will now discuss a program that reads the file *num.txt*, written by our last program, OUTNUM, to compute the sum of the integers in this file. This program would not be very interesting if we made it suitable only for files with exactly ten integers. Instead, we will make the program more general and more realistic: it will work for any text file which contains integers separated by white-space characters. If it encounters an invalid character, such as a letter, it will print an error message and the sum computed so far. If this happens, the rest of the input file will be ignored:

```
/* INNUM: This program reads integers from the file num.txt
          and computes their sum. It terminates as soon as
          an invalid character is encountered or the end of
          the file is reached.
*/
#include <stdio.h>
#include <stdlib.h>

int main()
{  FILE *fp;
   int sum=0, x;
   fp = fopen("num.txt", "r");
   if (fp == NULL)
   {  printf("File num.txt not available.\n");
      exit(1);
   }
   while (fscanf(fp, "%d", &x) == 1) sum += x;
   printf("The sum is: %d\n", sum);
   if (!feof(fp))
   {  printf("Invalid character read.\n");
   }
   fclose(fp);
   return 0;
}
```

Note the second argument, "r", in the call to **fopen**. In this case it is very desirable to verify after this call if the attempt to open the file has been successful. This is done for **fopen** in the same way as for **malloc**, as discussed in Section 5.6: each of these functions returns the value **NULL** if it fails to perform its task properly. In case of success, the return value is an address, which is different from **NULL**. In program OUTNUM we have not tested the value returned by **fopen** because a file opened with **"w"** may or may not exist. (Opening a file for output may fail only in rather unlikely circumstances, such as with an existing file for which we have no permission to write to; if this can happen, it would, of course, be wise to include the test under discussion.) An attempt to open a file with **"r"** will fail if the file does not exist. As this is by no means a far-fetched possibility, it is wise to include a test on the value returned by **fopen** whenever this function is used to open a file for input: it would be a very serious error if a call to **fscanf** (or to **fprintf**) took place with **NULL** as its first argument. The conditional statement (consisting of four lines) immediately after opening the file *num.txt* in program INNUM will now be clear.

The return value of **fscanf** (like that of **scanf**) is equal to the number of data items that have been read and assigned to variables. In our example this value should be 1. If the attempt to read an integer fails, **fscanf** returns either 0 or **EOF**. The latter value is returned if we try to read beyond the end of the file. If we had excluded the possibility for the file to contain invalid characters, the line

```
while (fscanf(fp, "%d", &x) == 1) sum += x;
```

would have been sufficient to form the sum of all integers in the file. If there are, for example, ten integers in the file, the call to **fscanf** is executed 11 times, so we deliberately try to read beyond the end of the file. There is no risk of obtaining run-time error messages or similar problems. As soon as a call to **fscanf** is unsuccessful, this function no longer returns 1 and the while loop terminates. Then, in case of a correct input file, the return value of **fscanf** is **EOF**. (Note that it would not be correct to omit the three characters **== 1** in the above program line, because besides the alternative 0 there is also the possibility for **fscanf** to return **EOF**, which is normally equal to –1 and would therefore be interpreted as 'true' if used as a logical value.)

If we have to include the possibility of invalid characters, we can use **feof**, as we did in program INNUM. This is normally a macro (not a function) defined in *stdio.h*. If it were a function, it would be declared as follows:

```
int feof(FILE *fp);
```

The value returned by **feof** is 0 if the end of the file has not yet been reached and nonzero if it has. If we apply program INNUM to the file produced by program OUTNUM, the end of the file is reached; this means that **feof** returns a nonzero value and **!feof(fp)** is equal to 0. In this case the output is

```
The sum is: 55
```

It is instructive to apply a program editor (or a text processor) to the file *num.txt*, to verify that this file contains one column with the integers 1 to 10. Inserting a letter just after the fifth line, for example, and running program INNUM once again, will cause a failure in the attempt to read the sixth integer. In that case **feof(fp)** is 0, so **!feof(fp)** is 1, and the output is

```
The sum is: 15
Invalid character read.
```

As you may have noticed, we do not really need **feof** in program INNUM, because **fscanf**, when failing to read an integer, returns either **EOF** or 0. We could therefore also have used the following method:

```
int sum=0, x, code;
...
while ((code = fscanf(fp, "%d", &x)) == 1) sum += x;
printf("The sum is: %d\n", sum);
if (code != EOF) {printf("Invalid character read.\n");}
```

Reading and writing single characters

The constant **EOF** is also useful in programs that read one character at a time. Program COPYTEXT copies a text file in this way. The file names are supplied as program arguments, discussed in Section 5.10. For example, if we want to copy file *aaa* to file *bbb*, we can write

```
copytext aaa bbb
```

Note the difference with redirection: we do not write **<aaa** and **>bbb** here. Although we could use the functions **fscanf** and **fprintf** with format string **"%c"**, we prefer the elementary macros **getc** and **putc** in this case for reasons of efficiency. These macros are similar to **getchar** and **putchar**, but they take a file pointer as an (additional) argument. Note that with **putc** this argument is the second. For example, we can write

```
ch = getc(fp); putc(ch, fp);
```

Program COPYTEXT shows clearly how to test for the end of the file. We will discuss this subject in more detail after having a look at the complete program:

```
/* COPYTEXT: This program copies a text file.
            Usage: COPYTEXT source destination
*/

#include <stdio.h>
#include <stdlib.h>

int main(int argc, char *argv[])
{   int ch;
    FILE *fpin, *fpout;
    if (argc != 3)
    {   printf("Type COPYTEXT, "
        "followed by a source and a destination.\n");
        exit(1);
    }
    fpin = fopen(argv[1], "r");
    fpout = fopen(argv[2], "w");
    if (fpin == NULL || fpout == NULL)
    {   printf("Can't read from %s or write to %s.\n",
                argv[1], argv[2]);
        exit(1);
    }
    while ((ch = getc(fpin)) != EOF) putc(ch, fpout);
    fclose(fpin); fclose(fpout);
    return 0;
}
```

The core of this program is the while-statement on the third line from the bottom. Repeatedly, a character **ch** is read by **getc** and written by **putc**. When the end of the input file is encountered, the call **getc(fpin)** fails and the value it returns is **EOF**. We have discussed in Section 8.1 why **ch** must have type **int** instead of type **char**.

Note that **getc**, like **getchar**, reads only one character, not an integer that may consist of several characters as type **int** might suggest. Another common misconception is the idea of EOF being a character actually read from the file. This is not the case. When **getc** returns EOF, this simply means that nothing could be read.

After using **getc** to read a character **ch** from the stream **fp**, we can undo this by writing

```
ungetc(ch, fp);
```

This statement puts **ch** back in the input buffer so it is read next time. We can do this for only one character, as with a buffer of length 1. For the sake of completeness it should be mentioned that both **putc** and **ungetc** return an **int** value, equal to the character **ch** in question or to EOF in case of an error.

Reading and writing a whole line

It is important to realize that after declaring, for example,

```
char str[100];
```

we cannot read a whole line by means of

```
code = fscanf(fp, "%s", str);
```

because, first, this statement would skip all leading white-space characters, and, second, it would stop reading as soon as it encountered a blank. Instead of **fscanf**, we can use the function **fgets**, which, together with a similar function for output, is declared in *stdio.h* as follows:

```
char *fgets(char *s, int n, FILE *fp);
int fputs(const char *s, FILE *fp);
```

The function **fgets** stops reading when **n**–1 characters have been read or when a newline character has been read, whichever happens first. In the latter case, the newline character is also stored in the array **s**; in both cases a null character is stored at the end. The function **fputs** does not write a newline character other than the one that may occur at the end of the array **s** (which is likely if this array has been filled by **fgets**.) The value returned by **fgets** is the address given as its first argument, unless the end of the file has been reached; in that case **fgets** returns NULL. The function **fputs** returns a nonnegative value in case of success or EOF if an error occurs.

In our example, we can now write, for example,

```
code = fgets(str, 80, fp);
```

The streams **stdin**, **stdout** and **stderr**

Three file pointers, also called *streams*, are immediately available, so we can use them without declaring them and without using **fopen** to assign values to them. They are

stdin	('standard input')	for the keyboard;
stdout	('standard output')	for the video display;
stderr	('standard error output')	for the video display.

We can now understand how the macros **getchar** and **putchar** are defined in *stdio.h*:

```
#define getchar() getc(stdin)
#define putchar(c) putc((c), stdout)
```

For example, the macro call

```
putchar(ch);
```

is expanded by the preprocessor with the following result:

```
putc((ch), stdout);
```

You may have noticed that we have not discussed a function (or macro) **ungetchar**, which would relate to **getchar** as **ungetc** relates to **getc**. Curiously enough, it is not available. However, this is not a serious problem, because we can write

```
ungetc(ch, stdin);
```

Another possibility is to define a macro **ungetchar** of our own:

```
#define ungetchar(c) ungetc((c), stdin)
```

Now that we are familiar with the standard streams **stdin** and **stdout**, we revert to the functions **fgets** and **fputs**, discussed a short while ago. Although at first sight these may seem to be generalized versions of the functions **gets** and **puts**, discussed in Section 5.7, there are some essential differences, not only because of their numbers of parameters but, less apparent and therefore more dangerous, in the way they deal with newline characters. You may find this confusing when using both kinds of functions at the same time. Fortunately, that is not necessary. Suppose you want to read a line from the keyboard and you prefer **fgets** to **gets**. Then you can simply write, for example,

```
fgets(str, 80, stdin);
```

In contrast to **gets**, this call to **fgets** stores a newline character, if read, in the array **str**. Analogously, you can use the following call to write the line stored in **str** (with a newline character stored at the end) to the video display by means of

```
fputs(str, stdout);
```

Rewinding a file

So far we have used *sequential access*: reading and writing was done in the way a magnetic tape is used; after opening a file we have used it either only for input or only for output. We will see in Section 8.6 that there is another way of using files, called *random access*. Here we mention two simple but useful ways of reading and writing, which, although still belonging to sequential I/O, offer some interesting new possibilities. First, we can close a file and open it again in the same program. This enables us, after having written data to a file, to go back to its beginning and read the data we have written ourselves. This method has the effect of 'rewinding' combined with switching from output to input mode. If this mode is to remain the same, we can rewind the stream **fp** more quickly as follows:

```
rewind(fp);
```

The append mode

Another extension to normal sequential access is the *append mode*, with **"a"** as the second argument of **fopen**. Suppose we want a program to implement a simple bulletin board: from time to time we want to add short messages to those that are already in the file *bulboard.txt*. If this file does not yet exist, it must be created. The following program can be used for this purpose:

```
// BULBOARD: This program adds a line, entered on the
//           keyboard, to the file bulboard.txt. This
//           file is created if it does not yet exist.
#include <stdio.h>

int main()
{  FILE *fp;
   char str[100];
   fp = fopen("bulboard.txt", "a");
   printf("Enter a one-line message:\n");
   fgets(str, 100, stdin);
   fputs(str, fp);
   fclose(fp);
   return 0;
}
```

8.5 'Binary Files'

The files discussed so far are so-called *text files*. They consist of variable-length lines of text and contain only characters. Examples of text files are C++ programs, as typed in by means of a program editor, and files with lines of numbers, such as, for example:

```
19 23
8
```

Not all files are used to store data in this way. For example, an object module, produced by a compiler, is a file which does not consist of characters and has no line structure. We call such files *binary* or *unformatted* files. Numbers, too, can be written to a file in the same (binary) format as they are stored in the computer's memory. For example, if we write the integer 19 in binary format to a file, it will not be represented by the two decimal digits 1 and 9 (possibly preceded by some blanks), but, if integers are two bytes long and each byte consists of eight bits, it is stored as the bit sequence

```
00000000 00010011
```

Note that a binary file consists of a sequence of bytes, as does a text file. Operating systems therefore normally do not distinguish between these two file types; we as users must make this distinction and remember which kind of type we are dealing with. We cannot simply print a binary file or load it with an editor as we do with text files.

To write data to binary files or to read data from them, we should add a **b** (short for binary) at the end of the second argument of **fopen**. Thus instead of **"r"**, **"w"**, **"a"**, or **"r+"**, **"w+"**, **"a+"**, to be discussed in the next section, we then write **"rb"**, **"wb"**, **"ab"**, **"r+b"**, **"w+b"**, and **"a+b"**. As said before, every file consists of a sequence of bytes. Assuming that, as usual, a byte consists of eight bits, we can store 256 distinct bit sequences in a byte. Now the essential difference between a binary file and a text file is the fact that in the former all these 256 bit configurations can occur, while with text files some of them may be reserved for special purposes. For example, with MS-DOS the value **0x1A** (or Ctrl-Z) in a text file will cause reading this file to terminate because it is interpreted as 'end of data'. In normal text files this value does not occur, but it may occur in binary files because the bytes in such files can be part of purely binary coded integers or floating-point numbers, which in principle can have all kinds of bit configurations. If we try to read a binary file as a text file, as, for example, program COPYTEXT in the last section would do, the occurrence of byte value **0x1A** would be used as an 'end of data' signal, which is most undesirable. This problem will not occur if we use the letter **b** in the second argument of **fopen**, as in

```
fp = fopen("binfile", "rb");
```

There is another problem, associated with going to the beginning of a new line. With MS-DOS, for example, this is achieved by using a combination of two characters:

Carriage Return =   **0x0D**   =   13
Line Feed   =   **0x0A**   =   10

As programmers, however, we use only one character, **'\n'** (= 0x0A = 10), to go to the beginning of a new line. Therefore, when our C program is writing this 'newline character', as we call it, actually the two byte values just mentioned are placed in the file, which is an exception to the rule that each character written by our program corresponds to one byte. Normally we do not have to bother about this phenomenon, because exactly its opposite occurs when we are reading from a text file: the two byte values 13 and 10 are read by, for example, a single call to **getc**, and the return value is **'\n'**. All this is the case if **"w"** and **"r"** are used as the second argument of **fopen**. On the other hand, if we use **"wb"** instead of **"w"**, every call to **putc** writes only one byte, and, analogously, after using **"rb"** every call to **getc** reads only one byte. In Section 8.6, when discussing random access, we will read and write data items by specifying their exact positions in files. It will be clear that this can reasonably be done only if we can determine these positions in a transparent and reliable way, so with random access we will consistently use binary files.

Now that we know the effect of **"rb"** and **"wb"**, we can use these strings not only for binary files, but also for text files, provided that we use two calls to **getc** and to **putc**, respectively, for each transition to a new line. We can now see that it makes sense to distinguish between text and binary *modes*, rather than between text and binary *files*: we can open *any* file in text mode with **"r"** and **"w"**, and in binary mode with **"rb"** and **"wb"**. Recall that it is not safe to use program COPYTEXT of Section 8.4 for binary files because of possible occurrences of byte values **0x1A** (= Ctrl-Z), which might be seen as 'end of data'. We only have to replace **"r"** with **"rb"** and **"w"** with **"wb"** to remedy this. These corrections are really advantageous, for although they make the program suitable for binary files, they do not affect its usefulness for text files! If the program counted how many bytes are copied, this count might be higher in the corrected program than in the original one, because of the different ways of dealing with newline characters.

The functions fread and fwrite

Now that we know how to read (and copy) a given binary file, we will see how we can generate such files ourselves. Remember that data have the same format in binary files as in memory. For example, assuming that integers take two bytes, we know that after

```
int i=257;     // or:  int i=0x0101;
```

the two bytes that represent **i** contain the following bit sequence:

```
0000 0001 0000 0001
```

If we now use, for example,

```
fprintf(fp, "%5d", i);
```

then five bytes (two blanks and the digits 2, 5, and 7) are written to the file with file pointer **fp**. For some applications, the conversion from the given two bytes to those five bytes is by no means necessary: it would then be simpler and more efficient to write the two bytes that represent **i** without any alterations. This can be done as follows:

```
fwrite(&i, sizeof(int), 1, fp);
```

When we want to read these two bytes later, we use the analogous statement

```
fread(&i, sizeof(int), 1, fp);
```

The four arguments of **fwrite** and **fread** are, in this order:

1. The start address of the memory area that contains the data to be written by **fwrite** or of the area that is to contain the data read by **fread**.

2. The number of bytes needed for each of the data elements that are written or read (see also the next point).

3. The number of data elements (such as integers, float-values, and so on) to be written or read.

4. The file pointer that identifies the file.

In the above examples, only one integer is written or read, and its size can best be given by means of the operator **sizeof**, discussed in Section 2.2. Instead of only one integer, we can write or read quite large amounts of data, as, for example, in

```
struct complicated { ... } table[1000];
...
fwrite(table, sizeof(complicated), 1000, fp);
```

The value returned by **fwrite** and **fread** is equal to the number of data elements that have been written or read. If nothing can be written or read, these functions return the value 0.

We must realize that **fwrite** and **fread**, though efficient, deprive us of the possibility of using a normal editor or a printer to see what data the files in question contain. If we want this possibility very much, we may decide to use **fprintf** and **fscanf** (and text files) rather than **fwrite** and **fread** (and binary files) for this reason, especially if the consequent loss of efficiency is not serious. However, there is an important class of applications that require using **fwrite** and **fread** for a reason other than efficiency, as the next section shows.

8.6 Random Access

We use the term *random access*, also known as *direct access*, if we are reading or writing data somewhere in the middle of a file, at a given position, without any restriction. With the opposite, sequential access, we always begin by reading or writing at the beginning of the file, then read or write the next data element, and so on. Besides using random access, we can also open a file in such a way that we can both read and write, which gives us the possibility of *updating* a file. For the latter, we must insert a plus sign in the second argument of **fopen**. It is highly recommended to use random access only in connection with binary files, so that, in that argument, we also use the letter **b**, which must be placed at the end. The following new strings, used as the second argument of **fopen**, open a file for update in binary mode:

"r+b"   Open an *existing* file for update: both reading and writing will be possible.
"w+b"   Create a *new* file for update: after writing data to it we can read these data from the file. If the file already exists, its old contents are lost.
"a+b"   Open a file for *append* and update: additional data can be written at the end of the file and then read and updated.

(If your operating system regards text mode and binary mode as identical, as is the case with UNIX, the letter **b** in these strings is not strictly necessary, but still recommended for reasons of portability.)

The bytes of a file are numbered 0, 1, 2, ... (so the third byte has number 2). We identify a byte position by means of the function **fseek**, which together with **ftell**, is declared in *stdio.h* as follows:

```
int fseek (FILE *fp, long offset, int fromwhere);
long ftell(FILE *fp);
```

The argument **fromwhere** is a code with 0, 1, and 2 as possible values. We may write them as symbolic constants, defined in *stdio.h* as shown below:

Name	Value	Meaning
SEEK_SET	0	Count from the beginning of the file
SEEK_CUR	1	Count from the current position
SEEK_END	2	Count from the end

In most cases we use SEEK_SET (or 0); in that case, **offset** is the absolute byte number (0L for the first byte, 1L for the second, and so on). When using SEEK_END, only negative **offset** values can identify existing bytes in the file.

The value returned by **fseek** is zero, unless something is wrong: it is nonzero in case of an error. We can therefore write

```
if (fseek(fp, position, SEEK_SET))
{  printf("Error in call to fseek");
   exit(1);
}
```

The function **ftell** returns the *current position*. Program LENGTH shows that we can use this function to determine the length of a file:

```
// LENGTH: This program determines the length of a file.

#include <stdio.h>

int main()
{  FILE *fp;
   char filename[51];
   printf("File name: "); scanf("%50s", filename);
   fp = fopen(filename, "r+b");
   if (fp != NULL)
   {  fseek(fp, 0L, SEEK_END);
      printf("Length: %ld bytes.\n", ftell(fp));
      fclose(fp);
   } else printf("File cannot be opened.\n");
   return 0;
}
```

This program illustrates that **0L** as the second argument of **fseek** (with **SEEK_END** as its third argument) corresponds to the position immediately after the final byte of the file. For example, with a file of five bytes the situation is as follows:

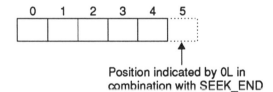

Position indicated by 0L in combination with SEEK_END

Since we count from 0, the number 5 denotes both the first position after the end of the file and the number of bytes in the file.

Note that program LENGTH does not read from or write to the file in question. Therefore the characters + and **b** in the second argument of **fopen** are not essential: with **"rb"**, **"r+"**, or **"r"** instead of **"r+b"** the program works equally well. If we use the letter **a** instead of **r**, the program still behaves in the same way for *existing* files. However, if no file with the given name exists, the letter **a** causes a new file (with length 0) to be created, while in that case the letter **r** leads to the message:

```
File cannot be opened.
```

Using the letter **w** instead of **r** or **a** is much worse, because in this case the program, when applied to an existing file, will destroy this.

A file-update example

Using **fseek** is more interesting if we really want to read and write. Let us use a very simple example. A club has members each of whom has a member number. These numbers are relatively small, so we can use them as record numbers in a file. Remember that *structures*, as used in C and C++, are often called *records*. A member's record will only contain his or her name and year of birth. (In a real situation it is most likely that there will be other data as well, such as the member's address. Adding such additional items here would not make the example more interesting for our purpose.) Each name will be stored in an array of 40 elements. When a member leaves the club, his or her number becomes available for a new member who may join the club. Program MEMBERS can be used to create and maintain a file with member records. The member numbers are used to locate the records and therefore need not be stored: we use the (binary) file *club.bin* like an array, with member numbers corresponding to subscript values. Some more explanation follows after the program, which can be used both to create and to update the file *club.bin*:

```
/* MEMBERS: With a given member number, the member's name and
            year of birth can be entered to create or update
            the file 'club.bin'.
*/
#include <stdio.h>
#include <stdlib.h>
#include <string.h>
#include <ctype.h>

void file_error(void)
{  printf("There is a problem with the file 'club.bin'.\n");
   exit(1);
}

int main()
{  FILE *fp;
   int nr, code;
   long pos, filelength, i;
   char answer;
   struct rec {char name[40]; int year;} r;
   fp = fopen("club.bin", "r+b");
   if (fp == NULL) fp = fopen("club.bin", "w+b");
   if (fp == NULL) file_error();

   for ( ; ; )
   {  printf("\nMember number (or STOP): ");
      if (scanf("%d", &nr) < 1 || nr < 0) break;
      pos = (long)nr * sizeof(rec);
      if (fseek(fp, 0L, SEEK_END)) file_error();
      filelength = ftell(fp);
```

```
            for (i=filelength; i<pos+sizeof(rec); i++)
               code = putc('\0', fp);
            if (code == EOF) file_error();
            if (fseek(fp, pos, SEEK_SET)) file_error();
            if (fread(&r, sizeof(rec), 1, fp) != 1)
               file_error();
            if (r.name[0] == '\0') answer = 'Y'; else
            {  printf(
                  "Name: %s   Year of birth: %d\n", r.name, r.year);
               printf("Update? Y/N): ");
               scanf(" %c", &answer);
               answer = toupper(answer);
                  // To upper case, see Section 12.2
            }
            if (answer == 'Y')
            {  printf("Name and year of birth (or 0 0): ");
               scanf("%s %d", r.name, &r.year);
               if (r.name[0] == '0') r.name[0] = '\0';
               if (fseek(fp, pos, SEEK_SET)) file_error();
               if (fwrite(&r, sizeof(rec), 1, fp) != 1)
                  file_error();
            }
         }
         fclose(fp);
         return 0;
      }
```

Program MEMBERS is not *robust*, that is, there are not enough checks in it to make it react satisfactorily to incorrect input data. In practice, such checks are highly desirable, but improving the program in this respect is more difficult than you may expect. It would also make the program more difficult to understand and therefore obscure the subject we are discussing. It is more comprehensible in its present form, especially in connection with the following demonstration:

```
Member number (or STOP): 123
Name and year of birth (or 0 0): Smith 1961

Member number (or STOP): 419
Name and year of birth (or 0 0): Johnson 1965

Member number (or STOP): 87
Name and year of birth (or 0 0): Williams 1963

Member number (or STOP): 419
Name: Johnson   Year of birth: 1965
Update? Y/N): y
Name and year of birth (or 0 0): Shaw 1959
```

```
Member number (or STOP): 419
Name: Shaw    Year of birth: 1959
Update? Y/N): n

Member number (or STOP): stop
```

As mentioned before, random file access is similar to using arrays. Instead of writing an expression between square brackets, we use **fseek**. The second argument of this function is a byte number derived from the record number. Program MEMBERS first tries to open the file *club.bin* for input. If this file does not yet exist, this attempt fails. In many other programs, we would in that case print an error message and terminate program execution, but here we once again try to open the file, but this time for output. Although it is very unlikely for this attempt to fail as well, a test has again been included. When the user, as requested, enters a member number, this is examined to see if it is small enough to be used as the number of an existing record. For example, if the maximum record number used so far is 10, a given new member number 20 cannot immediately be used as a basis for the second argument of **fseek**, but we must first extend the file. The latter is done here by means of a for-statement, in which **putc** adds a sufficient number of null characters at the end of the file. On the other hand, if the given record number is small enough to correspond to a record inside the file, **putc** is not called. Note that such an extension is only possible with a file, not with an array. (As discussed in Section 5.6, we can use a pointer instead of an array and extend the 'array length' by means of **realloc**, but this may involve much copying work, which is not the case when we are extending a file!).

Perhaps the most important point that should be noted in program MEMBERS is that a file is updated by calling **fseek** twice, namely just before calling each of the functions **fread** and **fwrite**. Omitting many details, we can write the simplified program structure as follows:

```
for (...)
{  ...                            // Compute position.
   fseek(fp, pos, SEEK_SET);      // Set file position.
   fread(&r, sizeof(rec), 1, fp); // Read record.
   ...                            // Update record in memory.
   fseek(fp, pos, SEEK_SET);      // Set file position.
   fwrite(&r, sizeof(rec), 1, fp);// Write record.
}
```

Even if program MEMBERS were extended with appropriate tests for the correctness of its input data, it is not likely to be a practical program, because it is more convenient for a club administration to use member names than member numbers as 'keys'. One way of doing this, with names as a basis for computing the positions where records are to be stored, is by using a method called *hashing*. This method is explained by means of C program text in *Programs and Data Structures in C*, listed in the Bibliography.

Exercises

In each of the following exercises, the names of the files involved are to be read from the keyboard after an appropriate request from your program. The exercises are formulated in a slightly abbreviated form. For example, *Print xxx* should actually be read as *Write a program that prints xxx*.

8.1 Print the longest line of a given text file.

8.2 A given text file contains only words, separated by white-space characters. Read a positive integer n from the keyboard. Count how many distinct words there are in the file, unless there are more than n. In the latter case, just print the text *Limit exceeded*. (Do not confuse the number of distinct words with the total number of words in the file; the latter number may be greater than n.)

8.3 The text of a given file has been typed by someone with little typing experience: comma characters in the file may not be followed by a blank. Copy the file to a corrected version in which each comma is followed by a blank. (If there is already a blank after a comma, you must not insert another one.)

8.4 Two text files are given, each of which contains a sequence of integers in increasing order. Merge these files to obtain an output file in which all numbers read from the original files occur in increasing order.

8.5 As 8.4, but with words in alphabetic order instead of integers in increasing order.

8.6 Examine if there is a file with a name read from the keyboard. If not, create such a file and write n zeros to it, where n is also read from the keyboard. If the file already exists, repeatedly read an integer k (less than n) from the keyboard to update the integer in position k in the file, according to directions given by the user. After reading the integer in the kth position, print it, and give the user the opportunity to replace it with another integer. The positions are numbered from 0. Use binary I/O and random access.

8.7 A text file contains records, each consisting of a name of at most 25 characters and an integer. Read this text file to build a binary file with the same records in alphabetic order of the names. After this, print the contents of the binary file.

9

Stream I/O

9.1 Streams

The input and output facilities proposed by B. Stroustrup, the designer of C++, are very different from standard I/O, discussed in the preceding chapter. A complication is that *stream I/O*, which is the usual term for these facilities, has been subject to rather drastic changes.

This chapter is based on declarations in *iostream.h*, which we include by writing

```
#include <iostream.h>
```

This line causes the shift operators >> and << (discussed in Section 3.3), to be overloaded for input and output operations. With these operators used for the latter purposes (not related to shift operations), we call their first operands *streams*. We use streams to indicate where input data is to be found and where output data is to be written. There are four standard streams, which are immediately available:

cin	The standard input stream.
cout	The standard output stream.
cerr	The standard error output stream, to be used for error messages.
clog	A buffered version of **cerr**, more suitable for large amounts of error messages.

The advantage of **cerr** over **clog** is that output buffers are flushed each time **cerr** is used, so that the output is sooner available on the external device (which, by default, is the video screen). On the other hand, with large amounts of messages, the buffered version **clog** is more efficient.

The type of **cin** is a class, called **istream**. Similarly, the streams **cout**, **cerr**, and **clog** have type **ostream**. Both **istream** and **ostream** are declared in the header file *iostream.h* as derived classes of another class, **ios**, also declared in this header file. As we know, this means that all members of **ios** are also members of **istream** and **ostream**.

9.2 Output

We will discuss output (also called *insertion*) by using the well-known stream **cout** as an example. Since all facilities for **cout** are also available for other output streams, including those created by ourselves, everything dealt with here is also relevant to file output, to be discussed in Section 9.4.

The standard left-shift operator, <<, is overloaded: if its left operand has type **ostream**, it denotes an output operation instead of 'shift left'. In this case, its precise meaning also depends on its right operand. As discussed in Section 3.5, the << operator is left-associative. For example, if both the value of variable **ch** and an equal sign are to be 'printed', we can write

```
cout << ch << '='
```

which means

```
(cout << ch) << '='
```

In Section 6.8, we saw that

```
s = u + v;
```

where **s**, **u** and **v** are class objects, is simply a convenient notation for

```
s = u.operator+(v);
```

Analogously, the expression

```
cout << ch
```

can be written as

```
cout.operator<<(ch)
```

Although the latter is rather cumbersome to write, it shows very clearly that **operator<<** is a member function of class **ostream** (which is the type of **cout**). The return value of this function is a reference to the object (**cout**) written in front of the dot. It follows that the type of **cout << ch** is the same as that of **cout**, namely **ostream**. This explains that the expression **cout << ch** can be followed by <<. It is very fortunate that the compact operator notation can be used instead of a function call, for otherwise we would have to use the statement

```
(cout.operator<<(ch)).operator<<('=');
```

instead of simply

```
cout << ch << '=';
```

Precedence of the << operator

To avoid incomprehensible error messages or incorrect results, we must bear in mind that << is an operator with a given precedence. Since the arithmetic operators have higher precedence than <<, we can write, for example,

```
cout << i + j << ' ' << i - j;
```

However, as we have seen in Section 3.6, there are many operators whose precedence is lower than that of <<. We must therefore not forget to use parentheses in statements such as

```
cout << (a < b);
cout << (code & mask);
cout << (a < b ? a : b);
```

Built-in inserter types

The type of *expression* in

```
cout << expression
```

is called an *inserter type*, because it determines which of all the << operator functions is actually to be used to 'insert' the value of *expression* in the output stream. For example, if this type is **char**, the << operator that is actually used is the **char** *inserter*; if this type is **int**, another << operator is used, namely the **int** inserter, and so on. In general, if the above *expression* has type **T**, the << operator used here is the **T** inserter, and **T** is the inserter type. The following built-in inserter types are supported:

char (**signed** and **unsigned**)
short (**signed** and **unsigned**)
int (**signed** and **unsigned**)
long (**signed** and **unsigned**)
const char*
float
double
long double
void* (displays an address in hexadecimal form)

After the declarations

```
int i;
long l;
double d;
```

the stream-I/O statements

```
cout << i;
cout << l;
cout << d;
```

give the same results as the following standard-I/O statements:

```
printf("%d", i);
printf("%ld", l);
printf("%g", d);
```

Besides the << operator, there are also some more primitive output facilities in the form of the **ostream** member functions **put** and **write**. If we want to output only one character, say, stored in the variable **ch**, we can write

```
cout.put(ch);
```

instead of

```
cout << ch;
```

Note that this **put** function is similar to the **putchar** macro in standard I/O. Another rather low-level stream output function is **write**, which corresponds to the **write** function of standard I/O. With a given address **a** (which may be the name of an array), we can use

```
cout.write(a, n)
```

to write **n** consecutive bytes, starting at address **a**. With this **write** function, zero bytes do not act as string terminators. This **write** function will actually be more useful for output to files on disk than for screen output. Rather than in connection with **cout**, it will be used with similar stream objects for files, as we will see in Section 9.4.

Manipulators for output

When we are using <<, normally as many positions are used as are needed to represent value of the right-hand operand. For example, with **i** = 7, the output produced by

```
cout << i;
```

takes only one position, while it would take four positions with $i = 8243$. When printing a table, we normally want columns with right-aligned numbers. This can be done by using a so-called *manipulator*, **setw**. For example, we can write

```
#include <iostream.h>
#include <iomanip.h>
...
i = 10;
cout << setw(3) << i << setw(7) << i * i * i;
```

to print i in three and i^3 in seven positions. In this example the output would be

```
b10bbb1000
```

where each *b* denotes a space character. If the width given by **setw** is too small to accommodate the output data, as many positions are used as are required. In other words, the minimum number of positions are used with the default width 0. For example, the output of

```
cout << setw(3) << 12345;
```

will be

```
12345
```

and it would not make any difference if, instead of **3**, we wrote **0, 1, 2, 4** or **5** as an argument of **setw**, or if we simply omitted **setw(3) <<**.

To use manipulators with parameters, as we did with **setw**, we must use the header file *iomanip.h* in addition to *iostream.h*. After we have used a manipulator to output an item, the default width 0 is restored.

Besides **setw**, there are some more manipulators. Here is a list of manipulators that we can use for output:

setw(n)	Set field width to **n**
setfill(ch)	Set fill character to **ch**
dec	Use decimal conversion (default)
hex	Use hexadecimal conversion
oct	Use octal conversion
endl	Insert newline (can be used instead of '\n')
ends	Insert null character (to terminate a string)
flush	Flush output stream (output of data from buffer)
setbase(n)	Set conversion base to **n** (8, 10, 16)
setprecision(n)	Set floating-point precision to **n** digits
setiosflags(l)	Set format bits specified by the **long** argument **l**
resetiosflags(l)	Reset format bits specified by the **long** argument **l**

Only for manipulators that have parameters do we have to use the header file *iomanip.h*. The manipulators **dec**, **hex**, **oct**, and **setbase(n)** change the conversion base and leave it changed. For example, the following statement prints both i and j in hexadecimal form:

```
cout << hex << i << ' ' << j;
```

The manipulator **setiosflags** enables us to specify all kinds of formatting requirements by setting certain bits, called *format state flags*, in its argument l. Fortunately, we can do this by using names that are easy to remember. In the class **ios**, the format states are declared as follows:

```
public:
enum
{   skipws     = 0x0001, // Skip white-space on input
    left       = 0x0002, // Left-adjust output
    right      = 0x0004, // Right-adjust output
    internal   = 0x0008, // Pad after sign or base indicator
    dec        = 0x0010, // Decimal conversion
    oct        = 0x0020, // Octal conversion
    hex        = 0x0040, // Hexadecimal conversion
    showbase   = 0x0080, // Show base indicator
    showpoint  = 0x0100, // Show decimal point (floating)
    uppercase  = 0x0200, // Upper case hexadecimal output
    showpos    = 0x0400, // Show '+' with positive integers
    scientific = 0x0800, // Scientific notation, e.g.1.2345e2
    fixed      = 0x1000, // Fixed point, e.g. 123.45
    unitbuf    = 0x2000, // Flush all streams after insertion
    stdio      = 0x4000, // Flush stdout and stderr after
                         // insertion
}
```

Since each of these states is coded in a bit of its own, we can combine several of them, using the bitwise-OR operator |. Class **ios** is declared in the header file *iostream.h*, so we can immediately use the above enumeration constants, provided that we write **ios::** in front of them. The latter is essential; an identifier such as **fixed** would otherwise be unknown. We can now use the same name for other purposes: if we define a variable **fixed** there will be no confusion with **ios::fixed**.

Aligning floating-point numbers in tables

In Section 2.5 we used standard I/O in program TABLE. Here is an equivalent program, based on stream I/O and manipulators:

```
// TABLE1: A table with numbers properly aligned.

#include <iostream.h>
#include <iomanip.h>

int main()
{   cout << " x           f(x)\n\n"
         << setiosflags(ios::fixed) ;
    for (int i=20; i<=40; i+=2)
    {   double x = i/10.0;
        cout << setw(3) << setprecision(1)
             << x << " "
             << setw(15) << setprecision(10)
             << (x*x + x + 1/x) << endl;
    }
    return 0;
}
```

As in Section 2.5, the output of this program is as shown below:

```
 x          f(x)

2.0     6.5000000000
2.2     7.4945454545
2.4     8.5766666667
2.6     9.7446153846
2.8    10.9971428571
3.0    12.3333333333
3.2    13.7525000000
3.4    15.2541176471
3.6    16.8377777778
3.8    18.5031578947
4.0    20.2500000000
```

To prevent this table from looking like

```
 x          f(x)

 2               6.5
 2        7.494545455
...           ...
```

the following use of **setiosflags** in program TABLE1 is essential:

```
setiosflags(ios::fixed)
```

The setf function

Instead of using the **setiosflags** manipulator, we can use the **setf** member function of class **ostream** to specify **ios::fixed**. This is hardly an advantage, but let us nevertheless briefly discuss **setf** for the sake of completeness. If we wanted to use **setf** in program TABLE1, we would replace

```
cout << " x              f(x)\n\n"
      << setiosflags(ios::fixed) ;
```

occurring just before the for-loop, with

```
cout << " x              f(x)\n\n";
cout.setf(ios::fixed, ios::floatfield);
```

What we can write as the first argument of **setf** depends on the second, as shown below:

Possible first arguments of setf	*Second argument*
`ios::fixed, ios::scientific`	`ios::floatfield`
`ios::dec, ios::doc, ios::hex`	`ios::basefield`
`ios::left, ios::right, ios::internal`	`ios::adjustfield`

We could also have used the two lines

```
cout.setf(ios::dec, ios::basefield);
cout.setf(ios::right, ios::adjustfield);
```

in program TABLE1, but they are superfluous because decimal base and right adjustment are used by default.

Another example of using manipulators

Manipulators are easy to use and in most cases we prefer them to the **setf** function. We should bear in mind that the **setw** manipulator affects only the immediately following output operations. By contrast, the settings specified by the manipulators **precision**, **setfill, dec, hex, oct, setbase, setiosflags** and **resetiosflags** remain in effect until further notice. Let us use the following table as an example:

Left justified		Right justified		Hexa- decimal	
5	125	5	125	0X5	0X7D
6	216	6	216	0X6	0XD8
7	343	7	343	0X7	0X157
8	512	8	512	0X8	0X200
9	729	9	729	0X9	0X2D9
10	1000	10	1000	0XA	0X3E8

This table was produced by the following program:

```
// MANIP: A demonstration of some manipulators.

#include <iostream.h>
#include <iomanip.h>

int main()
{   cout << endl
         << setiosflags(ios::showbase | ios::uppercase)
         << "Left            Right        Hexa-\n"
         << "justified     justified        decimal\n";
    for (int i=5; i<=10; i++)
    {   cout << dec << setiosflags(ios::left)
             << setw(5) << i << setw(8) << i * i * i

             << setiosflags(ios::right)
             << setw(2) << i << setw(8) << i * i * i

             << hex << setw(8) << i
             << setw(8) <<    i * i * i << endl;
    }
    return 0;
}
```

Note that we have to use **setw(8)** three times after **setw(2)**, to make each of the last three columns of the table appear in eight positions. By contrast, we need not repeat the **hex** manipulator for the last column of our table because we used it for the second last column so it is still in effect. This program also illustrates the use of the bitwise OR operator in this line of the **main** function:

```
<< setiosflags(ios::showbase | ios::uppercase)
```

For example, the very last number of this table is displayed as **0X3E8** (being the value 1000 in hexadecimal representation). If we had omitted the above program line, we would have obtained **3E8** instead. If we had only omitted | **ios::uppercase**, we would have obtained **0x3e8**.

Alignment of strings in tables

We have demonstrated the alignment of strings in tables in program ALIGN2, at the end of Section 5.7. In that program, left alignment of a column of strings is realized by **setiosflags(ios::left)** and this is followed by **resetiosflags(ios::left)** for the subsequent right alignment of a column of numbers.

Writing our own manipulators

We can define manipulators ourselves. This is very simple for manipulators that have no parameters: all we have to do is to write a function that has a 'reference to **ostream**' parameter and returns a similar result. This parameter, say **s**, is then used in the function for the desired output operation, which has the form

```
s << ...
```

and this whole expression provides the reference to an **ostream** that our manipulator function is to return, as program MYMANIP demonstrates:

```
// MYMANIP: A manipulator defined by ourselves.

#include <iostream.h>

ostream &mymanip(ostream &s)
{  static int count; // Initialized to 0.
   return s << "count = " << ++count << ' ';
}

int main()
{  cout << "This is output of my own manipulator:" << endl
        << mymanip << "(first time)\n"
        << mymanip << "(second time)\n";
   return 0;
}
```

In this demonstration program, the manipulator **mymanip** simply counts how often it is used and prints the count value. This gives the following output:

```
This is output of my own manipulator:
count = 1 (first time)
count = 2 (second time)
```

At first sight such a manipulator definition seems to be just another new language construct, to be learnt by heart rather than to be understood. However, this is not the case. Appendix C shows how this way of defining a manipulator fits into the C++ language.

So much for defining manipulators that do not take arguments. It is also possible to define manipulators that do, and again, no new language elements are required to accomplish this. The C++ class concept provides us with all the tools we need to define manipulators both with and without parameters. Since this subject is rather technical and possibly not essential for most C++ programmers, we will not discuss this subject here, but rather refer to Appendix C.

Inserters for user-defined types

So far, we have only used built-in inserter types, such as **char**, **int**, **float**, and so on. Everything we did with the << operator could also be done with the **printf** functions of standard I/O. We will now discuss an important advantage of << over **printf**, namely the possibility of applying << to types of our own by means of operator overloading. For example, with objects of type **vector** discussed in Chapter 6, we can overload the output operator <<, as shown in program USERINS:

```
// USERINS: A user-defined inserter
//          (for type 'vector').
#include <iostream.h>

class vector {
public:
   vector(float x=0, float y=0){xx = x; yy = y;}
   friend ostream &operator<<(ostream &s, vector &v);
private:
   float xx, yy;
};

ostream &operator<<(ostream &s, vector &v)
{  return s << "x = " << v.xx << "   y = " << v.yy << endl;
}

int main()
{  vector u(2, 4), v;
   cout << "u:   "; cout << u;
   cout << "v:   "; cout << v;
   return 0;
}
```

The most interesting statements in this program are **cout << u;** and **cout << v;** in the **main** function. They use our own operator <<, to output the vectors **u** and **v**. The output of this program is:

```
u:   x = 2   y = 4
v:   x = 0   y = 0
```

9.3 Input

The right-shift operator >> is overloaded in the header file *iostream.h*. If its first operand has type **istream** (also defined in this header file) its meaning is input, or, more technically, *extraction*. For example, if x has type **float**, the statement

```
cin >> x;
```

reads a numeric value from the standard input stream, which is usually the keyboard, and assigns it to x. This can be done because **cin** is declared in *iostream.h* as being of type **istream** and because there is a **float** *extractor* **>>**. The type of the expression that follows **>>** is the *extractor type*. The expression **cin >> x** (deliberately written without a semicolon) yields a reference to the **istream** object **cin**, so that it can in turn be used as the first operand of a **>>** operator, as in

```
(cin >> x) >> y
```

and so on. Since **>>** is left associative, the parentheses in this expression are superfluous and are therefore usually omitted.

When we are using **>>** for built-in types, any leading white-space characters are skipped. As for reading exactly one character, whether it is white-space or not, this can be done by means of a **get** member function:

```
char ch;
cin.get(ch);
```

In many applications we want to read one character in a loop until some terminating character is read. As we get one character too many in this way, there is a need for 'putting it back' into the input stream. This can be done by writing, for example,

```
cin.putback(ch);
```

Class **istream** also has another **get** member function to read strings. For example, if we have a **char** array **str** with at least 40 elements, we can write

```
cin.get(str, 40);
```

This call reads at most 39 characters, which are placed into **str**, followed by a null character. We can also use a third argument, of type **char**, which has '\n' as its default value. It indicates that reading characters is to terminate as soon as this character (given as the third argument or '\n' otherwise) has been read, that is, if this happens before 39 characters have been read. The terminating character, if found, is still available in the input stream, so it will be encountered when the next item is read.

The latter aspect is very inconvenient is we want to read several lines of text. For example, the fragment

```
cin.get(str1, 40);   // O.K.
cin.get(str2, 40);   // ???
```

is not practical. In the first statement, the terminating newline character is detected but not read. The second then immediately encounters it, so reading terminates as soon as it begins, and the empty string (consisting of '\0') is placed in **str2**. One way to solve this problem is by inserting

```
cin >> ws;    // Skip white-space characters.
```

between the above two calls. As we will see shortly, **ws** is a standard manipulator for input. It will be clear that this solution is not particularly elegant.

Fortunately, there is also the **istream** member function **getline**, which we have already briefly discussed in Section 5.7. The following fragment will be more useful than the similar one above:

```
cin.getline(str1, 40);   // O.K.
cin.getline(str2, 40);   // O.K.
```

As with **get**, a third argument can be supplied in case a terminating character other than '\n' is desired. Function **getline** not only *detects* but also *reads* the terminating character, so in a subsequent call to this input function it will be no longer in the way.

It is not necessary to use a terminating character. If we want to read exactly 40 bytes, irrespective of their values, and to store them into **str**, without appending a null character, we can use the **read** member function, to be discussed in Section 9.4:

```
cin.read(str, 40);
```

Built-in extractor types

The following built-in extractor types are supported:

char (**signed** and **unsigned**)
short (**signed** and **unsigned**)
int (**signed** and **unsigned**)
long (**signed** and **unsigned**)
char* (to read strings)
float
double
long double

In general, the format of numeric input data must be the same as that used in C++ programs, except for suffixes, as **L** and **F** in **123L** and **3.4F**, which must not be used. When reading strings, any leading white-space characters are skipped; the next non-white-space characters are read and stored until another white-space character is found. A final null character is then appended. The character that follows the final character of the input item (a number, a character, or a string) is still in the input buffer, so that it will be encountered in the next input operation.

Manipulators for input

There are several manipulators for input. The header file *manip.h* must be included for
any manipulator that has a parameter:

setw(n)	Set field width to **n**
ws	Skip any white-space characters
dec	Use decimal conversion (default)
hex	Use hexadecimal conversion
oct	Use octal conversion
setiosflags(l)	Set the format bits specified by the **long** argument l
resetiosflags(l)	Reset the format bits specified by the **long** argument l

As we have seen in Section 5.7, we can use the **setw** manipulator as follows:

```
char buf[40];
cin >> setw(40) >> buf;
```

In this way, reading terminates when 39 characters, followed by '\0', have been placed
in **buf**, unless a white-space character is encountered sooner. (Recall that, first, any
leading white-space characters are skipped and, second, any white-space character
terminates the process of reading normal characters.)

The **ws** manipulator 'eats' white-space characters. Recall that we have already
demonstrated it in our above discussion about the input functions **get** and **getline** for
strings.

The **dec**, **hex** and **oct** manipulators enable us to use not only decimal but also
hexadecimal and octal numbers as input.

Possible argument values of **setiosflags** and **resetiosflags** are the *format state flags*
discussed in Section 9.2. For example, we can write

```
cin >> resetiosflags(ios::skipws);
```

if we want to reset the flag for skipping white-space characters (which is set by
default). After this, using the **char** variable **ch**, we can write

```
cin >> ch;
```

to read exactly one character, which may be a white-space character. As we have seen,
this can also be done by means of the statement

```
cin.get(ch);
```

which does not skip any leading white-space characters.

Extractors for user-defined types

We can overload the operator >> for types defined by ourselves, in the same way as
for the operator <<. For example, if we are using type **vector**, declared as in Section 9.2,
we can define a **vector** *extractor* >> as follows:

```
istream &operator>>(istream& s, vector& u)
{   float x, y;
    s >> x >> y;
    u = vector(x, y);
    return s;
}
```

With this operator function, we can read a number pair by using >> only once, as in

```
vector v;
cin >> v;
```

9.4 File I/O

For input from and output to files on disk, we can use **ifstream** and **ofstream**, which
are derived classes with **istream** and **ostream** as their base classes, respectively, and
declared in the header file *fstream.h*. Figure 9.1 shows how the I/O classes discussed
in this chapter are related. The base class **ios** was mentioned in Section 9.1. Class
fstream, derived from **ifstream** and **ofstream**, will be discussed shortly.

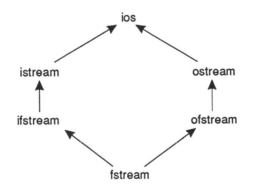

Figure 9.1. Classes for stream I/O

The class **ifstream** inherits the extraction operations from **istream**, while **ofstream** inherits the insertion operations from **ostream**. For example, the following program copies file *aa* to file *bb* and counts how many characters are copied:

```
// COPYAABB: This program copies characters from file aa to
//           file bb.
#include <fstream.h>
#include <stdlib.h>

int main()
{   char ch;
    int n=0;
    ifstream ff("aa", ios::nocreate); // See note below.
    if (!ff) {cout << "Cannot open aa for input\n"; exit(1);}
    ofstream gg("bb");
    if (!gg) {cout << "Cannot open bb for output\n"; exit(1);}
    while (gg && ff.get(ch)) {gg.put(ch); n++;}
    cout << n << " characters copied.\n";
    return 0;
}
```

The header file *iostream.h* is included in the header file *fstream.h*, so we need not include it ourselves if we include the latter file. The stream **ff** is opened and associated with file *aa* by defining it as an object of class **ifstream** in the above way, that is, by calling a constructor of this class. The second argument, **ios::nocreate**, is required with Microsoft Visual C++. With this compiler, omitting this argument would cause the creation of an empty file *aa* if this file did not already exist (even though the file is opened for input). Using **ios::nocreate** for input files may be superfluous with other C++ compilers, but it will not cause any problems. If file *aa* contains the contents

```
XYZ
PQR
```

with two newline characters, then after copying these contents to file *bb* the following line is displayed:

```
8 characters copied.
```

If you use MS-DOS, note that with this operating system a newline character is represented by two characters (carriage return and line feed), so the files *aa* and *bb* actually consist of 10 bytes, which you can verify with the DIR command. This way of dealing with newline characters applies to stream opened in the (default) *text mode*. By contrast, we can open streams in *binary mode,* as will be discussed shortly.

Note that the streams **ff** and **gg** are used after the operator **!** and before the operator **&&**, where we normally use expressions of type **int**, denoting truth values. This is possible because (a) there is a conversion function, similar to one discussed in

Section 6.10, which converts stream type to pointer type, and (b) pointers can be used as truth values, as we have seen in Section 5.6.

Opening and closing a stream

As follows from our discussion in Section 6.7, the declaration of a class variable, such as **ff** in

```
ifstream ff("aa", ios::nocreate);
```

invokes a constructor for the class **ifstream**. Since the principle of 'default arguments' is applied, we may omit a file name (*aa*) here, so that we can associate the stream **ff** with a file later by using the member function **open**. There is also a member function **close**, so we can close a stream and re-open it later:

```
ifstream ff;                       // No file opened yet.
...
ff.open("aa", ios::nocreate);  // Open file aa.
...
ff.close();                        // Close file aa.
...
ff.open("aaa", ios::nocreate); // Open file aaa.
```

As you will expect, the same facilities are available for the class **ofstream**. The second argument of **open**, the *open mode*, is optional. The default arguments are **ios::in** for **ifstream** and **ios::out** for **ofstream**. These modes and some others are defined in class **ios** as follows:

```
public:
enum open_mode
{   in       = 0x01, // Open for reading
    out      = 0x02, // Open for writing
    ate      = 0x04, // Seek to eof upon original open
    app      = 0x08, // Append mode: all additions at eof
    trunc    = 0x10, // Truncate file if already exists
    nocreate = 0x20, // Open fails if file doesn't exist
    noreplace= 0x40, // Open fails if file already exists
    binary   = 0x80  // Binary (not text) file
};
```

As these hexadecimal values show, each of the values **in**, ..., **binary** is represented by a bit of its own, so that we can apply the bitwise-OR operator | to them. For example, we can use the following lines if we want to open file *aa* in binary mode for both input and output with the proviso that the open operation must fail if the file does not already exist:

```
fstream ff;
ff.open("aa", ios::in | ios::out |
               ios::binary | ios::nocreate);
```

Stream **ff** has type **fstream**, which is a class derived from both **ifstream** and **ofstream**. Note the use of **ios::**. Because the symbolic constants **in**, **out**, and so on, are defined in class **ios**, there would be no conflict of names if we used the same names (without **ios::**) for other purposes in our program. Class **ios** is declared in *iostream.h*, which is implicitly made available by including *fstream.h*. Streams opened in binary mode, as **ff** in the above example, read byte by byte rather than character by character. If we used the binary mode in program COPYAABB (adding **ios::binary** as a second argument in the definition of both **ff** and **gg**) with the same input file *aa* as used in our example, the final value of the count variable **n** would be 10 instead of 8 (with MS-DOS, that is).

In the above fragment, the definition of **ff** and opening this stream are done separately. These two actions can be combined into one:

```
fstream ff("aa", ios::in | ios::out |
               ios::binary | ios::nocreate);
```

9.5 Random Access; Error States

The binary mode, introduced in the previous section, is especially useful in connection with *random access* to files. This is because we want to count bytes rather than characters, and, as we have seen, not every character corresponds to one byte. The **fstream** member functions to be used for random access are **seekg** for input and **seekp** for output. As the final letters of these function names indicate, we distinguish between a *get position* for input and a *put position* for output.

Suppose we open file *ff* as we did at the end of the previous section. Since this file is opened for both input and output, there is a 'get position' and a 'put position'. With *sequential access*, as used so far, these positions are initially at the beginning of the file and gradually move towards its end as we are using input and output operations, respectively. With *random access*, however, we can choose any position in the file as its current get position or put position. For example, the statement

```
f.seekg(i);
```

sets the current get position of stream **f** to **i**. This argument **i** has type **long** and is in fact a byte number, counting from 0 for the first byte of the file. There is a similar stream member function **seekp** for output. Alternatively, we can use another argument, which specifies the position relative to which we must count, using a **long** argument **offset**:

```
f.seekg(offset, ios::beg);
f.seekg(offset, ios::cur);
f.seekg(offset, ios::end);
```

For the first, the second and the third of these statements, an offset 0 refers to the beginning, the current position, and the end, respectively. With **ios::end**, real file positions are obtained by using negative **offset** values. Again, **seekg** is to be used for input. The function **seekp**, for output, can also have two arguments, with the same meaning.

There are also two member functions, **tellg** and **tellp**, to determine the current get and put positions. For example, we can write

```
long posget = f.tellg(), posput = f.tellp();
```

(If we like, we can use type **streampos** instead, which by means of **typedef** is declared as being equivalent to **long** in the header file *iostream.h*.)

Program UPDATE demonstrates the use of random access. It asks the user to enter a nonnegative (possibly long) integer n, which will be the number of **long int** values to be written in the file *info*. First, the values 0, 10, 20, ..., $10(n-1)$ are sequentially written to the file. If this file already exists, it is 'truncated', that is, its old contents are destroyed. Then the user is requested to enter another nonnegative (long) integer i, less than n. The ith stored value (counting from 0) is then displayed, and we are requested to enter an increment value, by which the displayed value will be increased. Before and after this updating action, the file contents are displayed, so that you can see what happens. Let us begin with a demonstration:

```
Demonstration of updating a binary file.
How many long ints are to be written? 4
0
10
20
30
Enter a nonnegative integer less than 4: 2
20
Enter increment: 7
0
10
27
30
```

In this case the integer position are numbered 0, 1, 2, 3, so entering 2 implies that the third integer, 20, is to be updated. With increment 7, its new value is 27. Program UPDATE contains some new elements, to be discussed shortly:

```cpp
// UPDATE: Updating a file by using random access.
#include <fstream.h>
#include <stdlib.h>
fstream f;

void display()
{  long x;
   f.seekg(0);
   for ( ; ; )
   {  f.read((char *)(&x), sizeof(x));
      if (f.eof()) break;
      cout << x << endl;
   }
   f.clear();
}

void check(int k)
{  if (! f.good())
   {  cout << "\nI/O error " << k << endl; exit(1);
   }
}

int main()
{  long n, i, x, incr;
   cout << "\n\nDemonstration of updating a binary file.\n";
   cout << "How many long ints are to be written? ";
   cin >> n;
   f.open("info", ios::in | ios::out | ios::binary |
                  ios::trunc); check(1);
   for (i=0; i<n; i++)
   {  x = 10 * i;
     f.write((char *)(&x), sizeof(x)); check(2);
   }
   display();
   do
   {  cout <<
      "Enter a nonnegative integer less than " << n << ": ";
      cin >> i;
   }  while (i < 0 || i >= n);
   f.seekg(i * sizeof(i), ios::beg);
   f.read((char *)(&x), sizeof(x)); check(3);
   cout << x << endl;
   cout << "Enter increment: "; cin >> incr;
   x += incr;
   f.seekp(i * sizeof(i), ios::beg);
   f.write((char *)(&x), sizeof(x)); check(4);
   display();
   return 0;
}
```

The stream member functions **read** and **write** are used for 'raw' (or 'binary') input and output: we use them if we want the internal and the external representation of data to be identical. These functions take two arguments: the begin address, which must be of type pointer-to-**char**, and the number of bytes to be read or written. Besides the actual input and output operations, some checks are performed, which we will discuss now.

Error states

In class **ios** (declared in *iostream.h*, which is included by *fstream.h*) there is a (protected) **state** member, the bits of which are called *status bits*. It can be consulted after I/O operations to check if these operations have been successful. For this purpose, the constants **ios::goodbit**, ..., **ios::hardfail**, defined as follows, can be useful:

```
public:
enum io_state
{   goodbit  = 0x00,    // No bit set: all is OK
    eofbit   = 0x01,    // At end of file
    failbit  = 0x02,    // Last I/O operation failed
    badbit   = 0x04,    // Invalid operation attempted
    hardfail = 0x80     // Unrecoverable error
};
```

One way to use these symbolic values is calling the member function **rdstate** to obtain the state, as, for example, in

```
f.write(str, n);
if (f.rdstate() == ios::hardfail)
{ ... // Unrecoverable I/O error
}
```

Instead, we can test the status bits by special member functions. These return an **int** value as specified below:

good( ) Returns nonzero if no error bits are set. Otherwise, it returns zero.

eof( ) Returns nonzero if **eofbit** is set. Otherwise, it returns zero.

fail( ) Returns nonzero if **failbit**, **badbit**, or **hardfail** is set. Otherwise, it returns zero.

bad( ) Returns nonzero if **badbit** or **hardfail** is set. Otherwise, it returns zero.

We can clear (or set) the error bits ourselves by calling the stream member function **clear**, declared as

```
void clear(int i=0);
```

Its argument, if present, will be assigned to the **state** member. Normally, we use this function to *clear* the error bits after we have found some of them to be set. Our program UPDATE calls the member functions **eof** and **clear** in the function **display**, at the top of the program. The member function **good** is called in our function **check**.

9.6 In-memory Format Conversion

When using standard I/O, the functions **sprintf** and **sscanf** are available for in-memory format conversion (see Section 5.11). Similar facilities are available with stream I/O. Suppose we have some numerical expression, say, x * x, and we want its value represented as a sequence of characters, in the same way as we would display it by writing

```
cout << x * x;
```

Instead of doing real output, we want the resulting text to appear in a string. Moreover, we want all formatting facilities, such as the **setw** and **setprecision** manipulators, to be available. The first part of program INMEMFC shows how this can be done. What we need is an object of type **ostrstream**, and we can use this in the same way as objects of type **ostream**. We also need to use the header file *strstream.h*, since class **ostrstream** is declared in this file.

```
// INMEMFC: In-memory format conversion.

#include <iostream.h>
#include <strstream.h>
#include <iomanip.h>
#include <string.h>

int main()
{   char str[80];
    float x = 2.5;
    // From binary to text (like sprintf):
    ostrstream oo(str, 80);
    oo << "Test:\n"                    // 6 characters
       << setfill('*') << setw(8)
       << setprecision(3) << x * x     // 8 characters
       << endl << ends;                // 1 character ('\n')
    cout << str << "Length: " << strlen(str) << endl;
    // 15 characters, followed by '\0': 16 positions used.

    // From text to binary (like sscanf):
    strcpy(str, "0.01234567 89");
```

```
        double y;
        int i;
        istrstream ii(str, 80);
        ii >> y >> i;
        cout << "\ny + i = " << setiosflags(ios::fixed)
             << setprecision(10) << y + i << endl;
        return 0;
    }
```

By writing

```
    ostrstream oo(str, 80);
```

we can use the object **oo** in the same way as **cout**, but the actual output is sent to the character array **str**, of length 80. The manipulator **ends** places a null character ('\0') at the end of the output string. The first three of the following output lines, produced by the program, show that a string of length 15, including two newline characters, is placed in array **str**:

```
    Test:
    ****6.25
    Length: 15

    y + i = 89.0123456700
```

So much for an alternative to **sprintf**.

As we know, it is the other way round with **sscanf**: we use it to read data from a character array into program variables. The stream solution to this problem, based on class **istrstream**, is also demonstrated by the second part of program INMEMFC and by the last line of the above output. With a character array **str**, containing data, we call the **istrstream** constructor in this way:

```
    istrstream ii(str, 80);
```

After doing this, we can use stream **ii** in the same way as we would use, say, **cin**. Instead of reading data from the keyboard, it is now read from array **str**.

Exercises

Solve the exercises given at the end of Chapter 8 by using the stream I/O facilities discussed in this chapter.

10

Standard Library Functions

Object modules, obtained by compiling source modules, can be grouped together in *libraries*, and we can instruct the *linker* to search these libraries. Most programmers do not *make* libraries but simply *use* them. It is not unusual for a C or C++ implementation to have a library with more than 500 functions. These include those which the American National Standards Institute (ANSI) has adopted as *standard library* functions for the C language. Since there are so many library functions, it is not always easy to find the one we need. Sometimes several candidates seem to be equally suitable to a particular problem. In such cases it is wise to look first in the standard library. Employing this library wherever possible increases program portability. This chapter lists this set of functions, along with some information about how to use them. They are available to both C and C++ programmers. Two aspects of the standard library are not discussed in this book: multi-byte characters and *locale* issues, which may be useful for those who use foreign languages such as Chinese.

The standard library functions are divided into groups; all functions that belong to the same group are declared in the same header file. Many of these functions have already been discussed in this book. They are also included in this chapter, often with references to previous sections. This chapter also includes many standard library functions that we have not discussed yet. Besides function declarations (or *function prototypes*), there is other useful information in the standard header files, such as macro definitions. Different C and C++ implementations need not have identical standard header files, but although the contents of these files may differ, they can be used in the same way. We will therefore focus on their use, not on their contents. The names of the standard header files, enclosed in angular brackets as used in our programs, are

```
<assert.h>   <ctype.h>    <errno.h>    <float.h>
<limits.h>   <math.h>     <setjmp.h>   <signal.h>
<stdarg.h>   <stddef.h>   <stdio.h>    <stdlib.h>
<string.h>   <time.h>
```

In our program modules, we may use **#include** lines for these header files in any order, and these lines may occur more than once.

This chapter may be useful as a reference. The header files just mentioned are therefore discussed in alphabetical order. To use a function or a macro, we want to know its number of arguments, their types, and the type of its return value. This information will be given in the form of function declarations, and this will be done even in case of macros.

10.1 Diagnostics: <assert.h>

`void assert(int expression);`

This is a macro. If *expression* is zero, an error message, such as

`Assertion failed:` *expression,* `file` *filename,* `line` *nnn*

appears, after which the program terminates execution. If **#define NDEBUG 1** occurs prior to **#include <assert.h>**, the call to **assert** is ignored.

10.2 Character Classification: <ctype.h>

In the following list, the declaration of each function is followed by a description of its return value:

`int isalnum(int ch);`   ≠ 0 (true) if **ch** is a letter or a digit (and 0 otherwise).
`int isalpha(int ch);`   ≠ 0 if **ch** is a letter.
`int iscntrl(int ch);`   ≠ 0 if **ch** is a control character.
`int isdigit(int ch);`   ≠ 0 if **ch** is a decimal digit.
`int isgraph(int ch);`   ≠ 0 if **ch** is a printable character, other than white-space.
`int islower(int ch);`   ≠ 0 if **ch** is a lower-case letter.
`int isprint(int ch);`   ≠ 0 if **ch** is a printable character, including a blank.
`int ispunct(int ch);`   ≠ 0 if **ch** is a printable character other than a letter, a digit, or a white-space character.
`int isspace(int ch);`   ≠ 0 if **ch** is a space, a form feed, a newline, a carriage return, a tab, or a vertical tab.
`int isupper(int ch);`   ≠ 0 if **ch** is an upper-case letter.
`int isxdigit(int ch);` ≠ 0 if **ch** is a hexadecimal digit.

There are also two functions to convert the case of letters:

`int tolower(int ch);`   The lower-case letter whose upper-case counterpart is **ch**. If **ch** is not an upper-case letter, the return value is **ch**.

`int toupper(int ch);`   The upper-case letter whose lower-case counterpart is **ch**. If **ch** is not an lower-case letter, the return value is **ch**.

For example, suppose that we want to convert **ch** if it denotes a lower-case letter; in that case we want its new value to be the corresponding upper-case letter. If **ch** does not denote a lower-case letter, it is not to be altered. We then write

```
ch = toupper(ch);
```

10.3 Error Numbers: <errno.h>

If we write

```
#include <errno.h>
```

in our program, then after an error occurs we can consult the value of the system variable **errno** to obtain more information about that error. Two symbolic constants are defined in *errno.h*:

EDOM   is assigned to **errno** in case of a domain error, as occurs, for example, if we try to compute **sqrt(–1)** (with **sqrt** declared in *math.h*).

ERANGE   is assigned to **errno** in case of a range error, as occurs, for example, if we try to compute **exp(1e8)**.

10.4 Floating-point Precision: <float.h>

We must be aware that the results of our computations may depend on our hardware. The header file *float.h* supplies us with detailed information about the floating-point arithmetic that is used. In this section the names that we use for this purpose are listed, together with their meaning, and, between parentheses, the minimum or maximum values considered acceptable by ANSI. To explain some new notions, we will first briefly discuss some fundamentals of the floating-point representation of numbers. Note that our discussion is only about principles: the floating-point format actually used on your machine may be slightly different from what is discussed below.
A real number x can be approximated by

$$x \approx m \times 2^n$$

where n is integer, and m satisfies the following condition to *normalize* the representation:

$0.5 \leq |m| < 1$ or $m = 0$ (in the latter case, we also have $n = 0$)

We call m the *mantissa* and n the *exponent* of the floating-point representation (m, n). Instead of 2, a different base, say, b, may be raised to the power n (in which case the number 0.5 in the normalization condition is replaced with $1/b$). This base is also known as the *radix* of the floating-point representation. The normalization condition makes the representation of x by the pair (m, n) unique (except for round-off errors). For example, with $x = 9/4$, we have

$$m = 9/16, \quad n = 2$$

Instead of x, both its (approximated) mantissa m and its exponent n are stored. Although x may have very large and very small absolute values, the numbers m and n that represent x can very well be stored in fixed numbers of bits. These numbers of bits determine both the precision and the maximum magnitude of x.

The above background information may be helpful in understanding the meaning of the following symbolic constants, defined in *float.h*:

FLT_RADIX   Radix of the floating-point representation; for example, 2 or 16.
FLT_ROUNDS   Floating-point rounding mode for addition.

Special information about type **float**:

FLT_DIG   Precision: number of decimal digits (at least 6).
FLT_EPSILON   Smallest number x such that $1.0 + x \neq 1.0$ (at most 10^{-5}).
FLT_MANT_DIG   Number of digits of the mantissa when this is written in the
                   number system with radix **FLT_RADIX**.
FLT_MAX   Maximum **float** value (at least 10^{37}).
FLT_MAX_EXP   Greatest n such that $\text{\textbf{FLT\_RADIX}}^n - 1$ can be represented.
FLT_MIN   Smallest positive normalized value of type **float** (at most 10^{-37}).
FLT_MIN_EXP   Smallest n such that 10^n can be normalized.

Special information about type **double**:

DBL_DIG   Precision: number of decimal digits (at least 10).
DBL_EPSILON   Smallest number x such that $1.0 + x \neq 1.0$ (at most 10^{-9}).
DBL_MANT_DIG   Number of digits of the mantissa when this is written in the
                   number system with radix **FLT_RADIX**.
DBL_MAX   Maximum **double** value (at least 10^{37}).
DBL_MAX_EXP   Greatest n such that $\text{\textbf{FLT\_RADIX}}^n - 1$ can be represented.
DBL_MIN   Smallest positive normalized value of type **double** (at most 10^{-37}).
DBL_MIN_EXP   Smallest n such that 10^n can be normalized.

10.5 Maximum Integer, etc.: <limits.h>

All elementary types for which no floating-point representation is used are sometimes called *integral* types. The header file *limits.h* supplies us with very useful information about these types:

CHAR_BIT	Number of bits in a **char** (at least 8).
CHAR_MAX	Maximum **char** value.
CHAR_MIN	Minimum **char** value.
INT_MAX	Maximum **int** value (+32767 or greater).
INT_MIN	Minimum **int** value (−32767 or less).
LONG_MAX	Maximum **long** value (+2147483647 or greater).
LONG_MIN	Minimum **long** value (−2147483647 or less).
SCHAR_MAX	Maximum **signed char** value (+127 or greater).
SCHAR_MIN	Minimum **signed char** value (−127 or less).
SHRT_MAX	Maximum **short** value (+32767 or greater).
SHRT_MIN	Minimum **short** value (−32767 or less).
UCHAR_MAX	Maximum **unsigned char** value (255 or greater).
UINT_MAX	Maximum **unsigned int** value (65535 or greater).
ULONG_MAX	Maximum **unsigned long** value (4294967295 or greater).
USHRT_MAX	Maximum **unsigned short** value (65535 or greater).

10.6 Mathematical Functions: <math.h>

In Section 4.7, we discussed a number of mathematical standard library functions. Here are their declarations once again:

```
double cos(double x);
double sin(double x);
double tan(double x);
double exp(double x);
double log(double x);
double log10(double x);
double pow(double x, double y);
double sqrt(double x);
double floor(double x);
double ceil(double x);
double fabs(double x);
double acos(double x);
double asin(double x);
double atan(double x);
double atan2(double y, double x);
double cosh(double x);
double sinh(double x);
double tanh(double x);
```

The header file *math.h* also declares four functions that are associated with floating-point representation, discussed in Section 10.4:

```
double ldexp(double x, int n);          Returns x · 2ⁿ.
double frexp(double x, int *exponent);  See below.
double modf(double x, double *ip);      See below.
double fmod(double x, double y);        See below.
```

As you can see, **ldexp** computes a floating-point number from its mantissa and its exponent. The opposite of this is done by **frexp**. For example, after the execution of

```
int n;
double x, mantissa;
x = ...;
mantissa = frexp(x, &n);
```

we have

$$x = mantissa \times 2^n$$

where

$$0.5 \le |mantissa| < 1 \qquad \text{if } x \ne 0$$
$$mantissa = n = 0 \qquad \text{if } x = 0$$

We can use **modf** to split a real number x into its integral part n and its fraction f. For example, consider the call to **modf** in

```
int n;
double x, f;
x = ...;
f = modf(x, &n);
```

After this call, the sum of n and f is equal to x, the signs of n and f are the same as that of x, and $|f| < 1$. For example, 123.456 is split into 123 and 0.456 in this way.

Our last function should not be confused with **fmod**, which computes the remainder when one floating-point number is divided by another. After

```
double a, b, r;
a = ...; b = ...;      // b unequal to 0
r = fmod(a, b);
```

the value of r is such that $a - r$ is a whole multiple of b, the sign of r is the same as that of a, and

$$0 \le |r| < |b|$$

For example, **fmod(2.8, 1.1)** is equal to 0.6 (= 2.8 − 2 × 1.1).

Besides the function declarations mentioned above, we also find the definition of the following symbolic constant in *math.h*:

HUGE_VAL   A very large positive value of type **double**.

10.7 Non-local Jumps: <setjmp.h>

Suppose that function **main** calls function **f**, which in turn calls function **g**. If we leave **g** in the normal way, the jump back will not be directly to **main** (but, instead, to **f**). However, there is a language facility to realize such a jump from **g** back directly to **main**. In general, this facility enables us to jump back from a low-level function (such as **g**) directly to a higher-level function (such as **main**), from which, possibly through other functions (such as **f**), a call to that low-level function was activated. The tools to be used for this purpose are a standard type, **jmp_buf**, defined in the header file *setjmp.h*, and two functions (possibly implemented as *macros*):

```
int setjmp(jmp_buf env);
```
     Save state information, including the current position, in **env**, for use by **longjmp**.

```
void longjmp(jmp_buf env, int val);
```
     Restore the state as stored in **env**; use the position stored there to perform a jump back to the **setjmp** call.

If **setjmp** is executed in the normal, sequential way, it returns 0; if it is executed as a result of executing **longjmp** (which jumps back to **setjmp**) it returns the (nonzero) value **val**, the second argument of **longjmp**. This enables us to tell which case applies. The following complete program illustrates all this. In accordance with the beginning of this section, **main** calls **f**, which in turn calls **g**. It depends on the input data whether or not **longjmp** is executed:

```
// SETJMP: Demonstration of setjmp and longjmp.
#include <stdio.h>
#include <setjmp.h>
jmp_buf position;
void f(void), g(void);

int main()
{  if (setjmp(position) == 0)
      f();
   else printf(
   "Jumped back directly from the middle of g.\n");
   printf("Ready.\n");
   return 0;
}
```

```
void f(void)
{  g();
   printf("Function f completed.\n");
}

void g(void)
{  char ch;
   printf(
   "Do you want to jump back directly to main? (Y/N): ");
   scanf(" %c", &ch);
   if (ch == 'Y' || ch == 'y')
      longjmp(position, 1);
   printf("Function g completed.\n");
}
```

Note how the value returned by **setjmp** is used. The first time this value is 0. If and when **longjmp** is executed, **setjmp** returns 1, because this was the second argument in the call to **longjmp**.

10.8 Special Situations: <signal.h>

The header file *signal.h* contains the following function prototypes:

int raise(int sig);
    'Send signal **sig**'; the return value is 0 if this call is successful and nonzero otherwise. See also **signal**.

void (*signal(int sig, void (*handler)(int)))(int);
    Specify the action that is to be performed immediately if and when 'signal **sig** is sent' by **raise**.

A call to **signal** looks considerably simpler than the above declaration of this function. The first argument, **sig**, can take the following values, defined in *signal.h*:

SIGABRT	The program has been terminated abnormally, as, for example, by means of a call to the function **abort**, mentioned in Section 10.12.
SIGFPE	An arithmetic error, such as, for example, division by zero, has occurred.
SIGILL	An illegal instruction has been executed.
SIGINT	An interrupt has occurred.
SIGSEGV	An attempt has been made to access memory that is not available.
SIGTERM	There has been a request to terminate the program..

So much for the first argument of **signal**. The second argument, **handler**, can be the name of a function of our own. Instead, we can also write:

SIG_IGN	Ignore the signal.
SIG_DFL	Perform the default action, as defined by the implementation.

The value returned by **signal** is the second argument, **handler**, unless an error has occurred. In that case the return value is **SIG_ERR**, also defined in *signal.h*.

10.9 Variable-length Argument Lists: <stdarg.h>

We are already familiar with two methods (namely default arguments and function overloading, discussed in Sections 4.5 and 4.8, respectively) to define functions that can be called with different numbers of arguments, so that we can write, for example, **f(a)** and **f(a, b)**. These two methods are available only in C++. There is a third method, which is also available in plain C. It is more general than the others, in that the function declaration does not limit the number of arguments. On the other hand, it does not provide for argument checking and conversion, as the others do.

We will consider the beginning of a function, **fun**, the first three parameters, **c**, **x**, and **k** of which have the types **char**, **float**, and **int**, respectively. In total, the number of arguments is $3 + n$ ($n \geq 0$). The first three arguments supply **fun** with information to determine how many arguments follow and what the type of each of these is. Then we write the first line of function **fun** as follows:

```
int fun(char c, float x, int k, ...)
```

Note that this should be taken literally, including the three dots. If we want a separate declaration of **fun**, this takes the same form as this line followed by a semicolon.

We then introduce a variable, traditionally called **argp**, of type **va_list** (defined in *stdarg.h*). Thus, at the beginning of **fun** we declare:

```
va_list argp;
```

This variable **argp** will act as a pointer to the next argument to be used. This process is initialized by executing the following macro call:

```
va_start(argp, k);
```

This expresses that **argp** is to point to the argument that follows the one that corresponds to parameter **k**. In order to obtain the value of the argument pointed to by **argp**, we must not use the normal notation ***argp**, but, instead, we write:

```
va_arg(argp, type)
```

where *type* is the type of the argument pointed to by **argp** (which means that *type* is also the type of this whole macro call). Thus, we can call **va_arg**, for example, as follows:

```
y = va_arg(argp, double);
```

As an important side effect, **va_arg** also alters **argp**, so that it points to the next argument, and so on. Therefore **va_arg** will in practice be called in a loop. After the termination of this loop, the following macro call is to be executed:

```
va_end(argp);
```

A complete program that uses variable-length argument lists is given below. The number of arguments used in calls to the function **sum** is unlimited. It is essential that these arguments (except for the first) have type **double**, as the given floating-point constants are. The first argument has type **int**. It specifies how many arguments of type **double** follow, so that function **sum** can compute their sum:

```
// VARARG: Variable-length argument lists.
#include <stdarg.h>
#include <stdio.h>

int main()
{   double sum(int n, ...); // Literal program text!
    printf("%f\n", sum(1, 9.87));
    printf("%f\n", sum(5, 10.0, 20.0, 30.0, 40.0, 50.0));
    return 0;
}

double sum(int n, ...)     // Literal program text!
// n is the number of arguments that follow.
{   va_list argp;
    float s=0;
    va_start(argp, n);
    while (n--) s += va_arg(argp, double);
    va_end(argp);
    return s;
}
```

10.10 Special Types: <stddef.h>

The following two special types are defined in the header file *stddef.h*:

size_t   The type of the value returned by the operator **sizeof**.
ptrdiff_t   The type which can always safely be used for the difference of two pointer values (that is, of two addresses).

In Sections 2.2 and 5.1, it was suggested that both **sizeof** and pointer differences have type **int**. Although in many cases we can use type **int** to store such values, more bits may be needed than are provided by this type. For example, 32767 is the largest **int** value with most compilers for MS-DOS. Since this may be too small for the difference of two pointer values, we may be inclined to use either type **unsigned** or type **unsigned long** instead. For example, **unsigned** happens to be the right choice for Borland C++, but for other compilers **unsigned long** may be required. To make our programs portable, we use neither of these two alternatives, but rather **size_t**. A **typedef** declaration in the header file *stddef.h* takes care that the right type is taken. With Borland C++ this declaration reads

```
typedef unsigned size_t;
```

There is a similar **typedef** declaration for **ptrdiff_t** in *stddef.h*. With Borland C++, **ptrdiff_t** can be **long** or **int**, depending on the 'memory model'.

10.11 Input and Output: <stdio.h>

We have dealt with the most important functions for standard I/O in Chapter 8 and elsewhere. The present section lists their declarations once again, with a reference to the sections that give more information about them. Then we will discuss some more standard I/O functions.

Many I/O functions make use of type **FILE**, defined in *stdio.h*. We have access to files (on disk) by using file pointers of type pointer-to-**FILE**, or type **FILE***, for short. There are three standard file pointers, also called *streams*, namely **stdin**, **stdout**, and **stderr**. They are normally used for input from the keyboard, output to the video display, and the display of error messages, respectively.

The following lines with function declarations also contain references to the sections that give more information about these functions (and macros); note that type **size_t**, discussed in the previous section, is used for **fread** and **fwrite**:

```
FILE *fopen(const char *filename, const char *mode);      // 8.4
int fclose(FILE *fp);                                      // 8.4
int fscanf(FILE *fp, const char *format, ...);            // 8.4
int fprintf(FILE *fp, const char *format, ...);           // 8.4
int scanf(const char *format, ...);                       // 8.3
int printf(const char *format, ...);                      // 8.2
int getc(FILE *fp);                                       // 8.4
int putc(int ch, FILE *fp);                               // 8.4
int ungetc(int ch, FILE *fp);                             // 8.4
int getchar(void);                                  // 8.1 and 8.4
int putchar(int ch);                                // 8.1 and 8.4
char *gets(char *s);                                      // 5.7
int puts(const char *s);                                  // 5.7
```

```
char *fgets(char *s, int n, FILE *fp);                    // 8.4
int fputs(const char *s, FILE *fp);                       // 8.4
size_t fread(void *bufptr, size_t size, size_t nobj, FILE *fp);
                                                          // 8.5
size_t fwrite(const void *bufptr, size_t size,
    size_t nobj, FILE *fp);                               // 8.5
int fseek(FILE *fp, long offset, int fromwhere);          // 8.6
long ftell(FILE *fp);                                     // 8.6
void rewind(FILE *fp);                                    // 8.4
int feof(FILE *fp);                                       // 8.4
int sscanf(char *s, const char *format, ...);             // 5.11
int sprintf(char *s, const char *format, ...);            // 5.11
```

The following functions have not yet been discussed:

```
int fgetc(FILE *fp);
```
Analogous to **getc**, but implemented as a function, not as a macro.

```
int fputc(int ch, FILE *fp);
```
Analogous to **putc**, but implemented as a function, not as a macro.

```
FILE *freopen(const char *filename, const char *mode, FILE *fp);
```
You can use this function for a stream **fp** that has been opened by means of **fopen**, to alter its physical file name or its mode. You can also use it to associate one of the streams **stdout, stdin,** or **stderr** with a real file. For example:

```
    fp = freopen("result.dat", "w", stdout);
```

After the execution of this statement, **printf** will write output data to the file *result.dat* instead of to the video display. The return value is equal to the third argument, unless an error occurs; in that case it is **NULL**.

```
int fflush(FILE *fp);
```
A call to this function is defined only if **fp** is being used for output. It then flushes the buffer: any output data that still is in the output buffer is actually written to the external device, such as a disk. This is done automatically when a program terminates normally and when **fclose** is called. The return value is normally 0; it is **EOF** if an error occurs.

```
FILE *tmpfile(void);
```
Creates and opens a temporary file in the mode **"w+b"**; this file is automatically deleted when the program terminates normally. The return value is a file pointer, or **NULL** if the file cannot be opened.

```
char *tmpnam(char s[L_tmpnam]);
```
After a call to this function, **s** contains a string different from all existing file names. The start address of **s** is returned. As many as **TMP_MAX** distinct file

names can be generated. The symbolic constants **L_tmpnam** and **TMP_MAX** are defined in *stdio.h*.

`int remove(const char *filename);`
Deletes a file with the given name. If this is indeed possible, **remove** returns 0; if not, it returns a nonzero value.

`int rename(const char *oldname, const char *newname);`
Renames a given file, and returns 0, unless renaming is not possible; in that case **rename** returns nonzero.

`int setvbuf(FILE *fp, char *buf, int mode, size_t size);`
Sets the buffering method for the stream **fp**. If **buf** is equal to **NULL**, memory space for a buffer is created automatically; otherwise **buf** is used as a buffer. (If **buf** is local to a function, do not forget to close the file in question before that function is left.) There are the following possibilities for **mode**:

_IOFBF	complete buffering;
_IOLBF	line buffering for text files;
_IONBF	no buffering.

(These three symbolic constants are defined in *stdio.h*.) The buffer size is given by the fourth parameter, **size**. Normally, 0 is returned; in case of an error, the return value is nonzero.

`void setbuf(FILE *fp, char *buf);`
If **buf** is **NULL**, the stream **fp** will be unbuffered. If **buf** is equal to a real address, the call

```
setbuf(fp, buf);
```

has the same effect as

```
setvbuf(fp, buf, _IOFBF, BUFSIZ);
```

(The symbolic constant **BUFSIZ** is defined in *stdio.h*.

`int fgetpos(FILE *fp, fpos_t *ptr);`
The current position in the stream **fp** is written into ***ptr**. Type **fpos_t** is defined in *stdio.h*. (Unlike **ftell**, which uses a byte number, **fgetpos** uses a more technical representation of the position in a file. (See also **fsetpos**.) The return value is 0, unless an error occurs; in that case it is nonzero.

`int fsetpos(FILE *fp, const fpos_t *ptr);`
The stream **fp** is positioned at the point given by **ptr**; see also **fgetpos**. The return value is 0, unless an error occurs; in that case it is nonzero.

```
int ferror(FILE *fp);
```
Returns nonzero if an error has occurred in an I/O operation on stream **fp**. (The occurrence of errors is registered in *status indicators*, such as **errno**, mentioned in Section 10.3.)

```
void perror(const char *s);
```
Prints **s**, together with an implementation-dependent error message that corresponds to the value of **errno**; see also Section 10.3.

```
void clearerr(FILE *fp);
```
Clears the error indicator and the end-of-file indicator for the stream **fp**. For example, if **feof(fp)** returns nonzero and the call **clearerr(fp)** is executed, then immediately after the latter call **feof(fp)** will return 0.

The following functions can be used in functions that have variable-length argument lists, as discussed in Section 10.9:

```
int vprintf(const char *format, va_list argp);
int vfprintf(FILE *fp, const char *format, va_list argp);
int vsprintf(char *s, const char *format, va_list argp);
```

Here is a complete program to demonstrate how **vprintf** can be used:

```
// VPRDEMO: A program to demonstrate vprintf.

#include <stdio.h>
#include <math.h>
#include <stdarg.h>

void myprintf(char *format, ...)
// The above three dots are literal program text!
{ va_list argp;
  printf("\nHere is output text:\n");
  va_start(argp, format);
  vprintf(format, argp);
  va_end(argp);
  printf("\nThis concludes the output text.\n");
}

int main()
{ myprintf("The square root of 2 is approximately %7.5f.",
           sqrt(2.0));
  return 0;
}
```

Like the standard output function **printf**, our own function **myprintf** has a format string as its first argument, which is followed by as many arguments as there are conversion specifications in that format string.

10.12 Miscellaneous: <stdlib.h>

The header file *stdlib.h* declares functions that are useful for various purposes:

`double atof(const char *s);`
> If the string **s** contains a valid character representation of a number, then this number, converted to type **double**, is returned. If not, **errno** is given a nonzero value; see Section 10.3.

`int atoi(const char *s);`
> As **atof**, except that **s** is converted to type **int**.

`long atol(const char *s);`
> As **atof**, except that **s** is converted to type **long**.

`double strtod(const char *s, char **endp);`
> Converts the beginning of string **s** to type **double**. If **endp** is not **NULL**, the address of the first character that follows the converted substring is assigned to ***endp**. In case of an error, **errno** is given a nonzero value; see Section 10.3.

`long strtol(const char *s, char **endp, int base);`
> Converts the beginning of string **s** to type **long**. If **endp** is not **NULL**, the address of the first character that follows the converted substring is assigned to ***endp**. If **base** satisfies $2 \le base \le 36$, the number in **s** is assumed to be written in the number system with radix **base**. If **base** is greater than 10 (but not greater than 36) the letters **A**, **B**, ... (or **a**, **b**, ...) act as the digits 10, 11, ..., **base**–1. If **base** is 0, the assumed radix is 16 if **s** starts with **0X** or **0x**, 8 if **s** starts with 0 not followed by **X** or **x**, or 10 in all other cases. In case of an error, **errno** is given a nonzero value; see Section 10.3.

`unsigned long strtoul(const char *s, char **endp, int base);`
> As **strtol**, except that the beginning of string **s** is converted to type **unsigned long**.

`void abort(void);`
> Causes abnormal program termination, as if by **raise(SIGABRT)**; see Section 10.8.

`void exit(int status);`
> Causes normal program termination; any open files are closed, as if the program terminates normally without calling **exit**. The use of the argument **status** is system dependent; its normal values are 0 for 'success' and 1 for 'failure'. Instead of 0 and

1, the symbolic constants **EXIT_SUCCESS** and **EXIT_FAILURE**, defined in *stdlib.h*, may be used.

int atexit(void (*fcn)(void));
Registers the function **fcn**, so that the latter will be called when the program (normally) terminates. The return value is nonzero if the registration cannot be made. If you register more than one function in this way, the most recently registered one is executed first, and so on, as the following example shows:

```
// ATEXIT
#include <stdio.h>
#include <stdlib.h>

void ready(void)
{  printf("Ready.\n");
}

void almost_ready(void)
{  printf("Almost ready.\n");
}

int main()
{  atexit(ready);
   atexit(almost_ready);
   printf("Not ready.\n");
   return 0;
}
```

The output of this program is

```
Not ready.
Almost ready.
Ready.
```

int system(const char *s);
The string **s** is passed to the command processor of the operating system, so that it will be interpreted and executed as a command. The value returned by **system** is system dependent.

char *getenv(const char *name);
If there is an 'environment variable' **name** in the operating system, the value of this variable is returned; if not, **NULL** is returned. Details are system dependent.

int abs(int n);
Returns the absolute value of its argument **n**. Remember, **abs** can be used only for **int** arguments. See also **labs** and **fabs**.

long labs(long n);
Returns the absolute value of its **long** argument **n**.

`div_t div(int num, int denom);`

Performs the integer division **num/denom** and computes both the quotient and the remainder. The return value is a structure of type **div_t**, defined in *stdlib.h* as follows:

`typedef struct {int quot, rem;} div_t;`

The quotient and the remainder will be found in the **quot** and **rem** members, respectively. (As with most machines the quotient and the remainder can be obtained in one divide instruction, these two results may be computed more efficiently by this **div** function than by the two C operators / and %, for which two divide instructions would be required.)

`ldiv_t ldiv(long num, long denom);`

As **div**, except that type **long** is used for the numerator **num** and the denominator **denom**. The quotient and the remainder also have type long: type **ldiv_t** is defined in *stdlib.h* as

`typedef struct {long quot, rem;} ldiv_t;`

`int rand(void);`

Returns a nonnegative pseudo-random integer, not greater than **RAND_MAX**; this symbolic constant is defined in *stdlib.h* and is not less than 32767. See also **srand**.

`void srand(unsigned int seed);`

Specifies that **seed** is to be used as the initial value in the process of generating pseudo-random numbers by means of successive calls to **rand**. If we do not call **srand**, that initial value is 1. We can use **srand** if the same pseudo-random number sequence is to be generated more than once: for each sequence, we call **srand** with the same argument, prior to entering the loop in which calls to **rand** generate the elements of that sequence. On the other hand, we may want to write a program that generates a sequence of pseudo-random numbers that is different each time the program is executed. Then each time the seed value must be different. This can be achieved by using the function **time** (to be discussed in Section 10.14), because this function supplies us with a different value each time the program is executed. We will apply this principle in connection with our discussion of the functions **bsearch** and **qsort** below.

The following functions have been dealt with in Section 5.6. (Note the use of **size_t**, discussed in Section 10.10.)

```
void *malloc(size_t nbytes);
void *calloc(size_t nobj, size_t objectsize);
void *realloc(void *p, size_t nbytes);
void free(void *p);
```

Finally, there are two functions with very complicated declarations:

```
void *bsearch(const void *key, const void *base,
              size_t n, size_t width,
              int (*fcmp)(const void *, const void *));

void qsort(void *base, size_t n, size_t width,
           int (*fcmp)(const void *, const void *));
```

Fortunately, using these functions is simpler than their declarations suggest. Function **bsearch** is for *binary search*: a sorted array **base** is searched for a given **key**. We can use function **qsort** to sort an array by means of the *quicksort* method. For both functions, the elements of array **base** can have any type and there are **n** such elements, each consisting of **width** bytes. Because of the general nature of these functions, we have to supply our own compare function, which has in common with the string compare function **strcmp** that the test results 'less than', 'equal to', and 'greater than' should result in return values that are negative, zero, and positive, respectively. We will demonstrate these functions and some others in a program that performs the following tasks:

1. It generates and prints an array **a** of 10 random integers, ranging from 0 to 9.
2. It sorts array **a** in increasing order and prints the result.
3. It asks the user to enter an integer; the sorted array **a** is searched for that integer. If it is found, its position is displayed; otherwise, the message **Not found.** is displayed.

Note that the calls to **qsort** and **bsearch** are much simpler than the declarations of these functions in program STDFUN:

```
// STDFUN: Demonstration of some standard library functions,
//         including qsort and bsearch.
#include <stdlib.h>
#include <iostream.h>

int comparefun(const void *p1, const void *p2)
{  return *(int *)p1 < *(int *)p2 ? -1 :
           *(int *)p1 > *(int *)p2;
}

void printarray(char *str, int *a, int n)
{  int i;
   cout << str << endl << "i   = ";
   for (i=0; i<n; i++) cout << i << "  ";
   cout << endl << "a[i] = ";
   for (i=0; i<n; i++) cout << a[i] << "  ";
   cout << endl;
}
```

```
int main()
{  const int n=10;
   int a[n], i, x, *p;
   srand((unsigned int)time(NULL));
   for (i=0; i<n; i++) a[i] = rand() % n;
   printarray("Before sorting:", a, n);
   qsort(a, n, sizeof(int), comparefun);
   printarray("After sorting:", a, n);
   cout << "Enter an integer: ";
   cin >> x;
   p = (int *)bsearch(&x, a, n, sizeof(int), comparefun);
   if (p == NULL) cout << "Not found.\n"; else
   cout << "Found as a[" << p - a << "].\n";
   return 0;
}
```

Besides sorting an array of numbers, we can also sort an array of pointers to strings for which memory has been allocated by **new** or **malloc**. In this case the compare function is rather tricky, as the following fragment demonstrates:

```
int cmp(const void *p, const void *q)
{  return strcmp(*(char **)p, *(char **)q);
}
...
char *a[N];
...  // Make each a[i] point to a null-terminated string
qsort(a, N, sizeof(char *), cmp);
```

In function **cmp**, parameters **p** and **q** contain *addresses* of pointers to characters, not these pointers themselves. This explains the casts **(char **)**. Since **strcmp** accepts pointers to characters (not pointers to pointers) dereferencing is required, hence the asterisks preceding these casts. If we wrote **strcmp((char *)p, (char *)q)** in function **cmp**, the compiler would not complain, but generate wrong code, mistaking array **a** for an array of characters instead of an array of pointers.

10.13 String Functions: <string.h>

The following functions have been discussed in Section 5.5:

```
size_t strlen(const char *s);
int strcmp(const char *s1, const char *s2);
int strncmp(const char *s1, const char *s2, size_t maxlen);
char *strcpy(char *dest, const char *src);
char *strncpy(char *dest, const char *src, size_t maxlen);
char *strcat(char *dest, const char *src);
char *strncat(char *dest, const char *src, size_t maxlen);
```

The header file *string.h* also declares the following string functions:

`char *strchr(const char *s, int ch);`
    Returns the address of the first occurrence of character **ch** in string **s**, or **NULL** if **ch** does not occur in **s**.

`char *strrchr(const char *s, int ch);`
    Returns the address of the *last* occurrence of character **ch** in string **s**, or **NULL** if **ch** does not occur in **s**.

`size_t strspn(const char *s1, const char *s2);`
    Returns the length of the longest possible prefix of **s1** consisting of characters that also occur in **s2**.

`size_t strcspn(const char *s1, const char *s2);`
    Returns the length of the longest possible prefix of **s1** consisting of characters that *do not* occur in **s2**.

`char *strpbrk(const char *s1, const char *s2);`
    Searches **s1** (starting at **s1[0]**) for a character that also occurs in **s2**. If such a character is found, its address is returned; if not, the return value is **NULL**.

`char *strstr(const char *s1, const char *s2);`
    Searches **s1** (starting at **s1[0]**) for a substring identical with **s2**. If this substring is found, its start address is returned; if not, the return value is **NULL**.

`char *strerror(int errnum);`
    Returns (the address of) a string that contains an error message belonging to the current value of **errnum**. See also Section 10.3.

`char *strtok(char *s1, const char *s2);`
    Consider the call **strtok(s1, s2)**. Then a *token* is a substring of **s1** consisting of characters that do not occur in **s2**; an additional requirement is that a token cannot be a substring of a longer token. An example will make this clear. Consider the call **strtok("!ABC.;DEF", ";?.!/")**. Here we have precisely two tokens, namely **ABC** and **DEF**. The value returned by **strtok(s1, s2)** is the address of the first token in **s1**. After this initial call (in which **s1** was not **NULL**), we can write a loop in which the call **strtok(NULL, s2)** occurs; each time, **strtok** returns the next token in the string **s1** supplied in the initial call. If no more tokens are to be found, **strtok** returns **NULL**. Each time a token is found in **s1**, the first character that follows this token is overwritten by the null character, as the following program demonstrates:

```
// STRTOK: This programs demonstrates the strtok function.

#include <string.h>
#include <stdio.h>
```

```
    int main()
    {  char *p, s[] = "31/12-1999---23.59 h";
       int n=0, len, i;
       len = strlen(s);
       p = strtok(s, " /.,;-");
       while (p != NULL)
       {  printf("%s;", p);
          p = strtok(NULL, " /.,;-");
       }
       for (i=0; i<=len; i++) if (s[i] == '\0') n++;
       printf(
       "\nThere are now %d null characters in array s.\n", n);
       return 0;
    }
```

This program produces the following output:

```
31;12;1999;23;59;h;
There are now 6 null characters in array s.
```

The following functions manipulate byte sequences that are not necessarily strings.
Remember that a string ends with a null character, on which most functions rely. The
following do not. They can therefore also deal with byte sequences that may contain
null characters in any positions.

```
void *memcpy(void *dest, const void *src, size_t n);
```
Copies **n** bytes from **src** to **dest** and returns **dest**. The result is undefined if **src** and
dest overlap.

```
void *memmove(void *dest, const void *src, size_t n);
```
The same as **memcpy**, except that **src** and **dest** may overlap.

```
int memcmp(const void *s1, const void *s2, size_t n);
```
The same as the well-known function **strncmp** (discussed in Section 5.5), except
that comparing characters does not terminate if a null character is encountered.

```
void *memchr(const void *s, int ch, size_t n);
```
Returns the address of the first occurrence of character **ch** in s[0], ..., s[n–1], or
NULL if **ch** does not occur in this sequence.

```
void *memset(void *s, int ch, size_t n);
```
Assigns **ch** to all elements s[0], ..., s[n–1], and returns s.

10.14 Time and Date: <time.h>

The types **time_t** and **clock_t** are defined in the header file *time.h* to represent the time as a number. These types may be defined, for example, as **long**. Bearing this in mind will be helpful in understanding the following function declarations:

```
time_t time(time_t *pt);
```
Returns the current calendar time, expressed in seconds; the return value may be the time elapsed since January 1st 1970, 0.00 h GMT. If the time is not available, −1 is returned. If **pt** is not **NULL**, the return value is also assigned to ***pt**.

```
double difftime(time_t t2, time_t t1);
```
Returns the difference t2 − t1, expressed in seconds.

```
clock_t clock(void);
```
Returns the processor time used since the beginning of program execution. This time is expressed in *ticks*. The number of ticks per second is given by the symbolic constant **CLK_TCK**, defined in *time.h*. It follows that a tick is 1/**CLK_TCK** seconds, and that the quotient **clock( )/CLK_TCK** gives the processor time in seconds. If the time is not available, the return value is −1.

To make the time available in other forms, type **tm** is defined in *time.h* as follows:

```
struct tm
{  int tm_sec;    // Seconds (< 60) after the minute
   int tm_min;    // Minutes (< 60) after the hour
   int tm_hour;   // Hours (< 24) since midnight
   int tm_mday;   // Day of the month (≤ 31)
   int tm_mon;    // Month: 0 = Jan., ..., 11 = Dec.
   int tm_year;   // Years since 1900
   int tm_wday;
      // Day of the week: 0 = Sunday, ..., 6 = Saturday
   int tm_yday;
      // Day of the year: 0 = Jan. 1st, 31 = Feb. 1st
   int tm_isdst; // Daylight Saving Time:
      //  Positive: Daylight Saving Time in effect
      //  0:        Daylight Saving Time not in effect
      //  Negative: The information is not available
};
```

The following functions are based on this type. The functions **localtime**, **gmtime**, **asctime**, **ctime** return the addresses of static objects, which may be overwritten by subsequent call to these functions.

```
tm *localtime(const time_t *pt);
```
Converts the time ***pt**, as returned by **time**, into local time.

```
tm *gmtime(const time_t *pt);
```
Converts the time *pt, as returned by **time**, into Universal Coordinated Time (UTC). It returns **NULL** if UTC is not available.

```
char *asctime(const tm *pt);
```
Converts the time available in the structure *pt into a string of the form

```
Fri Jul 14 09:06:43 1990\n\0
```

```
char *ctime(const time_t *pt);
```
Returns a string similar to the one returned by **asctime**, but based on the time available in *pt (as returned by **time**). Thus, **ctime(pt)** is equivalent to **asctime-(localtime(pt))**.

```
time_t mktime(tm *pt);
```
Converts the local time given in *pt into calendar time in the same representation as used by **time**.

```
size_t strftime(char *s, size_t smax, const char *fmt,
                const tm *pt);
```
Formats the date and time information given in *pt into s, according to the format string **fmt**, which can contain special conversion specifications listed below. Like **sprintf**, discussed in Section 5.11, **strftime** places the resulting string into a memory area the address of which is given by its first argument, **s**. No more than **smax** characters are transmitted to **s**. If **smax** is too small to place all characters that are generated into **s**, the return value is 0; otherwise it is the number of characters placed into **s**, excluding the null character, which is written at the end. Ordinary characters in **fmt**, not belonging to conversion specifications, are copied into **s**. The following conversion specifications can be used:

%a	Abbreviated weekday name.
%A	Full weekday name.
%b	Abbreviated month name.
%B	Full month name.
%c	Date and time.
%d	Two-digit day of the month (01-31).
%H	Two-digit hour (24-hour clock) (00-23).
%I	Two-digit hour (12-hour clock) (00-12).
%j	Three-digit day of the year (001-366).
%m	Two-digit month (01-12).
%M	Two-digit minute (00-59).
%p	AM or PM.
%S	Two-digit second (00-59).
%U	Two-digit week number with Sunday as the first day (00-53).
%w	Weekday, where 0 is Sunday (0-6).
%W	Two-digit week number with Monday is the first day (00-53).
%x	Date.
%X	Time.

%y   Two-digit year without century (00-99).
%Y   Year with century.
%Z   Time zone name, or no characters if no time zone.
%%   Character %.

As you can see, these conversion specifications are quite different from those used for
sprintf. Note also that, unlike **sprintf**, **strftime** has a fixed number of arguments: all
conversion specifications refer to the same structure, the address of which is given as
the last argument. The order of the conversion specifications in the format string may
be different from the order of the members in that structure.

Since most of the functions discussed in this section have addresses as arguments,
we will often have to use the operator **&**. Some of these functions are used in the
following demonstration program:

```
// TIMEDEMO: Demonstration of time and date functions.
#include <time.h>
#include <stdio.h>

int main()
{   tm s; time_t t; char str[80];
    time(&t);
    s = *localtime(&t);
    printf("\nTime in structure s (of type tm):\n");
    printf("sec=%d min=%d hour=%d mday=%d mon=%d year=%d\n",
            s.tm_sec, s.tm_min, s.tm_hour, s.tm_mday,
            s.tm_mon, s.tm_year);
    printf("wday=%d yday=%d isdst=%d\n",
            s.tm_wday, s.tm_yday, s.tm_isdst);
    printf("Time obtained by asctime            : %s",
            asctime(&s));
    printf("The same result obtained by ctime: %s",
            ctime(&t));
    printf("The following lines contain data "
            "obtained by using strftime:\n");
    strftime(str, 80, "Time: %M minutes after %I o'clock %p\n"
                      "Day:   %A, %B %d, 19%y", &s);
    printf("%s\n", str);
    return 0;
}
```

At the moment this program was executed, the result was as follows:

```
Time in structure s (of type tm):
sec=0 min=17 hour=11 mday=18 mon=9 year=94
wday=2 yday=290 isdst=1
Time obtained by asctime            : Tue Oct 18 11:17:00 1994
The same result obtained by ctime: Tue Oct 18 11:17:00 1994
The following lines contain data obtained by using strftime:
Time: 17 minutes after 11 o'clock AM
Day:   Tuesday, October 18, 1994
```

11

Templates

11.1 Introduction

In this chapter (and in the next one) we will discuss some advanced language concepts, which did not belong to the original version of C++ and may still not be supported by some compilers. Templates, the subject of this chapter, makes it easy for us to make our program code more general with regard to data types. Suppose, for example, that we write a function to swap the values of two **int** variables. Later, we may want a similar function for two **float** values. Templates enable us to write only one function that can be used for both purposes. Another example is a general class for, say, a binary tree. Templates provide a convenient means to write such a class without specifying the type of the data that we want to store in the nodes of the tree.

We are by now very familiar with function parameters. These represent values of a given type. Templates also have parameters, but these do not represent *values* but rather *types*.

11.2 Function Templates

The following program demonstrates a function template. It first swaps the values of two **int** variables and then those of two **float** variables:

```
/* FTEMPL: A function template for swapping the values
           of two objects of a given, arbitrary type.
*/
#include <iostream.h>

template <class T>
```

```
void swap(T &x, T &y){T w = x; x = y; y = w;}

int main()
{   int i=1, j=2;
    swap(i, j);   // Now i = 2 and j = 1.
    float u = 3.4, v = 5.6;
    swap(u, v); // Now u = 5.6 and v = 3.4.
    cout << i << " " << j << " " << u << " " << v << endl;
    return 0;
}
```

Since the sizes of int and float objects may be different, it is hard to understand that a single function should be able to perform both swapping tasks. Actually, this is not the case. Although we write only one function template here, two distinct functions will be generated, as if we had written these ourselves:

```
void swap(int &x, int &y){int w = x; x = y; y = w;}
void swap(float &x, float &y){float w = x; x = y; y = w;}
```

Consider this line in program FTEMPL:

```
template <class T>
```

Curiously enough, we find the keyword **class** here, even though we are not using any classes at all. The identifier **T** in this line can be replaced with another one: it is a parameter denoting a type. This parameter **T** is used in the text that follows , which looks like a normal C++ function:

```
void swap(T &x, T &y){T w = x; x = y; y = w;}
```

The two lines together specify that **swap** is not a normal function but rather a *template*. The function **swap(int, int)** shown above is generated by the call **swap(i, j)** while the **swap(float, float)** function is generated by the call **swap(u, v)**. If there had been another call, say, **swap(m, n)** with **m** and **n** of type **int**, there would still be only two **swap** functions, but there would be three if **m** and **n** in this latest call had been of type **char**, and so on. These two arguments **m** and **n** must, of course, be lvalues, and they must be of the same type.

Templates and separate compilation of modules

You may wonder if we can write a template in one program module and use them in another. Since the compiler will deal with only one module at a time, it can expand a function template into the actual functions only if calls to these functions occur in the same module. Consequently, if we want to declare a template in file A and use it in file B, then in file A there must be calls similar to those in file B. For example, we could write the following (unrealistic) program, consisting of files A and B:

File A:

```
template <class T>
void swap(T &x, T &y){T w = x; x = y; y = w;}

static void dummy()
{  int i, j; swap(i, j);
   float u, v; swap(u, v);
}
```

File B:

```
#include <iostream.h>
template <class T>void swap(T &x, T &y);

int main()
{  int i = 1, j = 2; swap(i, j);
   float u = 3.4, v = 5.6; swap(u, v);
   cout << i << " " << j << " " << u << " " << v << endl;
   return 0;
}
```

This example is very unsatisfactory: the **dummy** function, defined in file A, is not called at all. Yet we need it because it tells the compiler what calls to swap functions will be needed.

Fortunately, there is a better solution. The first two lines of file A form a *declaration*, not a *definition*. In other words, although part of it looks like a function definition, it is only a model for such a definition and the compiler will not convert it into executable code. Consequently, it is perfectly all right if we place this template declaration in a header file. Recall that we should use header files for declarations, not for definitions, as we have discussed in Section 4.11. The following program also consists of two modules A and B; they both use the same header file *swap.h*. Because of its simplicity, this program is not realistic either, but it shows very well how we can use a template in several modules:

Header file *swap.h*:

```
template <class T>
void swap(T &x, T &y){T w = x; x = y; y = w;}
```

File A:

```
#include "swap.h"
void f(float &v1, float &v2)
{  swap(v1, v2);
}
```

File B:

```
#include <iostream.h>
#include "swap.h"

int main()
{   int i = 1, j = 2; swap(i, j);
    float u = 3.4, v = 5.6;
    void f(float &v1, float &v2);
    f(u, v);
    cout << i << " " << j << " " << u << " " << v << endl;
    return 0;
}
```

Using more than one template argument

Like functions, templates can have more than one argument. This is interesting if we want to use more than one generalized type. Suppose, for example, that we want to compute $x = a^n$, where n is a nonnegative **int** value. If a has type **double** then so has x, but if a has type **int** we want x to be **long int** and avoid floating-point arithmetic. We want to use a function template **power** for both purposes. The following program shows how this can be done:

```
// POWERS: Two power functions resulting from a template.
#include <iostream.h>

template <class basetype, class resulttype>
resulttype power(basetype a, int n, resulttype &x)
{   x=1;
    for (int i=1; i<=n; i++) x *= a;
    return x;
}

int main()
{   double x1; power(10.0, 15, x1); cout << x1 << endl;
    long x2; power(2, 17, x2); cout << x2 << endl;
    long x3; cout << power(2, 20, x3) << endl;
    return 0;
}
```

This program demonstrates that a template argument can also be used as a return-value type. The third parameter of **power** seems superfluous. After all, we return the resulting power by means of a return-statement, so it looks silly to use the third parameter for this purpose as well. However, the C++ language demands that every template argument be used in the argument types of a function template. Here we need **resulttype** as a template argument; if we gave the function template **power** only two parameters, **a** and **n**, then **resulttype** would not be used in the argument types of the function template, which would be incorrect. Note that the first and the second calls to **power** ignore the value returned by this function, while the third uses it. Incidentally, this program produces the three output lines

```
1e+15
131072
1048576
```

showing the values of 10^{15}, 2^{17} and 2^{20}, respectively.

11.3 Class Templates

Object-oriented programming is about designing and using classes. If we have two or more classes that are almost identical, it will be desirable to generalize them in the same way as with function templates: instead of the classes themselves we write a *class template*, which is a model for the actual class declarations. For example, suppose that we want to use vectors in the same way as we did in Chapter 6, but this time we want to use two vector types: one with **int** and the other with **float** coordinates x and y. Since operations such as vector addition is done in the same way, it would be awkward if we had to write two almost identical classes. The following program shows how to use a class template for this purpose:

```
// CLTEMPL.CPP: Demonstration of a class template.
#include <iostream.h>

template <class T>
class vector {
public:
    vector(T x=0, T y=0){xx = x; yy = y;}
    void printvec()const;
    friend vector<T>
       operator+(vector<T> &a, vector<T> &b);
private:
    T xx, yy;
};

template <class T>
void vector<T>::printvec()const
{   cout << xx << "     " << yy << endl;
}

template <class T>
vector<T> operator+(vector<T> &a, vector<T> &b)
{   return vector<T>(a.xx + b.xx, a.yy + b.yy);
}
```

```
int main()
{   vector <int> iu(1, 2), iv(3, 4), isom;
    vector <float> fu(1.1, 2.2), fv(3.3, 4.4), fsom;
    isom = iu + iv;
    fsom = fu + fv;
    isom.printvec();
    fsom.printvec();
    return 0;
}
```

This program computes the vector sums

$(1, 2) + (3, 4) = (4, 6)$
$(1.1, 2.2) + (3.3, 4.4) = (4.4, 6.6)$

which explains this output:

```
4        6
4.4        6.6
```

As with a function template, discussed in the previous section, a class template begins with

template < *template-argument-list* >

which here has the form

template <class T>

The idea is that the actual type to be used for **T** will be specified later. In the template-declaration, we write **T** to denote this type. In the **printvec** and the **operator+** functions, we use the notation **vector<T>** to indicate that **vector** is not a class name but that an additional type **T** is required. In other words, **vector** is a parameterized type with **T** as its parameter. In this example, **T** will denote either **int** or **float**, as you can see in the **main** function. Here we find the so-called *template-class-names* **vector <int>** and **vector<float>**, which provide the actual types to be used for **T**. They are two distinct classes, as if we had written these ourselves, using distinct names, such as **vector_int** and **vector_float**.

The template-argument-list, mentioned above, can consist of more than one item, each of which is either a type-argument, that is, the keyword **class** followed by an identifier, or an *argument declaration* as used in function declarations. An example of the latter is **int n**. Using only such an argument declaration, we can write, for example,

```
template <int n>
class floatsequence {
    ...
    float r[n];
};
```

We can now use, for example, sequence **a** of 100 floats and sequence **b** of 200 floats as follows:

```
floatsequence<100> a;
floatsequence<200> b;
```

This might seem similar to writing

```
float a[100], b[200];
```

but here we have no class, so we cannot benefit from member functions, derivation and so on. It makes more sense to compare our **floatsequence** variables **a** and **b** with variables of the same names defined below:

```
class floatseq {
public:
    floatseq(int n){p = new float[n]; len = n;}
    ...
private:
    float *p;
    int len;
};

floatseq a(100);
floatseq b(200);
```

The main difference between the types **floatsequence** and **floatseq** is the way memory is allocated; it depends on your application and your computer system which is to be preferred. It should also be noted that in **floatseq** we can replace 100 and 200 with any **int** expressions, while we can use only *constant* expressions for them in our **floatsequence** example.

Using argument declarations (such as **int n**) is more interesting if we combine them with type-arguments (such as **class T**), as in this example:

```
template <class T, int n, class S>
class sequence
{   ...
};
```

In this case, we must use template-class-names that match this template-argument-list; in other words, we must supply a type, a constant expression of type **int**, and again a type, int that order. An example of such a template-class-name is

```
sequence <int, 100, long>
```

To demonstrate this principle in a complete program, let us use a class template for two number sequences, one consisting of four **int** values (1, 3, 5, 7) and the other of three **float** values (0.3, 0.4, 0.5). There will be a member function **sum** to compute the sum of the sequences. The third template argument, **long**, in the above template-class-name, indicates the type of this sum.

```
// SEQUENCE: A class template with three arguments.
#include <iostream.h>

template <class T, int n, class S>
class sequence {
public:
    sequence(T start, T incr);
    S sum();
private:
    T r[n];
};

template <class T, int n, class S>
sequence<T, n, S>::sequence(T start, T incr)
{   for (int i=0; i<n; i++) r[i] = start + i * incr;
}

template <class T, int n, class S>
S sequence<T, n, S>::sum()
{   S s = 0;
    for (int i=0; i<n; i++) s += r[i];
    return s;
}

int main()
{   sequence<int, 4, long> a_int(1, 2);
    sequence<float, 3, float> a_float(0.3, 0.1);
    cout << a_int.sum() << " " << a_float.sum() << endl;
    return 0;
}
```

By writing the general form

```
T r[n];
```

in the template, and by using this template as we did in the **main** function, we actually have

```
int r[4];
```

in one generated class and

```
float r[3];
```

in the other. The corresponding class variables are **a_int** and **a_float**, and their constructor arguments indicate the start and increment values of the sequences. Since the program computes 1 + 3 + 5 + 7 and 0.3 + 0.4 + 0.5, its output is

```
16 1.2
```

11.4 A Quicksort Template

Traditionally, C (and C++) programmers use the standard library function **qsort** (see Section 12.12) to sort arrays of any type and any length. As a reasonable alternative, we will use a sort function of our own here, also based on the Quicksort method and applicable to arrays of any type and any length. Actually, what we write is not a function but rather a function *template*, so more than one function can be generated from it. By placing the template in a header file, we can use it in several programs without duplicating source code:

```
// QS_TEMPL.H

template <class T>
void quicksort(T *a, int n)
{  int i, j;
   T x, w;
   do
   {  i = 0; j = n - 1;
      x = a[j/2];
      do
      {  while (a[i] < x) i++;
         while (a[j] > x) j--;
         if (i < j){w = a[i]; a[i] = a[j]; a[j] = w;}
      }  while (++i <= --j);
      if (i == j + 3){--i; ++j;}
      if (j + 1 < n - i)
      {  if (j > 0) quicksort(a, j + 1);
         a += i; n -= i;
      }  else
      {  if (i < n - 1) quicksort(a + i, n - i);
         n = j + 1;
      }
   }  while (n > 1);
}
```

The following demonstration program sorts two arrays, one of **int** elements and the other of elements of records. It uses the above header file:

```
// QS_TEMPL: Quicksort with templates.
#include <iostream.h>
#include <string.h>
#include "qs_templ.h"

class record {
public:
   record(int c=0, char *p=0):code(c)
   {  name = new char[strlen(p)+1];
      strcpy(name, p);
   }
   friend int operator<(record &r, record &s)
   {  return strcmp(r.name, s.name) < 0;
   }
   friend int operator>(record &r, record &s){return s < r;}
   friend ostream &operator<<(ostream &s, record &r)
   {  return s << r.code << " " << r.name << endl;
   }
private:
   int code;
   char *name;
};

int main()
{  int i;
   int a[8] = {234, 437, 12, 321, 14, 7, 100, 95};
   record b[5];
   b[0] = record(10, "Jim");
   b[1] = record(25, "Gregory");
   b[2] = record(35, "Mary");
   b[3] = record(17, "Arthur");
   b[4] = record(30, "Ella");
   quicksort(a, 8);  // Sort int array
   quicksort(b, 5);  // Sort record array
   for (i=0; i<8; i++) cout << a[i] << " ";
   cout << endl;
   for (i=0; i<5; i++) cout << b[i];
   return 0;
}
```

In the output of this program, you find one line for the sorted **int** array **a**, followed by five lines for the sorted **record** array **b**. The records, each containing a numeric code and a string, are sorted in alphabetical order of the strings:

```
7 12 14 95 100 234 321 437
17 Arthur
30 Ella
25 Gregory
10 Jim
35 Mary
```

This *quicksort* version is not the simplest possible, but it is a safe one. Instead of two recursive calls, only the one for the shorter subsequence is executed, to reduce the risk of stack overflow. A discussion of this aspect can be found in *Programs and Data Structures in C*. The **quicksort** template shown here is almost identical to a function (called **q_sort**) in that book, the only difference being the use of the template prefix and of type parameter **T** instead of type **int**.

Compared with the standard library function **qsort**, our **quicksort** template is easier to understand and to use because the 'less than' relation is represented here by the usual < operator rather than by a call to a separate compare function. For standard types, such as **int**, avoiding the overhead involved in calling such a compare function may also speed up the sorting process, as we will see in a moment. For types of our own, such as **record** in our example, we simply overload the < and > operators to define how comparisons are to be done.

C++, templates and speed

One of the most attractive aspects of C++ is that programs written in this language need not be less efficient than similar ones written in C. As mentioned above, the **qsort** standard library function is based on a compare function, which must also be used for standard types such as **int**. In view of the overhead involved in calling this compare function, we may wonder whether function **qsort** applied to an array of integers might be slower than using our **quicksort** template. The following program can be used to find an answer to this question:

```
// TIMESORT: Compare sorting times.
#include <iostream.h>
#include <stdlib.h>
#include <time.h>
#include "qs_templ.h"

const int MAX = 10000;
int a[MAX], a1[MAX];

int compare(const void* p, const void *q)
{  return *(int*)p - *(int*)q;
}

int main()
{  int i, length;
   long n, j;
   cout << "How often do you want to sort? "; cin >> n;
   cout << "How many elements in array?    "; cin >> length;
   if (length > MAX)
   {  cout << "At most " << MAX << ", please.";
      exit(1);
   }
   for (i=0; i<length; i++) a[i] = rand();
```

```
    clock_t t1, t2;

    // Our own function quicksort:
    t1 = clock();
    for (j=0; j<n; j++)
    {   for (i=0; i<length; i++) a1[i] = a[i];
        quicksort(a1, length);
    }
    t2 = clock();
    cout << "Time quicksort: "
         << (t2 - t1)/float(CLK_TCK) << " s\n";
    cout << "First and last array elements after sorting: "
         << a[0] << " " << a[length-1] << "\n\n";

    // The standard library function qsort:
    t1 = clock();
    for (j=0; j<n; j++)
    {   for (i=0; i<length; i++) a1[i] = a[i];
        qsort(a1, length, sizeof(int), compare);
    }
    t2 = clock();
    cout << "Time qsort: "
         << (t2 - t1)/float(CLK_TCK) << " s\n";
    cout << "First and last array elements after sorting: "
         << a[0] << " " << a[length-1] << "\n\n";

    return 0;
}
```

Note that this program uses our header file QS_TEMPL.H, which we have seen a short while ago. Here is a demonstration of this program, obtained by using the Borland C++ compiler:

```
How often do you want to sort? 100
How many elements in array?    10000
Time quicksort: 6.64 s
First and last array elements after sorting: 346 13125

Time qsort: 16.26 s
First and last array elements after sorting: 346 13125
```

As you can see, our **quicksort** template sorts much faster than the standard library function **qsort**. Any suspicion of templates necessarily leading to inefficiency is clearly unfounded.

12

Exception Handling

12.1 Errors and Exceptions

When writing large and complicated programs, one of the most difficult subjects is adequately dealing with errors that occur due to special circumstances. Examples of these are:

- Memory exhaustion.
- An input file cannot be opened.
- Division by zero due to incorrect input data.

In example programs, which we want to be easy-to-read, we sometimes omit checks to detect such errors. For example, in this book we have often seen code to read numbers from the keyboard or to allocate memory by using **new**, without checking if such attempts succeed. In practice such checks are highly recommended. If we have decided to write them in our programs, the question arises what to do if such tests fail. It would be best if, possibly assisted by the user, we could solve the problem and continue program execution. Sometimes this is too complicated and we prefer terminating the program by calling the **exit** function.

What is exception handling?

We often use the term *exception handling* when we actually mean *error handling*. The former is a generalization of the latter. In other words, every run-time error is an exception, but there are exceptions which we need not regard as an error. For example, if we try to assign a value greater than 255 to a **char** variable, only the eight least significant bits of that value will be used. By calling this situation an *exception*, we avoid any discussions whether or not it should be considered an error. We may define exception handling as 'dealing with run-time errors and other exceptional situations'.

Exception handling: where?

Besides thinking about *what* action to take in the case of an error, we must also discuss *where* to perform such an action. Suppose we have a **main** function which calls function **compute**, which in turn calls function **detail**. There are three levels in this example:

- **main**, the highest level;
- **compute**, the medium level;
- **detail**, the lowest level.

It may be desirable to react in **main** to an error occurring in **detail**. In general, if an error occurs at a low level we often want to deal with this error at a higher level. In other words, instead of

```
...
int main()
{  ... compute(...) ...
}

void compute(...)
{  ... detail(...) ...
}

void detail(...)
{  ...
   if (error) ...
   ...
}
```

we want to write something like this:

```
...
int main()
{  ...
   compute(...);
   if (error) ...
   ...
}

void compute(...)
{  ... detail(...)  ...
}

void detail(...)
{  ...
}
```

The error actually occurs in **detail**. However, since this function is invoked by a call to **compute** in the **main** function, we may as well regard this error as a failure of function **compute** and we may want to base an error message or any other action on this view. The traditional way of dealing with this problem is by letting both **detail** and **compute** return a status code, indicating success or failure. Alternatively, the functions **setjmp** and **longjmp** (see Section 13.7) are sometimes used for this purpose. Either solution may be undesirable because of its complexity or even be impossible. For example, if the above function **compute**, instead of being a **void** function, already had returned a value for a purpose other than its status. Errors may also occur in constructors, which do not return values at all. All this makes a special language construct for exception handling very desirable.

12.2 Using the Keywords try, catch and throw

Modern C++ compilers offer a very convenient means to solve the problem discussed at the end of the last section. It is based on three new keywords, **try**, **catch** and **throw**, which you can find in this program fragment:

```
...
int main()
{   ...
    try {compute(...);}
    catch (int i) { ... }
    ...
}

void compute(...)
{   ...   detail(...)   ...
}

void detail(...)
{   ...
    if (error) throw 123;
    ...
}
```

If an error occurs in function **detail**, the statement **throw 123;** is executed. As a result, this function is immediately left and program execution resumes in the compound statement { ... } following **catch(int i)** in the **main** function. In this compound statement, we can use **i**, whose value is 123. The compound statement just mentioned is not executed if the *error* expression in function **detail** is equal to zero. The following program is based on the above fragment:

```
// EXCEPT1: Example of exception handling

#include <iostream.h>
void compute(int i), detail(int k);

int main()
{  int x;
   cout << "Enter x: ";
   cin >> x;
   try {compute(x);}
   catch (int i) {cout << i << endl;}
   cout << "The End.\n";
   return 0;
}

void compute(int i)
{  cout << "Start of compute function.\n";
   detail(i);
   cout << "End of compute function.\n";
}

void detail(int k)
{  cout << "Start of detail function.\n";
   if (k == 0) throw 123;
   cout << "End of detail function.\n";
}
```

The output of this program depends on whether or not 0 is entered as input data. Here is a demonstration in which this is the case:

```
Enter x: 0
Start of compute function.
Start of detail function.
123
The End.
```

We say that in this case an *exception is thrown*. As you can see, the functions **detail** and **compute** are not completed.

If any other integer is entered, no exception is thrown and the demonstration will be similar to this one:

```
Enter x: 9876
Start of compute function.
Start of detail function.
End of detail function.
End of compute function.
The End.
```

This output shows that for nonzero **x** values all three functions are completed in the normal way and the compound statement following **catch(int i)** is skipped.

Although the keywords **try**, **catch** and **throw** are intended for exception handling, they could be used for just another flow of control: if in function **detail** we replaced == with !=, the 'exception would be thrown' for any nonzero input value.

To use exception handling in programs of our own, we must discuss a few points in some more detail. In program EXCEPT1, the line

```
catch (int i) {cout << i << endl;}
```

is called an *exception handler*, or simply, a *handler*, and a succession of at least one handler is known as a *handler-list*. A *try-block* is syntactically defined as

try *compound-statement handler-list*

It follows that

```
try {compute(x);}
catch (int i) {cout << i << endl;}
```

is an example of a try-block. In a try-block, at least one handler is required but there may be more. Instead of **(int i)** we could have written **(int)** here, provided we do not use **i** in the handler. Since this **i** can only have the value 123 in this example, we might as well have written

```
catch (int) {cout << "123\n";}
```

instead of the above handler.

The fragment

```
throw 123
```

is called a *throw-expression*, and it is an expression of type **void**. As usual, we obtain a statement by appending a semicolon. When an exception is thrown, control is transferred to a handler whose try-block was most recently entered and not yet exited. If there are several handlers in this try-block, the type of the expression following the **throw** keyword determines which one is taken. Program EXCEPT2 illustrates this.

If the user enters 0, an **int** exception is thrown and the first handler is executed. If he or she enters an nonzero integer, followed by a question mark, a **char** exception is thrown and the second handler is executed. If, instead, a nonzero integer is followed by a character other than a question mark, no exception is thrown. Finally, if 0? is entered, an **int** exception is thrown because of the order of the throw expressions in this program. Once control is transferred to a handler, there is no automatic return, so **throw '?'** will not be executed if **i** is zero.

```
// EXCEPT2: Two handlers in a try-block.
#include <iostream.h>

int main()
{  int i;
   char ch;
   cout << "Enter an integer, followed by some "
           "nonnumeric character:\n";
   try
   {  cin >> i >> ch;
      if (i == 0) throw 0;
      if (ch == '?') throw '?';
   }
   catch (int) {cout << "Zero entered.\n";}
   catch (char) {cout << "Question mark entered.\n";}
   cout << "The End.\n";
   return 0;
}
```

A handler can only be entered by throwing the corresponding exception, so at most one handler will be executed in this example, as the following four demonstrations illustrate:

```
Enter an integer, followed by some nonnumeric character:
0!
Zero entered.
The End.

Enter an integer, followed by some nonnumeric character:
2?
Question mark entered.
The End.

Enter an integer, followed by some nonnumeric character:
1!
The End.

Enter an integer, followed by some nonnumeric character:
0?
Zero entered.
The End.
```

In program EXCEPT2, the types (int and char) used in the throw expressions are the same as those of the handlers. Instead of standard types, we may also use types of our own. If a class D is derived from a base class B, a handler with type B is a match for a throw expression with an object of type D.

Try-blocks may be dynamically nested, as this example shows:

```
void f()
{  try {g();}
   catch(int) {...}
   catch(float) {...}
}

void g()
{  try {h();}
   catch(float) {...}
}

void h()
{  ...
   if (...) throw 1;
   if (...) throw 2.0;
   ...
}
```

Function **h** is called from a try-block in function **g**, which in turn is called from a try-block in function **f**. If **throw 1** is executed in function **h**, the **int** handler in **f** is invoked because there is no **int** handler in **g**. If **throw 2.0** is executed, however, a choice must be made between the **float** handlers in **g** and in **f**. In this case the **float** handler of **g** is taken because it is the one whose try-block was most recently entered and not yet exited.

If in function **h** an exception of any type other than **int** and **float** were thrown, there would be no matching handler. In that case the function **terminate** (to be discussed in Section 12.4) would be called.

12.3 Error Handling with new

Until recently, the **new** operator returned the value 0 (also known as **NULL**) if memory allocation failed. However, new compilers, such as Borland C++ 4.0 and higher, deal with memory this problem differently. This may be a real problem for existing C++ programs that we have to recompile. Fortunately, we can easily let the program behave in the way it did previously by inserting

```
#include <new.h>
```

and

```
set_new_handler(0);
```

in it, as we have done in Section 5.6.

The function **set_new_handler** can also have a pointer to a function (which may simply be the name of that function) as its argument. This function is a new-handler of our own. It must be a **void** function without parameters, and it is called if **new** fails. Here is a complete program to demonstrate this; when you run it, use a large integer as input data:

```
// NEW1: A new-handler of our own.
#include <iostream.h>
#include <stdlib.h>
#include <new.h>

void failing()
{   cout << "Memory allocation fails." << endl;
    exit(1);
}

int main()
{   struct chunk {char s[30000];} *p;
    int n;
    set_new_handler(failing);
    cout << "Enter an int value to make new operator fail: ";
    cin >> n;
    for (int i=0; i<n; i++) p = new chunk;
    return 0;
}
```

The call to **exit** in function **failing** is really necessary. If we omitted it, this function would return to its caller and **new** would be tried again, which would give rise to calling the **failing** function once again, and so on.

Default exception thrown by new

There is another way of dealing with failing memory allocation. If we do not call the **set_new_handler** function, the **new** operator, when failing, will throw an exception. With Borland C++, this is the **xalloc** exception, where **xalloc** is a class declared in the header file *except.h*. The following program, to be used with the compiler mentioned, is based on this **xalloc** exception, but otherwise similar to our previous program, NEW1:

```
// NEW2: Default exception for failing 'new' operator.
#include <iostream.h>
#include <stdlib.h>
#include <except.h>

void failing()
{   cout << "Memory allocation fails." << endl;
    exit(1);
}
```

```
int main()
{   struct chunk {char s[30000];} *p;
    int n;
    cout << "Enter an int value to make new operator fail: ";
    cin >> n;
    try
    {   for (int i=0; i<n; i++) p = new chunk;
    }
    catch (xalloc)        // Or catch(bad_alloc)?
    {   failing();
    }
    return 0;
}
```

There is a subtle difference between the programs NEW1 and NEW2. If, in the **failing** function of NEW2, we omit the call to **exit**, the program works almost in the same way: after printing the message, **failing** then returns to the **main** function and the program terminates normally. As we have seen, this is different in NEW1. Since some people are not happy with the rather cryptic name **xalloc**, this name will possibly be changed in the ANSI C++ standard. It has been suggested that **bad_alloc** would be a better name.

12.4 The set_terminate Function

As we have seen in Section 12.2, an exception handler is selected on the basis of its type. If there is no handler whose type matches the object of the throw-expression, the function **terminate** is called. By default, this **terminate** function calls the function **abort** so our program terminate abnormally. However, we do better by calling the function **set_terminate**, with another function, say, **my_terminate**, as its argument. The **terminate** function will then call **my_terminate**. Program TERMIN illustrates this:

```
// TERMIN: Using the set_terminate function.

#include <iostream.h>
#include <except.h>
#include <stdlib.h>

void my_terminate()
{   cout << "Could not find a matching handler.\n";
    exit(1);
}

void f()
{   throw "ABC";
}
```

```
int main()
{  set_terminate(my_terminate);
   try {f();}
   catch(int) {cout << "int handler.\n";}
   catch(char) {cout << "char handler.\n";}
   catch(float) {cout << "float handler.\n";}
   return 0;
}
```

This program cannot find a handler for type **const char***, which is the type of the object in the throw-expression. By calling **set_terminate**, we have specified what should happen in this case, so the function **my_terminate** will be called.

If (in complex programs) there are several calls to **set_terminate**, each such call will return the address of the function previously given to **set_terminate**, as indicated by comments in this fragment:

```
void f(){...}
void g(){...}
void h(){...}
...
int main()
{  void (*p)();
   p = set_terminate(f); // the address of terminate
   p = set_terminate(g); // the address of f
   p = set_terminate(h); // the address of g
   ...
}
```

12.5 Exception Specifications and set_unexpected

A function defined in the usual way can throw any exception. We can restrict the exceptions a function can throw by adding something to that function. For example, by writing

```
void f() throw (X, Y)
{  ...
}
```

function **f** can throw only the exceptions **X** and **Y**. An attempt by **f** to throw any exception other than **X** and **Y**, will cause a call to the function **unexpected**, which we will discuss in a moment. The suffix

```
throw (...)
```

as used here, is called an *exception-specification* and can list any number of exceptions. Only the exceptions listed can be thrown. In particular, this list can be empty. Function **g**, defined as

```
void g() throw()
{  ...
}
```

can therefore throw no exception at all. As we know, the opposite case, enabling any exception, is obtained by omitting this suffix altogether. So function **f** defined as

```
void f()
{  ...
}
```

can throw any exception.

Using the function set_unexpected

As mentioned above, there is a function **unexpected**, which will be called if a function throws an exception that is not listed in its exception-specification. By default, this function calls the **terminate** function (see Section 12.4), which in turn calls the **abort** function by default. However, we can make **unexpected** call a function of our own, supplied as an argument to function **set_unexpected**. The latter function is declared in *except.h*. Here is an example to show how this is done:

```
// UNEXPECT: An exception specification and set_unexpected.
#include <iostream.h>
#include <except.h>
#include <stdlib.h>

float f(float x) throw(int)
{  if (x == 0.0) throw "Division by zero.";
   return 1/x;
}

void g()
{  cout << "Function g executed.\n"; exit(1);
}

int main()
{  float x, y;
   cout << "Enter x: "; cin >> x;
   set_unexpected(g);
   try{y = f(x);}
   catch(const char *s){cout << s << endl;}
   cout << "y = " << y << endl;
   return 0;
}
```

If x is zero, function f throws an exception of type **const char***, while only **int** is listed in its exception-specification. The **unexpected** function will therefore be called in this case. Because of our call to **set_unexpected** in the **main** function, this call to **unexpected** will cause a call to function **g**. All this will not happen if x is nonzero, as these two demonstrations show:

```
Enter x: 0
Function g executed.

Enter x: 6
y = 0.166667
```

If (in complex programs) there are several calls to **set_unexpected**, each such call will return the address of the function previously given to **set_unexpected**. This is similar to the behavior of the **set_terminate** function, as discussed at the end of the previous section.

A

More Exercises

In addition to the exercises at the end of Chapters 1 to 9, here are some more recommended programming problems. As is usually the case in practice, you will have to choose yourself among several facilities of the C++ language that can be used to solve a given problem. Be economical with computer time and memory space. In particular, do not use arrays if you can easily do without them. These problems are approximately in increasing order of difficulty. The solutions to Exercises 42, ..., 47 are given at the end of this appendix.

1   When three numbers are given, it may or may not be possible to use them as the lengths of the sides of a triangle. Write a program to find this out for three real numbers read from the keyboard. If such a triangle exists, examine if it has an obtuse or a right angle.

2   Write a program which reads the three real numbers a, b, and c, to compute the real numbers x_1 and x_2 that satisfy the quadratic equation $ax^2 + bx + c = 0$, if such real numbers exist.

3   A sequence of positive integers is to be read from the keyboard, followed by a nonnumeric character. For each of the factors 2, 3, and 5, count how many of the integers that are read are multiples of that factor.

4   Write a program that reads a sequence of 20 integers to determine the smallest and the largest of them as well as the positions of these two elements in the sequence. In case they occur more than once, find the position of the first occurrence of the smallest number and that of the last occurrence of the largest number.

5   A sequence of real numbers, followed by a nonnumeric character, is to be read
     from the keyboard. Compute the sum of the 1st, 3rd, 6th, 10th, 15th, 21st, ...
     elements of this sequence.

6   A sequence of 20 integers is to be read from the keyboard. For each pair of
     successive integers in this sequence, compute the absolute value of their
     difference. The largest of these absolute values is to be printed.

7   A sequence of ten integers is to be read from the keyboard. Search this sequence
     for the first element that is equal to the tenth, and print the position of that first
     element. (If all elements are equal, that position is 1; if they are all distinct, it is
     10.)

8   Write a program that reads a positive integer n (not greater than 25), to print a
     table of n lines and n columns, which has the following form:

```
1   1   1    . . .    1
1   2   2    . . .    2
1   2   3    . . .    3
.   .   .             .
.   .   .             .
.   .   .             .
1   2   3    . . .    n
```

9   Write a program that reads a sample of n real values x_i, followed by a nonnu-
     meric character. The following numbers, used in statistics to characterize certain
     properties of the sample, are to be computed:

     a. The mean value: $(\Sigma x_i)/n$
     b. The variance: $\{(\Sigma x_i^2) - (\Sigma x_i)^2/n\}/(n-1)$
     c. The range: largest value – smallest value
     (Σx_i is the sum of all x_i; Σx_i^2 is the sum of all x_i^2.)

10   A given input file contains the values $x_1, y_1, x_2, y_2, ..., x_n, y_n$, in that order. Each
     pair (x_i, y_i) represents a point in the xy-plane. We want to compute the coefficients
     a and b of the equation

     $$y = a + bx$$

     which represents a *regression line*, that is, a straight line which fits 'best' through
     the n given points. Use the *method of least squares* by Gauss, according to which
     a and b are found as the solution of the following system of linear equations:

     $$an + b\Sigma x_i = \Sigma y_i$$
     $$a\Sigma x_i + b\Sigma x_i^2 = \Sigma 2x_i y_i$$

11   A ladder has a given length L. It is placed against a wall, and touches a box, which is a cube with height 1, as shown in Figure A.1. Compute the distance x between the box and the bottom of the ladder.

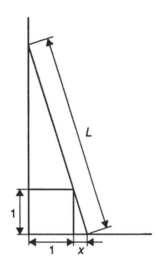

Figure A.1. Ladder and box

12   Both a real number x and an integer n are to be read from the keyboard. Compute the following sum, which is an approximation of the mathematical expression e^x ($e = 2.718281828459...$; $n! = 1 \times 2 \times ... \times n$):

$$1 + x + \frac{x^2}{2!} + \frac{x^3}{3!} + \cdots + \frac{x^n}{n!}$$

13   A file contains the positive integers k and n, followed by $k \times n$ real numbers in a table with k rows and n columns. Compute the arithmetic means of each of the n columns. The name of the input file is to be supplied as a program argument.

14   Write a program that reads two dates of the same (non-leap) year to compute how many days the second date falls after the first. The dates are given as four-digit integers $mmdd$. For example, 1231 is the last day of the year. Print the algebraic difference: the result is negative if the first given date falls after the second.

15   A file contains the integer n, followed by two sequences: first, n integers a_i and, second, n integers b_i. Compute $\Sigma \max(a_i, b_i)$, that is, the sum of the n larger values of each pair (a_i, b_i). The name of the input file is to be entered on the keyboard.

16   Count how many decimal integers occur in a given text file, and compute the sum of these integers. The integers may be separated by any nonnumeric characters. The name of the input file is to be supplied as a program argument. For example, the file consisting or the two lines shown below contains five integers, the sum of which is 1034.

```
123.111?abc200
500 100def
```

17   Write a program which reads a positive integer, doubles it, and prints the decimal digits of its result, separated by a blank. For example, if 3912 is read, the output is

```
7   8   2   4.
```

18   Write a program that reads an integer n and prints all possible sequences of n bits in which no successive zeros occur. For example, $n = 3$ leads to

```
010
011
101
110
111
```

19   Write a program that reads n, followed by the n^2 integers:

$$a_{11}, a_{12}, ..., a_{1n}$$
$$a_{21}, a_{22}, ..., a_{2n}$$
$$...$$
$$a_{n1}, a_{n2}, ..., a_{nn}$$

most of which are zero. Compute the largest absolute value $|i - j|$ for which a_{ij} is nonzero.

20   Write a program that sorts the real numbers $a_0, a_1, ..., a_{n-1}$, read from the keyboard, using the *straight selection* sorting method. It is given that n will be no greater than 25, so the n real numbers can be placed in an array. First, search the sequence for its smallest element and exchange this with a_0. Then, deal with the remaining sequence, starting with a_1, in the same way, and so on. When, finally, there is a remaining sequence of length 1, all elements in the array are in increasing order and can be printed. (Remember, this sorting method should be used only for sequences of moderate length, as in this example. For long sequences, the **qsort** standard function, discussed in Section 10.12, is much faster.)

21   Write a program which reads 25 positive integers $a_0, ..., a_{24}$, which are absolute frequencies. Show these in a graphical form known as a *histogram*. This should consist of 25 vertical bars, the jth bar ($0 \leq j < 25$) being a column of a_j letters **I**. The lower endpoints of all bars are to appear on the same horizontal line.

22   Write a program that reads a positive integer and writes it as a product of prime factors. For example, we have $120 = 2 \times 2 \times 2 \times 3 \times 5$.

23   Write a program which reads a sequence of integers, followed by a nonnumeric character, and counts how often each of the integers 0, 1, ..., 15 occurs in this sequence. Print the result in a table.

24   We are given 25 gears with the following numbers of teeth:

30	35	37	40	45
47	50	52	55	57
60	65	68	70	75
78	80	82	85	86
87	90	95	97	99.

In order to transmit power from one shaft to another, we need to use pairs of gears, as illustrated in Figure A.2. The left and the right gears have a and b teeth, respectively. In view of the allowed center distances d, the sum of the numbers of teeth must satisfy

$$130 \le a + b \le 140.$$

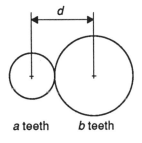

Figure A.2. Gears

Furthermore, we are only interested in pairs (a, b) that give a gear ratio $q = a/b$ satisfying $0.5 \le q < 1$. Write a program that produces a table of all allowed pairs (a, b), together with their gear ratios q:

a	b	q
.	.	.
.	.	.
.	.	.

(If you think this exercise too elementary, you can make it more interesting by requiring that the above lines be printed in increasing order of q.)

25 Write a program that looks for all occurrences of a given word in a given text file. Both the word (consisting of letters only) and the file name are supplied as program arguments. Print each line of the file in which the given word occurs.

26 We can write $8/35 = 1/(4 + 3/8)$. Applying the same process to $3/8$, we obtain $8/35 = 1/\{4 + 1/(2 + 2/3)\}$. We proceed in this way until the final plus sign is followed by the numerator 1. In our example, this is the case after another step, which gives $8/35 = 1/[4 + 1/\{2 + 1/(1 + 1/2)\}]$. We can represent such an expression, called a *continued fraction*, by listing all integers that occur in it except for all numerators 1. In this example we obtain 4, 2, 1, 2. Write a program which reads two positive integers a and b and computes the sequence representing the continued fraction for a/b.

27 Write a program which reads the positive integers $a_1, a_2, ..., a_n$ to find all pairs (i, j) for which the greatest common divisor of a_i and a_j is equal to 1. See also Exercise 4.5.

28 In a factory, there is a machine that examines a great many samples of, say, a liquid product. For each sample, the machine checks whether or not each of the elements $E_0, E_1, ..., E_7$ is present in the sample, and the eight answers are coded (as 1 for present and 0 for absent) in the bits $b_0, b_1, ..., b_7$ of a byte. All these bytes are written in the file *element.dat*. Write a program that reads this file, and, for each of the eight elements, counts how many times it has been present in the tested samples.

29 Write a program to approximate the value of x (between $\pi/2$ and π) that satisfies the following equation:

$$\sin x - x/2 = 0$$

Use the Newton–Raphson method (also known as the Newton method), which is a well-known numerical method for solving equations of the form $f(x) = 0$. Starting with some value x_0 as an approximation of the solution x, you repeatedly replace the approximation x_n with a better one, x_{n+1}, which is computed as:

$$x_{n+1} = x_n - f(x_n)/f'(x_n)$$

In our case we have $f(x) = \sin x - x/2$ and $f'(x) = \cos x - 1/2$. You can use, for example, $x_0 = 3$ as a start value. Find a termination condition yourself. The Newton–Raphson method can be explained as follows. We begin by drawing the tangent to the graph of f at point $(x_0, f(x_0))$, to find the point where this tangent intersects the x-axis. The x-coordinate of this new point is x_1. Then x_2 is derived from x_1 in the same way as x_1 has been derived from x_0, and so on.

30   Write a program that finds all prime numbers less than 100 000, using the 'sieve of Eratosthenes'. The smallest prime number is 2; furthermore, a positive integer n is a prime number if it is not a multiple of any smaller prime number. You can use an array of 12 500 bytes. As each byte contains eight bits, we can also regard this array as a sequence of $12\,500 \times 8 = 100\,000$ bits. Let us denote this sequence as

$$b_0, b_1, b_2, ..., b_{99999}$$

We want each bit b_i to be 0 if i is a prime number, and 1 if it is not. Initially we set $b_0 = b_1 = 1$ and $b_i = 0$ for all i greater than 1. As 2 is a prime number, b_2 remains 0. Obviously, no multiple of 2 is a prime number. We therefore place the value 1 into b_4, b_6, b_8, and so on. Similarly, b_3 remains 0, but we place 1 into b_6, b_9, b_{12}, and so on. Examining b_4, we find that it has already obtained the value 1, which means that 4 is a multiple of a smaller prime number; we then know that all multiples of 4 also have been set to 1; so the fact that b_4 is 1 means that we can immediately proceed to the next element, b_5. As this is 0, we do not alter it, but place the value 1 into b_{10}, b_{15}, b_{20}, and so on. We continue this process until all elements b_i have their correct values. Note that you can stop as soon as you have reached an element b_j such that $j^2 > 100\,000$. Write all prime numbers found in this way to the file *prime.dat*, and count how many there are. (The correct answer is 9592.) Also, print the greatest prime number that is less than 100 000.

31   With a given integer n, compute the nth element F_n of the Fibonacci sequence, which can be defined as follows:

$$F_0 = 0$$
$$F_1 = 1$$
$$F_n = F_{n-1} + F_{n-2} \qquad (n \geq 2)$$

For reasons of efficiency, do not use recursion. For some large values of n, also compare the quotient F_n/F_{n-1} with the following number:

$$\tau = 2 \cos 36° = (1 + \sqrt{5})/2 = 1.6180339887...$$

(Verify the fact that the sequence

$$..., \tau^{-2}, \tau^{-1}, 1, \tau, \tau^2, ...$$

is similar to the Fibonacci sequence in that the sum of any two successive elements is equal to the next element in the sequence.)

32   Write a program that can read any text file to check it with regard to parentheses and braces, which are allowed to occur only in pairs and arranged in the usual way. For example, the following is correct:

```
({(( ... )( ... ))}( ))
```

Note that all parentheses ( ) between the two braces { } are paired in the proper way. Incorrect examples are:

```
{()}
{}{}
```

33   Write a program that can read any text file to print both its longest and its second longest line. If several lines are candidates for being the longest, only the first is to be taken. The same applies to the second longest line.

34   Write a program with two program arguments, which are the names of input and output files. The input file contains text lines; all characters have the same width, say, 0.1 inch. We want to apply a process technically known as *justification* to this file. This means that, except for the final line of the file, all words that are at the end of a line are right aligned, so that the right margin of the page is made even. The modified version is to be written to the output file. The program is to read a line length (that is, the desired number of characters on each line of the output file) from the keyboard. You may regard all character sequences separated by blanks or newline characters as 'words'. These words are to be copied from the input file to the output file. Each line of the output file is to contain as many words as the given line length permits; the words are to be separated by at least one blank, but zero or more additional blanks are to be distributed as evenly as possible between the words to let the line exactly have its required length.

35   Write a program which reads the name of a text file from the keyboard to produce a *concordance* for all words in this file. All these words are to printed (only once) in alphabetic order, followed by the numbers of the lines on which they occur. Upper-case and lower-case letters are to be regarded as identical. For example, with the input file

```
To be or
not to be,
that is the question.
```

the following concordance is produced:

```
be        1  2
is        3
not       2
or        1
question  3
that      3
the       3
to        1  2
```

36   Write a program that examines if two given text files contain exactly the same words, regardless of their order and frequency. Two files, say, A and B, contain the same words if each word that occurs in A also occurs in B and each word of B also occurs in A.

37   Write a program to count how many times a given word, read from the keyboard, occurs in a given text file. Note that the word 'under' occurs only once in the following text:

```
The importance of understanding the
wise lessons presented in the book
under consideration is easily under-
estimated.
```

38   Write a program that reads a file containing a (possibly incorrect) C++ program. The program is to check that
      a. for each start (/*) of comment, its end (*/) is also present;
      b. for each start (") of a string, its end (") is also present.
      As usual in C++, a double slash (//), occurring outside a string, starts a comment that terminates at the end of the current line. A double quote in a comment, as in /* "ABC */, does not count as the start of the end of a string, nor are the character pairs /* and */ in a string (as in "ABC /*") related to comment. The double quote is also to be ignored if it occurs in a string, preceded by a backslash (as in "\""), or in a character constant (""). Neither strings nor comments can be nested. The double-quote pairs of a string must be on the same line, unless lines are continued by means of the backslash (\).

39   Write a calculator, with the operators + and *, for modulo n arithmetic. First the integer n is to be read, followed by an arithmetic expression in which integers less than n, operators and parentheses may occur in the usual way. An equal sign terminates the input. For example, with input

```
12
(11 + 3) * (4 + 9 + 2) + 8 =
```

the output is

```
2
```

Use the remainder of a division by n in each step, not only at the end. In this example, we have (11 + 3) % 12 = 2 and (4 + 9) % 12 = 1, so instead of the given expression we compute $2 \times (1 + 2) + 8$. With modulo 12 arithmetic, this is equal to 14 % 12 = 2.

40   Solve Exercise 5.8, the Josephus problem, once again; this time, use a *circular list*, which is a linear list the last element of which contains a pointer to the first. Use an element in the circular list for each person in the circle, and implement removing each kth person by deleting the corresponding element of the circular list.

41   Write a program that reads the following integers:

$$m, l_1, u_1, l_2, u_2, ..., l_m, u_m$$

The integers l_i and u_i are the lower and upper bounds of a 'running variable' r_i ($i = 1, 2, ..., m$). Print all distinct sequences $r_1, r_2, ..., r_m$, for which $l_i \le r_i \le u_i$. For example, with $m = 3, l_1 = 5, u_1 = 7, l_2 = 2, u_2 = 2, l_3 = 8, u_3 = 9$, the output will be

```
5    2    8
5    2    9
6    2    8
6    2    9
7    2    8
7    2    9
```

The following exercises, marked by asterisks, are more difficult than the previous ones. Their answers are therefore included in this book; they can be found after Exercise 47. Remember, however, you will benefit most from these problems if you seriously try to solve them yourself before consulting their answers.

42*   When working with binary trees, we want these to be more or less balanced, like trees in nature. A binary tree is said to be *perfectly balanced* if the number of nodes in its left subtree differs at most by 1 from that in its right subtree, provided that this also holds for every subtree of the given tree. If we are given a monotonic increasing sequence of numbers, and we know in advance the length of this sequence, we can build a perfectly balanced binary search tree to store these numbers. Write a program to realize this. Use an input file *num.dat*, which contains the sequence length n, followed by n integers in increasing order, and, after storing these in a perfectly balanced binary search tree, print this set of numbers in the form of that tree, rotated counterclockwise through 90°, that is, with the root on the left instead of on the top. For example, if the file *num.dat* contains

```
9
1    2    4    6    8    10 20 25 30
```

then the following output is required:

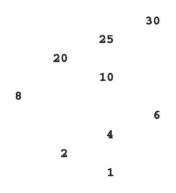

The root of this tree points to a node which contains the number 8, printed here on the left. The left and the right children of this node contain the numbers 2 and 20, respectively, and so on.

43* Write a program to solve the problem known as the *Towers of Hanoi*. There are three pegs, A, B, C, on which disks with holes in their centers can be placed. These disks have all different diameters. A larger disk must never be placed on top of a smaller one. There are n disks, numbered 1, 2, ..., n from the smallest to the largest. Initially all these disks, in the right order, are on peg A, so that pegs B and C are empty. The problem is to move all disks, one by one, from peg A to peg C, never placing a larger disk on a smaller one; peg B may be used as auxiliary. Write a program that reads n and prints the solution to this problem. If $n = 2$, for example, we want the following output:

```
Disk 1 from peg A to peg B.
Disk 2 from peg A to peg C.
Disk 1 from peg B to peg C.
```

44* Write a program which reads the positive integer n and generates all permutations of the sequence 1, 2, ..., n in increasing order. (What this means is explained below.) For example, with $n = 3$, the required output is:

```
1   2   3
1   3   2
2   1   3
2   3   1
3   1   2
3   2   1
```

If we regard each of these lines as a three-digit integer, we obtain 123, 132, 213, 231, 312, 321 in that order. As these numbers form a monotonic increasing sequence, we say that the above permutations are in increasing order.

45*   Write a program that reads the integers n and k and generates all combinations of k elements out of the integers 1, 2, ..., n. For example, if $n = 4$ and $k = 2$, the following output is required:

        1   2
        1   3
        1   4
        2   3
        2   4
        3   4

46*   The Eight Queens problem is to place eight queens on a chessboard so that no queen is attacking any other queen. It was investigated by C.F. Gauss in 1850, but he did not completely solve it. We generalize this problem to the n queens problem for an $n \times n$ board. Write a program that reads n (not greater than 10) and prints all solutions.

47*   Write a program for the Knight's Tour problem. As in the previous exercise, we are given an $n \times n$ board with n^2 squares. A knight, being allowed to move according to the rules of chess, is initially placed on the square in the lower-left corner of the board. In a tour of $n^2 - 1$ moves, the knight is to visit all other squares of the board exactly once. Present your solution in an $n \times n$ table consisting of the numbers 1, 2, ..., n^2, with 1 in the initial position of the knight, 2 in the square visited as a result of the first move, and so on. As for the integer n, read by your program, start with only the value 5: for higher values, such as 8, the program may be very time consuming. Here is a demonstration of the answer program, listed at the end of this Appendix, with $n = 7$:

```
Enter n, for an n x n board (for example, 5): 7

The following integers, arranged in the form of a board,
display the order in which the squares are visited:

   15 18 35  6 13 46 11
   36  7 14 17 10  5 44
   19 16  9 34 45 12 47
    8 37 30 21 26 43  4
   31 20 33 40  3 48 23
   38 29  2 25 22 27 42
    1 32 39 28 41 24 49
```

(This result was computed on a 486 PC in about 70 s.)

Answers to Exercises 42 to 47:

42   ```
       /* PERFBAL: This program builds a perfectly balanced
                    binary search tree.

           Input: The file num.dat, containing n, followed
                     by n integers in increasing order.
       */

       #include <fstream.h>
       #include <iomanip.h>
       #include <stdlib.h>
       ifstream numfile("num.dat", ios::nocreate);

       class tree {
       private:
           struct node {int num; node *left, *right;} *root;
       public:
           tree(int n=0);
           tree(node *p){root = p;}
           friend void printtree(tree t, int k);
       };

       tree::tree(int n)
       { if (n == 0) root = NULL; else
          { int nleft = (n - 1)/2,
                  nright = n - nleft - 1;
             root = new node;
             if (root == NULL)
             { cout << "Not enough memory.\n";
                exit(1);
             }
             root->left = tree(nleft).root;
             numfile >> root->num;
             root->right = tree(nright).root;
          }
       }

       void printtree(tree t, int k=0)
       { if (t.root != NULL)
          { k += 6;
             printtree(tree(t.root->right), k);
             cout << setw(k) << t.root->num << endl;
             printtree(tree(t.root->left), k);
          }
       }
       ```
       ```

```
int main()
{  if (!numfile)
   {  cout << "File num.dat cannot be opened.\n";
      exit(1);
   }
   int n;
   numfile >> n;
   tree t(n);
   cout << endl;
   printtree(t);
   return 0;
}
```

43   ```
        // HANOI: Solution to the Towers of Hanoi problem.
        #include <iostream.h>

        void Hanoi(char src, char aux, char dest, int n)
        /* A tower of n disks is moved from peg src to
           peg dest; peg aux may be used temporarily.
        */
        { if (n > 0)
           { Hanoi(src, dest, aux, n-1);
              cout << "Disk " << n << " from peg " <<
                        src << " to peg " << dest << '.' << endl;
              Hanoi(aux, src, dest, n-1);
           }
        }

        int main()
        { int n;
           cout << endl;
           cout << "Enter n, the number of disks: ";
           cin >> n;
           Hanoi('A', 'B', 'C', n);
           cout << endl;
           return 0;
        }
        ```

44      ```
        // PERMUT: Generating permutations in their natural order.
        #include <iostream.h>
        #include <iomanip.h>
        #include <stdlib.h>
        const int LEN=11;
        int n, r[LEN];

        void print()
        {  for (int i=1; i<=n; i++) cout << setw(3) << r[i];
           cout << endl;
        }
        ```

```cpp
void permut(int k)
/* Generate all permutations of the n - k + 1 integers
   r[k], r[k+1], ..., r[n].
*/
{  int i, j, aux;
   if (k == n) {print(); return;}
   for (i=k; i<=n; i++)
   {  /* For each i, a class of permutations is generated.
         Move r[i] to position k, and shift the (old)
         elements in the positions k, k+1, ..., i-1 one
         position to the right; in other words, rotate the
         elements in the positions k, k+1, ..., i one
         position to the right:
      */
      aux = r[i];
      for (j=i; j>k; j--) r[j] = r[j-1];
      r[k] = aux;
      permut(k+1); /* Recursive call  */
      /* Restore the old situation:   */
      for (j=k; j<i; j++) r[j] = r[j+1];
      r[i] = aux;
   }
}

int main()
{  cout << "\nEnter n ( < " << LEN << "): ";
   cin >> n;
   if (n >= LEN) {cout << "Too large.\n"; exit(1);}
   for (int i=1; i<=n; i++) r[i] = i;
   cout << "\nOutput:\n\n";
   permut(1);
   return 0;
}
```

45   // COMBIN: Generating combinations.

```cpp
#include <iostream.h>
#include <iomanip.h>
#include <stdlib.h>

const int LEN=100;
int n, k, r[LEN];

void print()
{  for (int i=1; i<=k; i++) cout << setw(3) << r[i];
   cout << endl;
}
```

```cpp
void combin(int m)
{   int i;
    if (m > k) print(); else
    for (i=r[m-1]+1; i <= n-k+m; i++)
    {   r[m]=i; combin(m+1);
    }
}

int main()
{   cout << "\nEnter n ( < " << LEN << "): "; cin >> n;
    if (n >= LEN) {cout << "Too large.\n"; exit(1);}
    cout << "Enter k ( < " << (n+1) << "): "; cin >> k;
    if (k > n) {cout << "Too large.\n"; exit(1);}
    cout << "\nOutput:\n\n";
    combin(1);
    return 0;
}
```

46
```cpp
// QUEENS: Solution to the n queens problem.
#include <iostream.h>
#include <iomanip.h>
#include <stdlib.h>

const int N=30;
int n, a[N], count=0;

void printsolution()
{   for (int k=1; k<=n; k++) cout << setw(2) << a[k];
    cout <<endl;
    count++;
}

int permitted(int k, int j)
/* This function examines if a queen in column k and
   row j is permitted with regard to all queens that
   are already in the columns 1, 2, ..., k-1.
*/
{   for (int kk=1; kk<k; kk++)
    if (a[kk] == j || abs(j-a[kk]) == k - kk) return 0;
    return 1;
}

void ok(int m)
// The columns 1, 2, ..., m are already O.K.
{   if (m == n) {printsolution(); return;}
    int k=m+1, j;
    for (j=1; j<=n; j++)
    if (permitted(k, j)) {a[k] = j; ok(k);}
}
```

```
    int main()
    {   cout <<
        "\nEnter n, the number of queens on an n x n board: ";
        cin >> n;
        if (n >= N) {cout << "Too large.\n"; exit(1);}
        cout << "Each of the following lines is a solution\n";
        cout <<
        "in the form of the row numbers for the columns\n";
        cout << "1 to " << n << ".\n\n", n;
        ok(0);
        cout << "\nThere are " << count << " solutions.\n";
        return 0;
    }
```

47
```
    // KNIGHT: A knight's tour on an n x n board.
    #include <iostream.h>
    #include <iomanip.h>
    #include <stdlib.h>

    const int N=10;
    int n, n2, a[N][N];
    // Array a is implicitly initialized with zeros.
    // Element a[i][k] denotes the square in row i and column k.

    void printsolution()
    {   for (int i=n; i>0; i--)      // The top row has number n
        {   for (int k=1; k<=n; k++) cout << setw(3) << a[i][k];
            cout << endl;
        }
    }

    void moveknight(int i, int k, int m)
    /* Try to place the knight on the square with row number
       i and column number k. If this is possible, that
       square is the mth square visited and we write m in
       the corresponding element of array a.
    */
    {   int m1=m+1;
        if (m > n2) {printsolution(); exit(0);}
        if (i > n || k > n || i < 1 || k < 1 || a[i][k] != 0)
            return;
        a[i][k] = m;
        /* The following recursive calls examine whether this
           move leads to a solution. If so, that solution will
           be printed and program execution will terminate.
        */
        moveknight(i+1, k+2, m1); moveknight(i+2, k+1, m1);
        moveknight(i+2, k-1, m1); moveknight(i+1, k-2, m1);
        moveknight(i-1, k-2, m1); moveknight(i-2, k-1, m1);
```

```
       moveknight(i-2, k+1, m1); moveknight(i-1, k+2, m1);
       a[i][k] = 0; /* Undo the move mentioned above if it did
                       not lead to a solution.
                 */
}

int main()
{   cout <<
    "\nEnter n, for an n x n board (for example, 5): ";
    cin >> n;
    if (n >= N) {cout << "Too large.\n"; exit(1);}
    cout << "\nThe following integers, arranged in "
            "the form of a board,\n";
    cout << "display the order in which the squares "
            "are visited:\n\n";
    n2 = n * n;
    moveknight(1, 1, 1); // Start in the lower-left corner.
    return 0;
}
```

ASCII Table

HEX	DEC	CHAR		HEX	DEC	CHAR		HEX	DEC	CHAR		HEX	DEC	CHAR
00	0	^@	NUL	20	32	SPACE		40	64	@		60	96	`
01	1	^A	SOH	21	33	!		41	65	A		61	97	a
02	2	^B	STX	22	34	"		42	66	B		62	98	b
03	3	^C	ETX	23	35	#		43	67	C		63	99	c
04	4	^D	EOT	24	36	$		44	68	D		64	100	d
05	5	^E	ENQ	25	37	%		45	69	E		65	101	e
06	6	^F	ACK	26	38	&		46	70	F		66	102	f
07	7	^G	BEL	27	39	'		47	71	G		67	103	g
08	8	^H	BS	28	40	(		48	72	H		68	104	h
09	9	^I	HT	29	41	)		49	73	I		69	105	i
0A	10	^J	LF	2A	42	*		4A	74	J		6A	106	j
0B	11	^K	VT	2B	43	+		4B	75	K		6B	107	k
0C	12	^L	FF	2C	44	,		4C	76	L		6C	108	l
0D	13	^M	CR	2D	45	-		4D	77	M		6D	109	m
0E	14	^N	SO	2E	46	.		4E	78	N		6E	110	n
0F	15	^O	SI	2F	47	/		4F	79	O		6F	111	o
10	16	^P	DLE	30	48	0		50	80	P		70	112	p
11	17	^Q	DC1	31	49	1		51	81	Q		71	113	q
12	18	^R	DC2	32	50	2		52	82	R		72	114	r
13	19	^S	DC3	33	51	3		53	83	S		73	115	s
14	20	^T	DC4	34	52	4		54	84	T		74	116	t
15	21	^U	NAK	35	53	5		55	85	U		75	117	u
16	22	^V	SYN	36	54	6		56	86	V		76	118	v
17	23	^W	ETB	37	55	7		57	87	W		77	119	w
18	24	^X	CAN	38	56	8		58	88	X		78	120	x
19	25	^Y	EM	39	57	9		59	89	Y		79	121	y
1A	26	^Z	SUB	3A	58	:		5A	90	Z		7A	122	z
1B	27	^[	ESC	3B	59	;		5B	91	[		7B	123	{
1C	28	^\	FS	3C	60	<		5C	92	\		7C	124		
1D	29	^]	GS	3D	61	=		5D	93	]		7D	125	}
1E	30	^^	RS	3E	62	>		5E	94	^		7E	126	~
1F	31	^_	US	3F	63	?		5F	95	_		7F	127	DEL

More About Manipulators

C.1 Manipulators without Parameters

We have seen in Section 9.2 how we can define manipulators without parameters. Program MYMANIP of that section is also shown below:

```
// MYMANIP: A manipulator defined by ourselves.
#include <iostream.h>

ostream &mymanip(ostream &s)
{   static int count; // Initialized to 0.
    return s << "count = " << ++count << ' ';
}

int main()
{   cout << "This is output of my own manipulator:" << endl
         << mymanip << "(first time)\n"
         << mymanip << "(second time)\n";
    return 0;
}
```

As we have seen, its output is as follows:

```
This is output of my own manipulator:
count = 1 (first time)
count = 2 (second time)
```

We will now see how this way of defining a manipulator fits into the C++ language. Remember that the expression

```
cout << mymanip
```

is actually a convenient notation for the following call to the **ostream** member function **operator<<**, in which **mymanip** is the argument:

```
cout.operator<<(mymanip)
```

Since the name of a function, not followed by an open parenthesis, gives the address of that function (see Section 5.12), this call makes sense only if there is a function **ostream::operator<<** that has a pointer to a function as its parameter. More precisely, this parameter type must be 'pointer to function taking an **ostream&** argument and returning an **ostream&**', for that is the type of this argument **mymanip**. There is indeed such a function; it can be found in the header file *iostream.h*, where, in class **ostream**, it may be defined like this:

```
ostream& operator<<(ostream& (*f)(ostream&))
{   return (*f)(*this);
}
```

Our expression **cout << mymanip** is apparently a call to this function, with argument **mymanip** corresponding to parameter **f** and **cout** corresponding to ***this**. The return-statement of this function implies that the value of **cout << mymanip** is equal to **mymanip(cout)**. We see that our manipulator function **mymanip** is called in this return statement, and that manipulators (without parameters) do not require any additional C++ language extensions at all.

Another possible solution

Even if there were no definition of **operator<<** (which takes a function as its argument) such as the one shown above in class **ostream**, we could have implemented the **mymanip** manipulator. To do this, we must realize that in

```
cout << mymanip
```

the identifier **mymanip** must be some object, of a specific type. As we have seen, this was a pointer type in our previous solution. Since function calls always contain parentheses, this occurrence of **mymanip** cannot represent a function call. It can be a variable, but not one of a standard type such as **int** because there are already **<<** operators for such types. We will therefore define a new class, and **mymanip** will be an object of this class. We need this class only to overload the **<<** operator, so there is no need to store any data in objects of such types. This may explain the curious fact that the following program is based on a class (**maniptype**) which does not have any members at all:

```
// MYMANIP1: A manipulator defined by ourselves.
#include <iostream.h>

class maniptype {} mymanip;

ostream& operator<<(ostream& s, maniptype m)
{   static int count; // Initialized to 0.
    return s << "count = " << ++count << ' ';
}

int main()
{   cout << "This is output of my own manipulator:" << endl
         << mymanip << "(first time)\n"
         << mymanip << "(second time)\n";
    return 0;
}
```

Although program MYMANIP1 has the same output as program MYMANIP, it is essentially different: the actual work is now done in an overloaded **operator<<** function, and **mymanip** is now a class object. The requirement that this rather funny class **maniptype** should be supplied in this program makes our first solution, demonstrated in program MYMANIP, preferable.

C.2 Defining Manipulators with Parameters

Besides manipulators without parameters, such as **hex**, we have also seen some that take an **int** argument. An example of those is **setprecision**. We will now see how such manipulators fit into the language, so we will be able to write manipulators with parameters ourselves. As an example, we will define the manipulator **horline()**. It displays a horizontal line consisting of minus signs, and it has an **int** argument indicating how many minus signs are to be displayed. For example, by writing

```
cout << horline(5) << "Ready.\n";
```

we will obtain the following output line:

```
-----Ready.
```

As usual, this new manipulator should be quite general in the sense that it can be used not only for **cout** but for any **ostream** object.

Since **horline(5)** has the syntactical form of a function with an **int** argument, we might try to define such a function, and make this function display the minus signs. However, it is not immediately clear what value type this function should return. Besides, no information about any output stream would be available in such a function: if we used **cout << '-'** in this function, its use would be restricted to **cout**. We therefore see that the actual output actions are to be done by an overloaded << operator. This suggests using a new type, different from all existing types so a new and unique function **operator<<** can be defined. Now the question arises how to determine the value of the **int** argument of **horline** in this new operator function. These two points lead to the idea of using a new class **horline**, with **horline(5)** being a constructor call. We can then store the value 5 in the object generated by this call. Here is a complete program that demonstrates all this:

```
// PARMANIP: Defining a manipulator with a parameter.
//   Both class 'horline' and operator<< are specific
//   for this manipulator.

#include <iostream.h>

class horline {
public:
   int n;
   horline(int nn):n(nn){}  // Use nn to initialize n.
};

ostream& operator<<(ostream& s, horline& h)
{  for (int i=0; i<h.n; i++) s << '-';
   return s;
}

int main()
{  cout << horline(5) << "Ready.\n";
   return 0;
}
```

An alternative solution

If we need only one manipulator with an **int** argument, the solution demonstrated by program PARMANIP is a simple and attractive one. However, if we wanted to use several manipulators of this kind, then, with this type of solution, we would have to write both a class and an **operator<<** function for each of them. It is possible to use only one class and one **operator<<** function, shared by all those manipulators, which are separate functions. This second solution (to the problem of defining manipulators with an **int** argument) is again based on the idea of using a pointer to a function. We will demonstrate this by defining two manipulators, **horline** and **square**, each having one **int** parameter *n*. While **horline** again draws a horizontal line of *n* minus signs, **square** draws a square of *n* × *n* asterisks, starting on a new line. Recall that in program PARMANIP we stored the manipulator's argument in a class object. We do this also in the following program, but this time we store the address of the manipulator function there as well.

```
// PMANIP1: Defining two manipulators,
//          each having an int parameter.
#include <iostream.h>

struct manip
{   int n;
    manip(*p)(int, ostream*);
};

ostream& operator<<(ostream& s, manip m)
{   m.p(m.n, &s);
    return s;
}

manip horline(int n, ostream *ps=0)
{   static manip m;
    if (ps == 0)
    {   m.n = n; m.p = horline;
    } else
    {   for (int i=0; i<n; i++) *ps << '-';
    }
    return m;
}

manip square(int n, ostream *ps=0)
{   static manip m;
    if (ps == 0)
    {   m.n = n; m.p = square;
    } else
    {   for (int i=0; i<n; i++)
        {   *ps << endl;
            for (int j=0; j<n; j++) *ps << '*';
        }
    }
    return m;
}

int main()
{   cout << horline(5) << square(4) << "\nReady.\n";
    return 0;
}
```

Here is the output of this program:

```
-----
****
****
****
****
Ready.
```

Since the manipulators **horline** and **square** are very similar, let us discuss only one of them, **horline**. This manipulator function is called in two different ways. The first call is

```
cout << horline(5)
```

and can be found in the **main** function. Since there is only one argument in this call, the value of **ps** in **horline** is zero. Then both the **int** argument value (5) and the address of the function **horline** itself are stored in the **manip** object **m**, defined here as a static variable. The return statement returns this object **m**. Then the **operator<<** is called. This function can find the **horline** function as **m.p** and the original **int** argument (5) as **m.n**, so it can call **horline** once again by executing

```
m.p(m.n, &s);
```

where **s** is the output stream. The two calls to **horline** are distinguished by the absence or presence of a second argument, **&s**. Since it is present in this second call, the stream address is available in **horline,** so the actual work of drawing a horizontal line can now be done.

Bibliography

Ammeraal, L. (1992) *Programs and Data Structures in C, Second Edition*, Chichester: John Wiley.

Coplien, J. O. (1992) *Advanced C++ Programming Styles and Idioms*, Reading, MA: Addison-Wesley.

Ellis, A. E. and B. Stroustrup (1990) *The Annotated C++ Reference Manual*, Reading, MA: Addison-Wesley.

Gorlen, K. E., S. M. Orlow, and P. S. Plexico (1990) *Data Abstraction and Object-oriented Programming in C++*, Chichester: John Wiley.

Gray, N. A. B. (1994) *Programming with Class*, Chichester: John Wiley.

Horstmann, C. S. (1991) *Mastering C++*, New York: John Wiley.

Kernighan, B. W. and D. M. Ritchie (1988) *The C Programming Language, Second Edition*, Englewood Cliffs, NJ: Prentice-Hall.

Lippman, S. B. (1991) *C++ Primer, Second Edition*, Reading, MA: Addison-Wesley.

Smith, J. D. (1990) *Reusability and Software Construction: C and C++*, New York: John Wiley.

Stroustrup, B. (1991) *The C++ Programming Language, Second Edition*, Reading, MA: Addison-Wesley.

Stroustrup, B. (1994) *The Design and Evolution of C++*, Reading, MA: Addison-Wesley.

Winder, R. (1993) *Developing C++ Software, Second Edition*, Chichester: John Wiley.

Index